ANDREW JACKSON IN CONTEXT

(A VOLUME IN FIRST MEN,
AMERICA'S PRESIDENTS SERIES)

OTHER BOOKS IN THE FIRST MEN, AMERICA'S PRESIDENTS SERIES
Barbara Bennett Peterson, Editor

**Theodore Roosevelt:
A Political Life**
Tom Lansford
2004. ISBN 1-59033-990-8

Citizen Lincoln
Ward M. McAfee
2004. ISBN 1-59454-112-4

**George Washington,
America's Moral Exemplar**
Barbara Bennet Peterson
2005. ISBN 1-59454-230-9

**President James K. Polk:
The Dark Horse President**
Louise Mayo
2006. ISBN 1-59454-718-1

**Franklin Delano Roosevelt,
Preserver of Spirit and Hope**
Barbara Bennett Peterson
2006. ISBN 1-60021-117-8

**John Quincy Adams:
Yankee Nationalist**
Paul E. Teed
2006. ISBN 1-59454-797-1

President Herbert Hoover
Don W. Whisenhunt
2006. ISBN 1-60021-476-2

**Chester Alan Arthur: The Life of a
Gilded Age Politician and President**
Gregory J. Dehler
2007. ISBN : 978-1-60021-079-2

**William Henry Harrison:
General and President**
Mary Jane Child Queen
2007. ISBN 978-1-60021-407-3

**Thomas Jefferson:
A Public Life, A Private Life**
David Kiracofe
2008. ISBN 978-1-60456-061-9

John Tyler: A Rare Career
Lyle Nelson
2008. ISBN-13: 978-1-60021-961-0

**James Madison: Defender of the
American Republic**
*Donald Dewey and
Barbara Bennett Peterson*
2009. ISBN: 978-1-60456-858-8

Andrew Jackson in Context
Matthew Warshauer
2009. ISBN: 978-1-60741-709-5

To Carl ~

ANDREW JACKSON IN CONTEXT

(A VOLUME IN FIRST MEN, AMERICA'S PRESIDENTS SERIES)

MATTHEW WARSHAUER

Nova Science Publishers, Inc.
New York

Copyright © 2011 by Nova Science Publishers, Inc.

All rights reserved. No part of this book may be reproduced, stored in a retrieval system or transmitted in any form or by any means: electronic, electrostatic, magnetic, tape, mechanical photocopying, recording or otherwise without the written permission of the Publisher.

For permission to use material from this book please contact us:
Telephone 631-231-7269; Fax 631-231-8175
Web Site: http://www.novapublishers.com

NOTICE TO THE READER

The Publisher has taken reasonable care in the preparation of this book, but makes no expressed or implied warranty of any kind and assumes no responsibility for any errors or omissions. No liability is assumed for incidental or consequential damages in connection with or arising out of information contained in this book. The Publisher shall not be liable for any special, consequential, or exemplary damages resulting, in whole or in part, from the readers' use of, or reliance upon, this material. Any parts of this book based on government reports are so indicated and copyright is claimed for those parts to the extent applicable to compilations of such works.

Independent verification should be sought for any data, advice or recommendations contained in this book. In addition, no responsibility is assumed by the publisher for any injury and/or damage to persons or property arising from any methods, products, instructions, ideas or otherwise contained in this publication.

This publication is designed to provide accurate and authoritative information with regard to the subject matter covered herein. It is sold with the clear understanding that the Publisher is not engaged in rendering legal or any other professional services. If legal or any other expert assistance is required, the services of a competent person should be sought. FROM A DECLARATION OF PARTICIPANTS JOINTLY ADOPTED BY A COMMITTEE OF THE AMERICAN BAR ASSOCIATION AND A COMMITTEE OF PUBLISHERS.

LIBRARY OF CONGRESS CATALOGING-IN-PUBLICATION DATA

Warshauer, Matthew, 1965-
  Andrew Jackson in context / Matthew Warshauer.
    p. cm.
  Includes bibliographical references and index.
  ISBN 978-1-61209-622-3 (softcover)
 1. Jackson, Andrew, 1767-1845. 2. Presidents--United States--Biography.
 3. United States--Politics and government--1815-1861. I. Title.
  E382.W286 2011
  973.5'6092--dc22
  [B]
                                                            2010051512

Published by Nova Science Publishers, Inc. ✦ New York

*To Barry H. Leeds, Connecticut State University
Professor of English, Emeritus,
and Norton Mezvinsky, Connecticut State University
Professor of History, Emeritus.
My teachers, mentors, colleagues, and friends.*

Contents

Foreword		ix
	Barbara Bennett Peterson	
Preface		xvii
Introduction		xix
Chapter 1	Jackson's Early Years: Lasting Trauma or Hardened Youth?	1
Chapter 2	The Nashville Frontier and Building a Reputation	19
Chapter 3	The Military Jackson: The Creek War	41
Chapter 4	The Military Jackson: Florida, New Orleans, Florida	61
Chapter 5	Jackson's March to the White House	87
Chapter 6	Presidency: The First Term	109
Chapter 7	Presidency: The Second Term	137
Chapter 8	Retirement	161
Conclusion		185
Bibliography		189
Index		203

Foreword

President of the United States of America is an official title sought by many and won by only a few individuals. Most American Presidents are of high merit and political acumen and reflected wisdom, leadership, and integrity. This series titled *First Men, America's Presidents* published by NOVA Science Publishers contains a book length biography of each President of the United States of America. Every book contains information on the President's early education, professional career, military service or political service prior to the presidency, interpretative discussion of both domestic and foreign policies during each presidency, and the conclusion of their political lives in public service. Every presidential biography in the NOVA series has been written by a professional historian or political scientist well versed in the field of presidential scholarship. The two major themes of this series are the character traits marking success in the presidency, and the changes in the office of the presidency through America's history. Character matters in all walks of life, but perhaps matters most within the character of the President of the United States.

The duties of the President of the United States are delegated through Article II of the Constitution of the United States of America, and from the successive laws passed by Congress over time. Each president takes the Oath of Affirmation:--"I do solemnly swear (or affirm) that I will faithfully execute the Office of the President of the United States, and will to the best of my Ability, preserve, protect and defend the Constitution of the United States." The president's duties and responsibilities under the Constitution are to serve as "Commander in Chief of the Army and Navy of the United States, and the Militia of the several States, when called into actual Service of the United States." The president may invite the counsel and opinions of his various department heads upon any subject related to the execution of the duties of their offices, either in writing or orally as has become the custom within the president's Cabinet. The president "shall have the power to grant Reprieves and Pardons for Offenses against the United States, except in Cases of Impeachment." Every president has realized that each must administer through constitutional principles, as each was elected by the voting majority of the people to be their chief executive through the Electoral College. Each president of the United States "shall have Power, by and with the Advice and Consent of the Senate, to make Treaties, provided two thirds of the Senators present concur." As the president directs both the domestic and foreign activities of the government, he has the power to "nominate and by and with the Advice and Consent of the Senate….appoint Ambassadors, other public Ministers and Consuls, Judges of the Supreme Court, and all other Officers of the United States, whose Appointments are not herein otherwise provided for, and which shall be established by law." The president also receives foreign ambassadors and officials on behalf of the American people. The president "shall have the Power to fill up all Vacancies that may happen during the Recess of the Senate, by granting Commissions which shall expire at the End of their next Session." The president under the Constitution shall give Congress a State of the Union address every year to acquaint them with his policy agenda and plans for the future. Usually in this address to Congress he recommends "to their Consideration such Measures as he shall judge necessary and expedient." Above all, the president of the United States "shall take Care that the Laws be faithfully executed, and shall Commission all the Officers of the United States." A strong role for the President had been envisioned by the Founding Fathers who rejected the obsolete Articles of Confederation and replaced the framework of government with the Constitution of the United States. Article II of the Constitution outlining the powers of the presidency provided that the office of the President would be held by one individual. It provided the President with enumerated powers including the power of the veto. And stipulated that the president's election would be above the control of the Congress to ensure the separation of powers and the system of checks and balances. It stipulated that the president, vice president, and all civil officers of the United States *must govern in the name of the American people* lest they "be removed from Office on Impeachment for, and Conviction of Treason, Bribery, or other high Crimes and Misdemeanors."

From Presidents George Washington through John Quincy Adams candidates for the presidency were selected in caucuses of senators and congressmen and then the state legislatures indirectly chose the president through the selection of Electors to the Electoral College. This system had worked for Washington, Adams, Jefferson, Madison and Monroe—they were statesmen who held wide appeal within Congress and the state legislatures and claimed to represent the people. But as demands for greater democracy in the election process were heard, the process was changed. In the outcome of the election of 1824, John Quincy Adams was chosen president by the Congressional House of Representatives under constitutional law after no candidate had received a majority of the electoral ballots in the Electoral College. Jackson, the candidate who had received the most popular votes was not chosen president and his supporters called for more direct popular participation and worked to introduce changes. Hence, the voting process was altered in the name of democracy. In the election of 1828 President Andrew Jackson triumphed after voting had been given directly to the people and removed from the state legislatures. Democracy further triumphed by the elimination of the congressional caucuses in naming presidential candidates and the holding of national political party conventions to name them instead, allowing greater voice and participation of the people. The institution of the party convention to nominate presidential candidates remains, although winners in various state primaries command party delegates to vote the choice of the people. The Presidency, molded by the character and designs of each president, oversees command, administration, diplomacy, ceremony, legislation, and public opinion. The modern strength of the Presidency is a reflection of the mighty power of the United States within a global world.

The majority of America's presidents have served for one four-year term or less as some died in office. Four presidents served out part of their predecessor's term and won subsequent re-election in their own right: Theodore Roosevelt, Calvin Coolidge, Harry S. Truman, and Lyndon Baines Johnson. Only one president, Grover Cleveland, was elected to two discontinuous terms of office and thus was both the twenty-second and the twenty-fourth president of the United States. Several outstanding presidents have been elected to two four-year terms or more. They were: George Washington, Thomas Jefferson, James Madison, James Monroe, Andrew Jackson, Abraham Lincoln, Ulysses S. Grant, Grover Cleveland, William McKinley, Woodrow Wilson, Franklin D. Roosevelt, Dwight D. Eisenhower, Richard Nixon, Ronald Reagan, William Jefferson ("Bill") Clinton, and George W. Bush. Only one president, Franklin D. Roosevelt, was elected for a third and fourth term. Eight presidents have achieved their office as a result of being the vice-president of a preceding president who died in office or resigned: John Tyler, Millard Fillmore, Andrew Johnson, Chester Arthur,

Theodore Roosevelt, Calvin Coolidge, Harry S. Truman, Lyndon Baines Johnson, and Gerald R. Ford. Additionally, John Adams, Thomas Jefferson, Martin Van Buren, Richard M. Nixon and George H.W. Bush also rose from the office of vice-president to president. Besides the vice-presidency as a stepping stone to the presidency, two thirds of the presidents elected had held congressional office earlier in their political careers such as Barack Obama, America's 44th President elected in 2008 who had served as a Senator from Illinois. Twenty presidents had served as Governors of states or territories before being elected. They were: Thomas Jefferson (Virginia), James Monroe (Virginia), Andrew Jackson (Florida), Martin Van Buren (New York), William Henry Harrison (Indiana), John Tyler (Virginia), James K. Polk (Tennessee), Andrew Johnson (Tennessee), Rutherford B. Hayes (Ohio), Grover Cleveland (New York), William McKinley (Ohio), Theodore Roosevelt (New York), William Howard Taft (The Philippines), Woodrow Wilson (New Jersey), Calvin Coolidge (Massachusetts), Franklin D. Roosevelt (New York), Jimmy Carter (Georgia), Ronald Reagan (California), William Jefferson Clinton (Arkansas), and George W. Bush (Texas). Some states with larger voting populations and hence more electoral votes have seen their native sons rise to the presidency of the United States. The American Presidents have come from both coasts, east and west, and from both the upper tier and the lower tier of states geographically, north and south. When elected, the president becomes the president of 'all the people', not just those of his political party. Since the president acts as America's commander in chief, the majority of the presidents of the United States have served in the U.S. military. George Washington, Andrew Jackson, William Henry Harrison, Zachary Taylor, Franklin Pierce, Ulysses S. Grant, Rutherford B. Hayes, James Garfield, Chester Arthur, Benjamin Harrison, and Dwight David Eisenhower served in the capacity of generals. James Monroe, John Tyler, Abraham Lincoln, William McKinley, Theodore Roosevelt, Harry Truman, John F. Kennedy, Lyndon Baines Johnson, Richard Nixon, Gerald R. Ford, Jimmy Carter, Ronald Reagan, George Herbert Walker Bush, and George W. Bush also served their country in military service at various ranks, and always with dedication. The youngest elected president was John F. Kennedy (1960) at forty-three. The youngest man to ever serve as president was Theodore Roosevelt who at forty-two assumed the office following William McKinley's assassination. The average age for an elected president was fifty-four. The oldest elected president was Ronald Reagan at sixty-nine (1980) and seventy-three (1984).[1]

---

[1] David C. Whitney and Robin Vaughn Whitney, *The American Presidents*, Garden City, New

One of the major features of American constitutional development has been the growth of the presidency both in power and prestige as well as in new Cabinet positions, departments and agencies under the control of the president. The Federal government has grown mightily in comparison with the States' governments since the inception of the Constitution. Increases in presidential powers have been occasioned by wars, depressions, foreign relations, and the agenda of the presidents themselves. Henry F. Graff, Emeritus Professor at Columbia University, described the office of the president as "the most powerful office in the world" in *The Presidents.* The Executive Office of the President (EOP) was created during the administration of President Franklin D. Roosevelt upon passage by Congress of the Reorganization Act of 1939. The EOP originally included the White House Office (WHO), the Bureau of the Budget, the Office of Government Reports, the National Resources Planning Board, and the Liaison Office for Personnel Management. In addition, wrote Henry F. Graff, the 1939 Act provided that an "office for emergency management" may be formed "in the event of a national emergency, or threat of a national emergency."[2] Today the White House Office has become "the political as well as policy arm of the chief executive." The larger, all encompassing Executive Office of the President has expanded through time to include a myriad number of departments in addition to the first five listed above and the president is advised by nearly 60 active boards, committees and commissions. During and immediately after World War II the following additional departments within the purview of the EOP were organized: Committee for Congested Production Areas, 1943-1944, War Refugee Board, 1944-1945, Council of Economic Advisers, 1946-, National Security Council, 1947-, and National Security Resources Board, 1947-1953. During the Cold War, additions to the EOP were made adding the following departments: Telecommunications Adviser to the President, 1951-1953, Office of the Director for Mutual Security, 1951-1954, Office of Defense Mobilization, 1952-1958, President's Advisory Committee on Government Organization, 1953-1961, Operations Coordinating Board, 1953-1961, President's Board of Consultants on Foreign Intelligence Activities, 1956-1961, Office of Civil and Defense Mobilization, 1958-1962, and National Aeronautics and Space Council, 1958-1993. By the Sixties, some of the earlier departments organized in the 1939 to 1960 decades were allowed to close, with newer agencies with a new focus and expanded technology taking their

---

York: Doubleday, 1993, pp. v-ix.
[2] Henry F. Graff, Editor, *The Presidents, New York: Charles Scribner's Sons*, Simon & Schuster Macmillan, 2nd edition, 1996, Appendix C pp. 743-745.

place. These newer agencies included: President's Foreign Intelligence Advisory Board, 1961-1977, Office of Emergency Planning, 1962-1969, Office of Science and Technology, 1962-1973, Office of Economic Opportunity, 1964-1975, Office of Emergency Preparedness, 1965-1973, National Council on Marine Resources and Engineering Development, 1966-1971, Council on Environmental Quality, 1969-, Council for Urban Affairs, 1969-1970, and Office of Intergovernmental Relations, 1969-1973. By the mid-Seventies, once again there was a general reorganization with some of the earlier departments and offices being swept away and replaced by newer agencies reflecting new presidential agendas. Many of the new agencies reflected the urgencies in domestic policies and included: the Domestic Council, 1970-1978, Office of Management and Budget, 1970-, Office of Telecommunications Policy, 1970-1977, Council on International Economic Policy, 1971-1977, Office of Consumer Affairs, 1971-1973, Special Action Office for Drug Abuse Prevention, 1971-1975, Federal Property Council, 1973-1977, Council on Economic Policy, 1973-1974, Energy Policy Office, 1973-1974, Council on Wage and Price Stability, 1974-1981, Energy Resource Council, 1974-1977, Office of Special Representative for Trade Negotiations, 1974-, Presidential Clemency Board, 1974-1975, Office of Science and Technology Policy, 1976-, Office of Administration, 1977-, and Domestic Policy Staff, 1978-1981. Many of the departments, councils and agencies organized as part of the Executive Office of the President by the late Seventies and early Eighties included: Office of Policy Development, 1981-, Office of the U.S. Trade Representative, 1981-, National Critical Materials Council, 1984-, Office of National Drug Control Policy, 1988-, National Economic Council, 1993-. By the 21st Century the EOP continued several effective agencies started earlier: Council of Economic Advisers 1946-, National Security Council 1947-, Council on Environmental Quality 1964-, Office of Management and Budget 1970-, Office of Science and Technology Policy 1976-, Office of Administration 1977-, Office of the U.S. Trade Representative 1981-, Office of Policy Development 1981-, and the Office of National Drug Control Policy 1988-. In addition to the White House Office of the president, the Office of the Vice President functions and is administered as part of the EOP.[3] At the turn of the millennium the department of Homeland Security 2001- was established by presidential Executive Order and administered by the

---

[3] Henry F. Graff, Editor, *The Presidents, New York: Charles Scribner's Sons*, Simon & Schuster Macmillan, 3rd edition, 2002, Appendix C pp. 743-747.

Executive Office of the President that continues to be evolutionary in response to new issues, demands, and events.

Capable presidents have responded to America's changing needs and responsibilities by retooling their administrations to meet new crises, opportunities, and challenges. This series *First Men, America's Presidents* published by NOVA explains the personal and public life of each President of the United States. Their qualities of character and leadership are aptly interpreted and offer strong role models for all citizens. Presidential successes are recorded for posterity, as are the pitfalls that should be guarded against in the future. This series also explains the domestic reasons and world backdrop for the expansion of the Executive Office of the President. The President of the United States is perhaps the most coveted position in the world and this series reveals the lives of all those successfully elected, how each performed as president, and how each is to be measured in history. The collective life stories of the presidents reveal the greatness that America represents in the world.

Dr. Barbara Bennett Peterson
First Men, America's Presidents NOVA Series Editor
Professor of History, Oregon State University (retired)
Emeritus Professor University of Hawaii
Former Adjunct Fellow East-West Center
Professor of History, California State University San Bernardino, Palm Desert

PREFACE

Publishing a book allows an author a wonderful opportunity to thank those who have been a part of their lives, either personally or intellectually, often both. This particular book has been in my head long before I ever had the opportunity to set it down on paper. During that "thinking about it" phase, I lectured on and debated Jackson with colleagues and students. Given Jackson's controversial actions and reputation, which in large part forms the core of this book, I was forced during my debates to think and rethink his role in early America. I am always struck by the degree to which people become passionate about whether or not Jackson was good or evil. No matter what side of that coin my colleagues and students came down upon, I have always learned from their perspectives. Thus my thanks to all who engaged the topic.

More specifically, I owe a debt of gratitude that can never be paid to Barry H. Leeds and Norton Mezvinsky, to whom this book is dedicated. They were my professors when I attended Central Connecticut State University as an undergraduate. Barry taught me American literature and Norton American history. They wrote letters of recommendation for my admission into graduate school, stayed in contact with me through those long years of work, and became my steadfast colleagues and friends when I returned to teach at my alma mater. They have been and will always be my mentors. Norton also read and commented on this manuscript.

I also owe thanks to my colleague John Tully, associate professor of history at CCSU and our department's social studies education coordinator. John is a gifted historian and teacher with an eye for explaining things clearly and his help has made this book better than it would have been otherwise. I am also indebted to Ann Toplovich, the director of the Tennessee Historical Society for her steadfast support of my work and for reading the manuscript.

The Historic New Orleans Collection, especially Priscilla and John Lawrence, have also been wonderful supporters and there is no place like New Orleans for lecturing on Jackson. Because I truly wanted this book to be accessible to students, I asked two of my former graduate students to read the manuscript and give me their thoughts. Robert Dowling, of Avon Old Farms School, and Joshua Reese, of Northwest Catholic High School (both in Connecticut), graciously accepted, and offered me excellent, constructive suggestions. Thanks also to the series editor Barbara Bennett Peterson for her always prompt responses to inquiries and fine organization of the entire *First Men* project.

Finally, I thank my wife, Wanda, and our three wonderful little girls, Emma, Samantha, and Jessica. They keep me grounded and incredibly happy.

INTRODUCTION

Historians disagree about Andrew Jackson. The most prolific Jackson scholar of the twentieth century, Robert V. Remini, has argued for years across the pages of more than a dozen books that Jackson was a "masterful" politician, a self-made man who worked his way to the presidency and proved that a common man could rise up in what had previously been a deferential, aristocratically based society. In doing so, Jackson, more than any other previous president, helped to further and secure the burgeoning democracy that had begun with the American Revolution. It was Jackson, as both a leader and as a symbol for the average man, who opened the possibilities and established the realities of mass democracy.[1]

Other historians, such as James C. Curtis and Andrew Burstein wholeheartedly disagree. To these scholars, Jackson was anything but a champion of democracy and "masterful" politician. He was, instead, a vainglorious, self-seeking, temperamental man who bullied his way through life, lashed out at those who opposed him and most certainly failed to possess the skills or the vision necessary to usher the United States into a new period in which democracy replaced the more aristocratic elements of American government and society.[2]

---

[1] See for example, Robert V. Remini, *Andrew Jackson* (New York: Twayne Publishers, 1966; republished Harper Perennial, 1999); *Andrew Jackson: The Course of American Empire* (New York: Harper & Row, 1977); *Andrew Jackson: The Course of American Freedom* (New York: Harper & Row, 1981); *Andrew Jackson: The Course of American Democracy* (New York: Harper & Row, 1984); this is by no means a complete list of Remini's works. For a recent continuation of this argument, see Sean Wilentz, *The Rise of American Democracy: Jefferson to Lincoln* (New York: W.W. Norton, 2005); Sean Wilentz, *Andrew Jackson* (New York: Henry Holt, 2005).

[2] James C. Curtis, *Andrew Jackson and the Search for Vindication* (New York: Harper Collins, 1976); Andrew Burstein, *The Passions of Andrew Jackson* (New York: Knopf, 2003); see

With such diametrically opposite representations of Andrew Jackson, how is one to determine who he really was and how his role as a general and seventh president of the United States impacted the nation? A seemingly simple question, historians have not done well in coming to a generally accepted conclusion. Nor is this merely a recent historical dilemma. During Jackson's own day he was an incredibly polarizing figure who sparked the development of the Second American Party System. It was around Jackson that, in the 1820s and 1830s, the Democratic and Whig parties formed and engaged in a mean-spirited partisanship that defined the Jacksonian Era. To his own party of Democrats, Jackson was ever the patriot-hero who defended the nation from enemies and unprincipled politicians bent on gaining power through corruption and special privilege. To Whigs, Jackson was "King Andrew I," a dangerous military chieftain who usurped presidential power and represented the real danger to the still fledgling republic.

The opposite views of Jackson were so extreme that even at his death in 1845 the two parties could not set aside the partisanship that gripped the period and come to a determination on what Jackson represented for the age. Citizens of the time seemed certain that future historians would draw final conclusions. "Soon, history, divested of the passions and interest with which he came in conflict, will do him justice, and all honor," reported the *Albany Argus* of New York. The *New York Herald* made similar predictions: "After the partisan passions and prejudices of the present generation shall have ceased to operate, posterity will pronounce a just and united judgment."[3] Benjamin M. Dusenbery, who in 1846 compiled the many funeral eulogies on Jackson, came to the same determination: "It can hardly be expected that the present generation will do justice to the character of Jackson."[4]

The partisanship of the Jacksonian Era has certainly passed, yet historians seem no closer to arriving at uncontested conclusions about the seventh president. The obvious question is why? How can historians draw such

---

also Michael Paul Rogin, *Fathers and Children: Andrew Jackson and the Subjugation of the American Indian* (New York: Alfred Knopf, 1975; reprint, Piscataway: Transaction Publishers, 1991, 2000).

[3] "The Death of Gen. Jackson," *Albany Argus*, 18 June 1845; "The Life, Public Services and Last Days of General Jackson," *New York Herald*, 18 June 1845. For more on responses to Jackson's death see, Matthew Warshauer, "Contested Mourning: The New York Battle over Andrew Jackson's Death," *New York History 87*, no. 1 (Winter 2006): 29-65; Matthew Warshauer, "Ridiculing the Dead: Andrew Jackson and Connecticut Newspapers," *Connecticut History 20, no. 1* (Spring 2001): 13-31.

[4] Benjamin M. Dusenbery, *Monument to the Memory of General Andrew Jackson: Containing Twenty-Five Eulogies and Sermons Delivered on the Occasion of His Death* (Philadelphia, Walker & Gillis, 1846), 32.

divergent views about the motivations and legacy of Andrew Jackson? Part of the answer obviously lay in Jackson himself. A man of amazing twists and contradictions, Jackson at times confounded even his closest friends and family. No author has done a better job of defining Jackson's complexity than his first professional biographer, James Parton, who in a three-volume work published in 1860, concluded,

> "Andrew Jackson, I am given to understand, was a patriot and a traitor. He was one of the greatest generals, and wholly ignorant of the art of war. A writer brilliant, elegant, eloquent, without being able to compose a correct sentence, or spell words of four syllables. The first of statesmen, he never framed a measure. He was the most candid of men, and was capable of the profoundest dissimulation. A most law-defying, law-obeying citizen. A stickler for discipline, he never hesitated to disobey a superior. A democratic autocrat. An urbane savage. An atrocious saint."[5]

Parton's study of Jackson was in part based on dozens of personal interviews with those who supported and battled the seventh president, and as such it accurately represented the complexities of the man. Most subsequent biographers have made good use of Parton's attempt to define Jackson, yet few have done a better job of getting at the seemingly baffling contradictions that made Jackson who he was. Still, they have tried. Robert Remini wrote in 1966 that Jackson was "full of sharp contrasts, angular twists, and sudden turns. He was impetuous and cautious, ruthless and compassionate, suspicious and generous. He was driven by ambition—a skillful, hardheaded political operator, enamored of power, and deeply involved in all the ambiguities and oblique maneuvers that are inevitable in the pursuit of power. He was a complex of towering ambition, fierce loyalties, and stern discipline." Other historians concurred on the difficulty of defining Jackson: Lorman Ratner noted, "for a man who saw himself, and has often been described as simple and straight forward, he seems especially hard to explain." John Belohlavek remarked that Jackson was "complex in his simplicity or perhaps simple in his complexity."[6]

Andrew Burstein, writing in 2003, described an equally problematic, though decidedly more negative, Jackson. Explaining the General's popularity

---

[5] James Parton, *The Life of Andrew Jackson, vol. 1* (New York: Mason Brothers, 1860), vii.
[6] Remini, *Andrew Jackson, 2*; Lorman A. Ratner, *Andrew Jackson and His Tennessee Lieutenants: A Study in Political Culture* (Westport: Greenwood Press, 1997), ix; John M. Belohlavek, *Let the Eagle Soar: The Foreign Policy of Andrew Jackson* (Lincoln: University of Nebraska Press, 1985), ix.

in the aftermath of the famous Battle of New Orleans in which Jackson won an unprecedented victory over the British at the end of the War of 1812, Burstein explained, "he became known to a grateful public as a man of endurance, unwavering will, and resolute action. Over the years, as the public got to know him better, they realized alternative meanings for endurance, will, and action: obstinacy, fierceness, and self-absorption. Which was Jackson? they pondered. Brave or unbalanced? Or both? Was he steel wrought in a fiery furnace, or an uncontrollable monster irresponsibly unleashed into the political world? Was he the ultimate democrat or the ultimate despot?"[7]

Burstein's final question, whether Jackson was a democrat or a despot, is more essential than even the author himself recognized. Burstein concluded, rather simplistically, that Jackson was little more than a despot, going even further by insisting that he was "a man of platitudes, a mediocre intellect with a glamorous surface." Essentially, "historical imagination has contrived" Jackson as a "romanticized figure," insisted Burstein, and "we can add [Jackson] to such story book heroes as Daniel Boone and Davy Crockett."[8]

The problem with Burstein's conclusions is that Jackson was not merely a "story book" hero. He was a real hero with very real victories and as a result he resonated with a large portion of the American public. His nationalism was intricately tied to that of the country. Jackson was also a powerful president who shaped, for good or bad, the direction of the Union. Moreover, it was not that historical imagination contrived Jackson's image so much as the political parties of his day shaped and directed his image based on their own views and desires for the future of their parties and the republic. Granted, Jackson's actions provided ample fodder for those who loved or hated him. That Jackson was a hero and a despot, a democrat and an autocrat, no serious historian of the period can deny, but one must also recognize the degree to which rabid partisanship influenced the perception of Jackson in his own day.

Those who championed the General focused upon his heroism, questioning in the 1828 presidential contest, "Who that has feelings of gratitude, and loves the land he dwells in, will fear to trust the directions and affairs of this country, to him, who has protected and defended, and saved it."[9] Opponents countered by focusing on Jackson's equally negative traits: "His conduct puts us in mind of the exasperated rhinoceros, wreaking his fury on every object that presents itself." Another writer denounced Jackson's

---

[7] Burstein, *The Passions of Andrew Jackson*, xiv.
[8] Burstein, *The Passions of Andrew Jackson* , 233.
[9] *The Letters of Wyoming, to the People of the United States, on the Presidential Election, and In Favour of Andrew Jackson* (Philadelphia: S. Simpson & J. Conrad, 1824), 87.

"vindictiveness and cruelty," noting that he possessed "a total want of talent or acquirements, suitable for civil office."[10]

These opposing views of Jackson accurately reflect the scholarship from the mid to late nineteenth through the twenty-first century. In 1948, Richard Hofstadter noted, "Historians have never been certain how much his policies were motivated by public considerations and how much by private animosities."[11] Writing an overview of Jacksonian scholarship in 1968, Charles Grier Sellers, Jr., insisted that Jackson historians "have been forced pretty substantially either into the Jackson camp or into the camp of Jackson's enemies." Quite aptly, Sellers began his essay by insisting that "Andrew Jackson's masterful personality was enough by itself to make him one of the most controversial figures ever to stride across the American stage." He also argued that much of what historians wrote about Jackson has determined as much if not more about their own "social and intellectual environments" as it did about Jackson's. Labeling the earliest Jackson biographers, such as James Parton and William Graham Sumner, as "Whig," Sellers explained that their aristocratic upbringings in many ways colored their perceptions of Jackson, especially as it related to the seventh president's championing of the Spoils System, or Rotation in Office, in which he insisted that any man should be able to serve in federal office, not just the well-born, privileged elite. Sellers insisted further that the rise of studies focusing on the foundations and influences of democracy, such as Frederick Jackson Turner's "The Significance of the American Frontier," sparked a deeper interest in the growth of democracy in the early republic. Hence works followed, such as John Spencer Bassett's *Life of Andrew Jackson* published in 1911, which lauded the seventh president as the champion of democracy. After Bassett's work came a succession of others, the pinnacle of which was the 1945 publication of Arthur M. Schlesinger, Jr's, *The Age of Jackson*. Sellers concluded, "the pro-democratic orientation that transformed Jacksonian historiography at the turn

---

[10] J. Snelling, *A Brief and Impartial History of The Life and Actions of Andrew Jackson* (Boston: Stimpson and Clapp, 1831), 95; *A History of the Life and Public Services of Major General Andrew Jackson* (n.p., 1828), 37; another writer stated, "that from the irritability of his constitution, and an untoward disposition, he does not control the first impulse of his temper, but has indulged in repeated acts of violence." See *An Address to the People of the United States, on the Subject of the Presidential Election: with a special reference to the nomination of Andrew Jackson, containing public sketches of his public and private character. --By a citizen of the United States* (n.p., 1828), 7.

[11] Richard Hofstadter, *The American Political Tradition, and the Men Who Made It* (New York: Knopf, 1948), 61.

of the century has continued to be the dominant influence on writings about the Jackson period ever since."[12]

Some twenty years after Sellers announced the dominance of the pro-Jackson camp, another historian, Douglas R. Egerton, writing in 1987, supported the conclusion: "the pro-Jackson partisans have not only returned to the field, they have very nearly won the battle." He noted in particular that Robert Remini's three-volume biography had "throw[n] down the gauntlet."[13]

The question of whether pro-Jackson scholars won the battle of the twentieth century regarding Jackson as the champion of democracy is debatable. That they did not win the war is without question. The latter half of the twentieth and early twenty-first century, in particular, witnessed the publication of works that challenged the interpretations of pro-Jackson scholars. Michael Paul Rogin focused on Jackson's treatment of Native Americans. James Curtis insisted that Jackson was so heavily scarred by the trauma of the American Revolution and the premature deaths of his brothers and mother that he "spent his life trying to prove his right to survival." Andrew Burstein agreed, claiming that Jackson was merely a vain, blustering, fiction of American popular imagination.[14]

The battle rages on with the recent publication of H. W. Brand's *Andrew Jackson: His Life and Times*, which does not really enter the foray of the historiographical war though it does present Jackson in a more positive light, and Sean Wilentz's *Andrew Jackson*, which again champions Jackson as a leader in bringing democracy to the forefront of America. Most recently, Jon Meacham's *American Lion: Andrew Jackson in the White House* offers a stirring, forceful account of Jackson's life and presidency that engages the politics of the era and portrays Jackson in a remarkably human light that few historians have captured.[15] Still, the question remains: can historians come to any accepted conclusions about Jackson and his influence, both negative and positive, on American government?

To a large extent, both sides of the Jackson battle have some valid arguments. Jackson's intensity allowed him to achieve greatness for himself

---

[12] Charles Grier Sellers, Jr., "Andrew Jackson versus the Historians," *Mississippi Valley Historical Review 44* (March 1968): 615-634.

[13] Douglas R. Egerton, "An Update on Jacksonian Historiography: The Biographies," *Tennessee Historical Quarterly 46* (1987): 79-85.

[14] Rogin, *Fathers & Children;* Curtis, *Andrew Jackson and the Search for Vindication*, ix; Burstein, *The Passions of Andrew Jackson*.

[15] H.W. Brand, *Andrew Jackson: His Life and Times* (New York: Doubleday, 2005); Wilentz, *Andrew Jackson*; Jon Meacham, *American Lion: Andrew Jackson in the White House* (New York: Random House, 2008).

and the nation, yet also act ruthlessly towards those who opposed him or endangered his vision for the nation's future. In a previous work I argued that from the very outset of Jackson's nationalist appeal, New Orleans, he embodied traits of heroism and despotism. One can readily see both by recognizing the glory in which Jackson achieved victory at the Battle of New Orleans and the tyranny which he used to achieve that victory by illegally declaring martial law and crushing civil liberties. Moreover, there are numerous examples of Jackson's magnanimity and mean spiritedness prior to the Battle of New Orleans. Consider his adoption of an orphaned Native American child in one moment and in another a frontier brawl on the streets of Nashville with Thomas Hart Benton and Jesse Benton.[16]

One can follow these contrasting traits of heroism and despotism throughout Jackson's life and presidency. Hence the reason that historians have continued to express a degree of confusion over Jackson's personality and an inability to draw agreed upon conclusions on what type of an individual and president he was. Certainly, some pro-Jackson historians have confronted the rougher, darker aspects of Jackson's personality. John Spencer Bassett noted quite clearly Jackson's "lack of education, his crude judgments in many affairs, his occasional outbreaks of passion, his habitual hatreds of those enemies with whom he had not made friends for political purposes, and his crude ideas of some political policies."[17] Nevertheless, the contrasting Jackson, the man of passion and the man of the people, has yet to be fully accepted by scholars.

One of the problems is that historians, especially those who depict only Jackson's negative qualities, perceive the contrasting traits of his character as mutually exclusive. In essence, one cannot be both a hero and a despot. If Jackson was brutal towards his enemies, brooked no tolerance when it came to matters of honor and the Union's survival, and failed to possess the more staid, learned qualities of his presidential predecessors, then he could not possibly, some scholars surmise, have embodied the skills and vision to shape the presidency and the nation. The reality, however, is that Jackson possessed all of these traits. He was James Parton's man of contradictions. Had Jackson merely been the apparent lunatic that some historians have depicted, he would have been utterly incapable of achieving success either militarily or politically. He would certainly have to be recognized as the luckiest president in American history.

---

[16] Matthew Warshauer, *Andrew Jackson and the Politics of Martial Law: Nationalism, Civil Liberties and Partisanship* (Knoxville: University of Tennessee Press, 2006).

[17] Bassett, *The Life of Andrew Jackson, vol. 1*, xi.

It is also important to note that though Jackson scholars have continued to debate his character and success as a president, historians overall have accorded him a great deal of respect. He has consistently been rated as one of the nation's top presidents from the time that historian Arthur M. Schlesinger first created a presidential poll in 1948, to those polls that came over the next forty years, as well as the one recently conducted by Schlesinger's son, Arthur M. Schlesinger, Jr., in 1997. Each and every one of the rankings has placed George Washington, Abraham Lincoln, and Franklin Delano Roosevelt in the category of greatness, and, in varying order, Thomas Jefferson, Jackson, James K. Polk, Theodore Roosevelt, Woodrow Wilson, and Harry S. Truman in the category of near greatness. It should also come as no surprise that one poll which measured both great and controversial presidents found Jackson to finish in both categories. Schlesinger, Jr., concluded, "Great presidents possess, or are possessed by, a vision of an ideal America. Their passion is to make sure the ship of state sails on the right course." Moreover, he wrote, "Great Presidents have a deep connection with the needs, anxieties, dreams of the people."[18]

Jackson unquestionably possessed such presidential qualities. Despite his passion, his penchant for grudges, his vanity, and his legendary temper, the seventh president, by the time he entered the White House, had a vision for America that furthered the growing democracy that was already underway since the Revolution. Even prior to becoming president he had an unyielding devotion to the preservation and expansion of the Union. These beliefs alone defy Andrew Burstein's notion that "Jackson had conceived no political direction for the country."[19] His political and military creed was the protection and expansion of a still fledgling and fragile Union. His political direction in the aftermath of the 1824 presidential election later included what he understood as the will of the people. As James Parton, who was no fan of many Jacksonian policies, wrote some one hundred and fifty years ago: "Andrew Jackson loved the people, the common people, the sons and daughters of toil, as truly as they loved him.... He was in accord with his generation. He had a clear perception that the toiling millions are not a class in the community, but *are* the community. He knew and felt that government

---

[18] Arthur M. Schlesinger, *Life Magazine, 25* (1 November 1948): 65-66; Robert K. Murray and Tim H. Blessing, "The Presidential Performance Study: A Progress Report," *Journal of American History 71, No. 3* (December 1983): 535-555; Arthur M. Schlesinger, Jr., "Rating the Presidents: Washington to Clinton," *Political Science Quarterly 112, No. 2* (Summer, 1997): 179-190.

[19] Burstein, *The Passions of Andrew Jackson*, book flap.

should exist only for the benefit of the governed; that the strong are strong only that they may aid the weak."[20]

This definition of democracy and Jackson's devotion to it is today in many ways as much a paradox as was Jackson himself. The democracy of this era did not include women, blacks, or Native Americans, certainly the weakest members of the "community" and the ones in most need of protection. Yet in Jackson's day and before, they were not included within the nation's understanding of democracy. These groups were not in Thomas Jefferson's thoughts when he framed the Declaration of Independence, which ultimately opened the gates of democracy with the idea that "all men are created equal." Jackson's democracy, built on this precept, did not consider the needs of any group other than white men. Understanding this fact, historians must evaluate the seventh president within the context of his own time.

One of the particularly difficult aspects of judging Jackson in the late twentieth and early twenty-first century is the changing ethical and cultural standards of the nation since the time that Jackson served as president. He was an unrepentant slaveholder and responsible for the 1830 Indian Removal Act that eventually resulted in the infamous 1838 Trail of Tears in which thousands of Cherokees died on their way west of the Mississippi River. These too are the legacies, however repugnant, of Andrew Jackson.

In today's America, a nation in which multiculturalism and racial tolerance is taught in our schools, Jackson stands up as a poster-child for all that was wrong with the United States of the nineteenth century. One can argue that for contemporary Americans it is Jackson's treatment of Native Americans for which he is most known. I have certainly found this to be the case for the many students in my courses. Internet petitions call for the removal of Jackson from the twenty dollar bill specifically because he "started a trend of genocidal policies against Indians; not only the mass murder of Indians, but the systematic destruction of a culture." Some scholars have agreed. Burstein refers to Jackson as a "destroyer of Indian cultures." Other sources note that today's Cherokees would rather carry two ten dollar bills than one bill which carries the image of the man who forced their removal.[21]

---

[20] Parton, *Life of Andrew Jackson*, 699.
[21] "Remove Jackson from the Twenty," http://www.petitiononline.com/2047/petition.html (accessed January 5, 2007); Burstein, *The Passions of Andrew Jackson, 6*; Christina Berry, "Andrew Jackson – The Worst President the Cherokee Ever Met," *All Things Cherokee*, http://www.allthingscherokee.com/atc_sub_culture_feat_events_020201.html (accessed January 5, 2007).

One simply cannot dismiss or condone Jackson's racist, culturally destructive policies. Yet we can contextualize them and judge the seventh president by the standards of his own time rather than by our far more multicultural accepting views that are a direct result of the Civil Rights upheaval of the 1950s through the 1970s. Whereas there were certainly some Americans who opposed the government's removal policy, the mass of Americans, especially those in the South and West, enthusiastically supported it. For their part, those in the Northeast had already effectively wiped out the tribes that had inhabited that region and thus some New Englanders in Jackson's day were free to express a rather ironic concern over the plight of Indians.[22]

The primary question for Jackson, with respect to Indians, is, was he attempting genocide or ethnic cleansing? Was his goal to wipe out Indian culture? Was he, as some have questioned, an American Hitler? Historians have debated this point and, as with all else regarding Jackson's record, disagreed.[23] While more will be said on Jacksonian Indian policy later in this book, it is nevertheless important for readers to begin thinking about that policy, and Jackson overall, within the context of the day in which he lived. As Sean Wilentz recently wrote, "All efforts to judge Andrew Jackson by political standards other than his own, and those of his time, are doomed from the start." Lorman Ratner made a similar plea, insisting, "Andrew Jackson's rise as a political leader can be understood best by placing him in the context of the political culture of which he was a part."[24]

For Jackson, battling Native Americans and ultimately removing them west of the Mississippi was not an attempt at genocide, nor was it an attempt to utterly destroy their culture. It was in Jackson's mind a policy of national defense, expansion, and resource attainment. Granted, that policy was racist

---

[22] Francis Jennings, *The Invasion of America: Indians, Colonialism, and the Cant of Conquest* (New York: W. W. Norton & Company, 1976); Francis Jennings, *Empire of Fortune: Crowns, Colonies and Tribes in the Seven Years War in America* (New York: W. W. Norton & Company, 1990); David Stannard, *American Holocaust: The Conquest of the New World* (New York: Oxford University Press, 1993).

[23] Carl Byker, "The Two Andrew Jacksons: Was 'Old Hickory' a Great President or an American Hitler?" *Los Angeles Times*, December 12, 2007; the following is a very limited overview of works on Jacksonian Indian policy: Rogin, *Fathers & Children*; Robert Remini, *The Legacy of Andrew Jackson: Essays on Democracy, Indian Removal, and Slavery* (Baton Rouge: Louisiana State University Press, 1988); Jeanne and David Heidler, *Old Hickory's War: Andrew Jackson and the Quest for Empire*, (Mechanicsburg: Stackpole Books, 1996); John Buchanan, *Jackson's Way: Andrew Jackson and the People of the Western Waters* (New York: John Wiley & Sons, 2001); Robert Remini, *Andrew Jackson and His Indian Wars* (New York: Viking, 2001); Burstein, *The Passions of Andrew Jackson*.

[24] Wilentz, *Andrew Jackson*, 6; Ratner, *Andrew Jackson and His Tennessee Lieutenants*, 1.

and utterly unfair, focusing soley on benefits to whites, but it was unquestionably about America's security and growth. Equally important, it was not a policy that began or ended with Andrew Jackson. One can reasonably argue that had Jackson never been born, the fate of Native Americans in the United States would have been no different. Perhaps the timing of removal might have changed, but the ultimate outcome would not.

The path for the indigenous peoples of the New World began with the arrival of Europeans, and their policy became the policy of Euro-Americans. Even Thomas Jefferson, who viewed Native Americans as people in a true state of nature and capable of being "civilized," understood that some Indians would have to move west of the Mississippi and those who attempted to fight the United States must be dealt with harshly:

> "Our settlements will gradually circumscribe and approach the Indians, and they will in time either incorporate with us as citizens of the United States, or remove beyond the Mississippi. The former is certainly the termination of their history most happy for themselves; but, in the whole course of this, it is essential to cultivate their love. As to their fear, we presume that our strength and their weakness is now so visible that they must see we have only to shut our hand to crush them, and that all our liberalities to them proceed from motives of pure humanity only. Should any tribe be fool-hardy enough to take up the hatchet at any time, the seizing the whole country of that tribe, and driving them across the Mississippi, as the only condition of peace, would be an example to others, and a furtherance of our final consolidation."[25]

One Jefferson scholar accurately reflected upon the third president's policy, explaining, "Jeffersonian legacy is ironic, given that Jefferson as a scholar, diplomat, and Secretary of State was an ardent supporter of Indian sovereignty and eventual citizenship. Yet these views were subordinated during his presidency to concerns of what we would term 'national security,' to preserve the Union, and to advance the interests and needs of his political party." Another scholar insisted that "When Jefferson became President, he set aside the restraints established by Washington and encouraged the rush of conquest into the West....'Indian policy' became simplified into two alternatives: removal or eradication. By 1804, those two courses of action

---

[25] Thomas Jefferson to Governor William H. Harrison, February 27, 1803, in The Writings of Thomas Jefferson, *Albert Ellery Bergh, ed., vol. 10*, (Washington, D.C.: The Thomas Jefferson Memorial Association, 1907), 368-373.

became ordained—one might say decreed—by a new sovereign gathering power in the South and West: King Cotton."[26]

Jefferson's fellow Virginian, James Monroe, concluded well before Jackson's presidency that Indians were not sovereign and should be removed beyond the Mississippi. In his "First Inaugural Address," Monroe insisted, "We have treated them as independent nations, without their having any substantial pretension to that rank....Their sovereignty over vast territories should cease." He followed up in his "Second Inaugural" by announcing, "The removal of the tribes from the territory which they now inhabit...would not only shield them from impending ruin, but promote their welfare and happiness."[27] These were the arguments that Jackson embraced. Clearly, he was not the sole architect, nor the originator of such a policy. Readers might also consider the extent to which American foreign policy to this very day, focused upon access to resources, expansion of U.S. markets, and the extension of democracy, and with it capitalism, has caused our government to interfere, often militarily, in the affairs of other nations. Jackson's era, much like our own, was consumed with violence and power, all in the rather paradoxical midst of fighting for liberty and democracy. We can also question the degree to which our government and nation has attempted to right the wrongs done to Native American in the aftermath of policies that for some three hundred years have crushed, corralled, and created poverty among their peoples. Andrew Jackson deserves rebuke for his beliefs and actions, but we must also recognize that in terms of those beliefs and actions he was, as with his visions of democracy, America's everyman. This is one reason why John William Ward, in his seminal work, *Andrew Jackson: Symbol for an Age*, insisted that the General was a representative and an embodiment of American nationalism.[28] Jackson's views were the views of most Americans and, paradoxically, built into his wider commitment to democracy. To a large degree, the expansion of American democracy relied upon the subordination of non-Americans. One could argue that in this regard little has changed, even in the aftermath of World War II.

---

[26] Stephen Bragaw, "Thomas Jefferson and the American Indian Nations: Native American Sovereignty and the Marshall Court," *Journal of Supreme Court History 31, no. 2* (2006): 155-180; see also, Anthony F.C. Wallace, *Jefferson and the Indians: The Tragic Fate of the First Americans* (Cambridge: Belknap Press, 1999); Roger G. Kennedy, *Burr, Hamilton, and Jefferson: A Study in Character* (New York: Oxford University Press, 1999), 241.

[27] James Monroe, "First Annual Message," March 4, 1817, "Second Annual Message," March 4, 1821, *The American Presidency Project*, http://www.presidency.ucsb.edu (accessed June 16, 2007);.

[28] John William Ward, *Andrew Jackson: Symbol For An Age* (New York: Oxford, 1953).

Jackson's racial proclivities can also be used to explain, though not justify, his support of slavery. Like so many of the nation's early leaders, Jackson embraced the slave system. At one time he owned upwards of one hundred and fifty slaves and never questioned the morality of doing so. Moreover, he did not emancipate a single slave at the time of his death. Without question, Jackson considered blacks inferior to whites. Again, to our contemporary sensibilities such views are anathema, but consider how long it took for most Americans to embrace the idea of racial equality and the degree to which race issues in America remain controversial today. One can reasonably argue that the racial divide between African and white Americans continues as a prominent dilemma in the United States. In terms of Jackson's treatment of and feelings for slaves, he can be reconciled as a typical paternal slaveholder.[29]

The primary point in understanding Jackson's treatment of Native American and slaves is that he was born into a world that embraced and for the most part condoned – in the South slave owning was a mark of status – the views that Jackson himself held. From the larger historical vantage point this does not mean that we should simply forget the negatives of the early republic and chalk them up to some simplistic notion that the Founders can be "let off the hook" for their reprehensible social views. Rather, the point is to understand that societies evolve; changes take place that, hopefully, result in the valuing of racial, cultural, and economic diversity. Drawing such conclusions does not approve the past. It allows us to learn from it and progress beyond it. To condemn without context is folly.

The issues that surrounded Jackson and were most controversial in his own day involved the president's battle against the Bank of the United States and the expansion of the burgeoning market economy, as well as the question of the Union's perpetuity in the Nullification controversy. Some historians have argued that the Bank War was the most substantial issue in Jackson's presidency.[30] Believing the bank to be unconstitutional, a monopoly, and too powerful an influence in the American economy, Jackson vetoed its re-charter by the Congress in 1832. In the rapidly growing market economy of the early republic, the veto was, as with everything that Jackson did, viewed in drastically different ways. Supporters believed that Jackson had saved them

---

[29] For more on Jackson's ownership of slaves see, Matthew Warshauer, "Andrew Jackson: Chivalric Slave Master," *Tennessee Historical Quarterly*, 65 (Fall 2006): 203-229.

[30] Marvin Meyers, *The Jacksonian Persuasion: Politics and Belief* (Stanford: Stanford University Press, 1957); Harry L. Watson, *Liberty and Power: The Politics of Jacksonian America* (New York: Noonday, 1990).

from the "Monster Bank," with its special governmental privilege and incredible economic power. Jackson's slaying of the bank was, for his followers, the ultimate devotion to the protection of the people. Opponents saw Jackson's veto as something else: personal, vengeful, economically short-sighted, and a prime example of the president's abuse of power and unfitness for the executive office. On this, too, historians have had difficulty coming to a general consensus. One must also recognize that, as with everything else regarding Jackson, the veto was highly politicized. The bank's re-charter was specifically pushed four years early by Jackson's political enemies, namely Henry Clay, so that it would coincide with the 1832 presidential election and thus harm Jackson's re-election.

Whereas historians who focus on the Bank War during Jackson's presidency are correct to highlight its importance, the Nullification crisis and the ensuing definition of Union that resulted from that conflict are equally important. When South Carolina held a convention in 1832 and determined that the tariff laws of the United States were no longer constitutional and would not be enforced within the state, insisting further that any attempt to implement the laws would result in secession, it sparked a crisis that debated and defined the meaning of Union. At no other time prior to the Civil War did Americans witness such a challenge to the nation's very existence or the power of its federal government. Jackson's stand, his devotion to Union, and the definition of that Union as outlined in his "Nullification Proclamation" are as crucial to understanding his presidency as is the Bank War and helps to further define his vision for the nation and his role as a constitutional thinker who defended the nation's perpetuity. None other than Abraham Lincoln, some thirty years later, lauded Jackson's views of Union when the Civil War rocked the nation. At that time, many of Lincoln's followers looked to Jackson as the great defender and insisted that a president with strength and conviction, another Jackson, was needed to preserve the nation.

For good or bad, readers should also be aware of the extent to which Jackson was at the forefront of presidential milestones. He was the first president born in a log cabin to common people, rather than within an aristocratic family. He was not well educated, as were most previous presidents. Jackson was also the first president (this was prior to his gaining office) to have killed another man in a duel. He was the first president to embrace the power of the veto, utilizing it more than any of the previous presidents combined. Jackson is also the first and only president in the nation's history to pay off the national debt, yet he also spent more on federal internal improvements than any of his predecessors combined. Finally, Jackson was the first president to have suffered an assassination attempt. In many ways these varying firsts further define Jackson's character and complexity.

In the end, historians and Americans may never agree on Andrew Jackson. In many ways, Jackson is an outstanding figure for students to engage and in doing so gain a better understanding of historical interpretation and the nature of historiography. Perhaps with continued investigation, especially the Jackson Papers project at the University of Tennessee, new information will be revealed that will help us to define more clearly and reassess Jackson's role in the early republic. My feeling, however, is that this is doubtful. After many carefully researched works on Jackson, historians are still unable to draw a consensus on his character and presidency. That I am attempting to engage in a balanced, context driven biography that takes seriously the arguments of both pro- and anti-Jackson scholars leaves me with no delusions about the potential success of such an endeavor. After teaching students about Jackson for many years, always with a mind towards presenting an objective assessment of his actions and personality, I inevitably get students who are impressed with his drive and determination, his devotion to the Union – and those who are repulsed by his vengeance, intolerance, and especially the actions that led to the Trail of Tears. It seems that on an almost gut level, people either identify with or are repulsed by Andrew Jackson. I imagine that the same was true in his own day. He was both horrific and heroic, and any attempt to focus on one without the other not only distorts Jackson, but the age that bears his name. In Jackson one can see both the good and the evil that was and is America. Understanding his motivations and beliefs may very well help us to understand our own.

Chapter 1

JACKSON'S EARLY YEARS: LASTING TRAUMA OR HARDENED YOUTH?

INTERPRETATION AND CONTEXT

In recent decades historians have focused intensely on the great trauma of Andrew Jackson's life. Surmising that the premature deaths of his brothers and mother during the American Revolution left Jackson suffering from survivor's guilt and scarred for life, some scholars theorize that as a result Jackson lashed out at anyone and anything that challenged his right to survive. James Curtis, for example, drew upon Freudian psychoanalysis to understand the death of Jackson's family, insisting, "The tragedy left deep scars on Andrew Jackson's personality," and "For the rest of his life, Andrew Jackson tried to resolve the awful anxieties of this adolescent trauma."[31]

Michael Paul Rogin joined Curtis in analyzing Jackson's youth, yet went even further down the psychoanalytical road by engaging such classic Freudian topics as Jackson's relationship with his mother, oral fixation, elements of sexual anger, and disturbances in the parasympathetic nervous system. He concluded,

> "Those with early tensions in the maternal tie, later traumas, or culturally created anxieties but nurturing relationships are particularly sensitive to primitive feelings of anger and loss. Aggression is often the servant of desire,

---

[31] Curtis, *Andrew Jackson and the Search for Vindication,* 11, 12; Curtis and Rogin even exchanged manuscripts prior to their publication, thanking one another in the acknowledgments.

instrumental to attain a love object. But a man in the grip of primitive rage wants vengeance for wounds to the core of the self. Sources of rage deriving from separation anxiety are intense, fantasy-ridden, and ego-destructive. They devour the self, and express fears of being devoured. The self experiences primitive rages as ego- and world-destroying; such rages are often called maddened. They characterize Jackson, and he gained his mature political power from his ability to sublimate them."

Rogin continued by insisting that Jackson's "childhood and adolescence, I believe, produced buried rage against his mother for at once dominating him, abandoning him, and denying him nurture."[32]

One of the key difficulties in embracing Curtis' and Rogin's theories are the very fact that they are so theoretical, based on a psychoanalytical technique that is predicated on contact and deep analysis of the actual subject. Jackson was long dead by the time these historians laid his corpse upon the therapeutic couch in an attempt to divine the inner demons of his youth. Indeed, Curtis admits, "No record of his exact thoughts exists, but his subsequent behavior suggests that he was consumed with anger and guilt." Rogin acknowledges the same difficulty: "We have, of course, no clinical evidence to root Jackson's rage in early childhood experience."[33] Nevertheless, these historians have utilized this tenuous, theory-dependant explanation to categorize all of Jackson's later actions as an adult. Other historians have embraced the theory.[34]

To be sure, there is little doubt that one's experiences in youth influence adult development, but it is naïve to assume that there is no ability on the part of the individual to come to grips with past problems and build one's life on that understanding. Indeed, every day we encounter those who have done so. The key question, then, is whether Jackson was able to rise above the tragedy of his adolescence. Essentially, were Jackson's early and later years primarily characterized by lasting trauma or hardened youth?

Oddly, one of the best histories of Jackson's early years has gone largely unnoticed by Jacksonian historians. In *Young Hickory: The Making of Andrew Jackson*, Hendrik Booraem engages in a detailed study of the young Jackson,

---

[32] Rogin, *Fathers and Children*, 45, 46; see chapter two, "Andrew Jackson: The Family Romance," in particular.

[33] Curtis, *Andrew Jackson and the Search for Vindication*, 10; Rogin, *Fathers and Children*, 45.

[34] The following is a very brief example: Cole, *The Presidency of Andrew Jackson*, x; John F. Marszalek, *The Petticoat Affair: Manners, Mutiny, and Sex in Andrew Jackson's White House* (New York: The Free Press, 1997), 13. See especially, chapter one. For an additional example of Jackson as the product of his orphaned youth, see Heidler and Heidler, *Old Hickory's War*, 18-19.

even traveling to Ireland in order to gain a better understanding of the clan culture that the Jacksons brought to America when they emigrated in 1765. And, indeed, it is in part an understanding of that culture which is imperative to fully understand Jackson. Of his early years and the penchant of some historians to claim that he was heavily influenced by trauma and that he was lost within his own community, Booraem states:

> "Some twentieth-century biographers have used Parton's data [James Parton's 1860 biography] to depict the young AJ either as a young psychopath, inarticulate and "choked with rage" (Rogin, 42), or as a backwoods country bumpkin, "cantankerous and extremely defensive," whose underlying pathology was masked…by "mimicry and crude levity" (Curtis, 8). Neither approach is tenable, even in terms of the little evidence that exists. Parton's account suggests that AJ was a boy favored by the adults of his community, from whom good things were expected; in no way the dull, slobbering bully that Rogin portrays. Curtis seems to blame AJ for the mores of the backcountry; crude levity and an appetite for fighting were part of Carolina Irish male behavior and in no way unique to AJ."[35]

Ultimately, Booraem does not dispute that Jacksons early years shaped his adulthood, even concluding that by the age of twenty-one Jackson was essentially the person he would be for the remainder of his life. The difference is that Booraem's Jackson was far more akin to James Parton's contradictory, complex man: "a willingness to challenge older and more powerful people, regardless of proprieties; an immense self-confidence in spite of a deficient education; a touchy concern about his personal image and public perceptions of his 'character'; an unhesitating resort to a quick, simple, and…violent method of handling a problem; and in the end, a levelheaded perception of reality."[36] This Jackson, as I have argued elsewhere, was supremely confident in his own abilities, to such a degree of vanity that he believed himself to always be right. This caused problems with his adult familial relationships, in his role as a military commander, and as president. The headstrong Jackson was an ambitious man of action whose military and political successes would most certainly have been impossible had he suffered the psychological impairment that some historians assert.[37]

No one can deny that Jackson's youth, including the trauma of his family's death, shaped his personality. Yet rather than crumbling into some

---

[35] Booraem, *Young Hickory*, note #18, 231.
[36] Booraem, *Young Hickory*, xii.
[37] Warshauer, *Andrew Jackson and the Politics of Martial Law*, 4-5.

sort of debilitated lunatic who constantly needed to prove himself, Jackson forged the already formidable young man he was before the deaths of his brothers and mother into an even more, sometimes overpowering person. Such a conclusion regarding Jackson's personality does not end disputes over the positive or negative results of his leadership – his role as a general and president can and should be debated. The primary point here is quite simple: it is simplistic and untenable to theorize that Jackson was so psychologically crippled that he was incapable of true leadership. It is essential for historians and readers to come to grips with the question of Jackson's "trauma" because it has been used to explain away otherwise complex issues that Jackson engaged as one of the nation's leading men, the Bank War and Nullification, for example.

THE EARLY YEARS

The basics of Jackson's youth are well known by historians. In 1765, his father and mother, Andrew and Elizabeth Hutchinson Jackson, embarked with their two small boys, Hugh and Robert, on the challenging and, hopefully, promising voyage from Ireland to America. The Jacksons certainly did not engage in a solitary endeavor into the wilds of the Carolina countryside. Betty Jackson's family, the Hutchinsons, which included six sisters, had settled en masse along the North/South Carolina border by the early 1760s. Though the Jacksons were in a new land, the clan ties that were an essential part of their Irish world were still firmly in place. More than one historian has noted in particular that we cannot begin to understand Jackson and the immediate circle of friends from his early years without comprehending the Ulster-Scot, or Scotch-Irish, world of their fathers and that cultural stability on the American frontier came from an earlier time and place.[38]

Upon arrival the Jacksons settled in the Waxhaw region, which straddled the boundary line between the two Carolinas. One difficulty of this fact has been the ever-disputed point of where exactly the young Andrew was born. Throughout his life, Jackson himself insisted it was South Carolina, but

---

[38] Booraem, *Young Hickory*, 2-3; Ratner, *Andrew Jackson and His Tennessee Lieutenants*, 8-9; Kerby Miller, *Emigrants and Exiles: Ireland and the Irish Exodus to North America* (New York: Oxford University Press, 1985); Charles Fanning, *New Perspectives on the Irish Diaspora* (Carbondale: Southern Illinois University Press, 2000); Patrick Griffen, *The People with No Name: Ireland's Ulster-Scots, America's Scotch-Irish, and the Creation of a British Atlantic World* (Princeton: Princeton University Press, 2001).

Hendrik Booraem notes that oral tradition persists that North Carolina was his birthplace. In any regard, what is clear is the fact that Jackson was born on March 15, 1767, at a time of family tragedy. A few months earlier his father had died suddenly. The Jackson family had been unable to adequately prepare the land on which they settled, and with two small children and a newborn, Betty Jackson retreated to the security of her sister Jane Crawford's home, where she and her boys resided for the next fourteen years.[39]

The possibility of such tragedies was one of the very reasons that Andrew, Sr., and Elizabeth had settled close by her relatives, so that the clan reliance critical to life in Ireland would also exist in America. James Curtis has asserted that due to Andrew, Sr.'s, death, Elizabeth and her sons were essentially thrown into a familial limbo – no home of their own, no clear father figure, perpetual guests in another's house. The difficulty in this account is two-fold: first, it is conjecture for which Curtis has no evidence. Second, it defies the reality of the clan network that had served the Ulster Scots, and so many other cultures, for centuries. Indeed, Booraem explained not only this point, but the importance of the Presbyterian church community in the Waxhaws as well as the understanding of the Jackson boys regarding their living situation: "To them the Crawford house was home and the Crawford boys were brothers."[40] There is simply no evidence to dispute this point and much to support it. Moreover, one should keep in mind that such clan support remained with Jackson throughout his life. As an adult he regularly took in and adopted his wife Rachel Donelson's nieces and nephews, as well as friends' and neighbors' children, providing them with a stable home. In doing so, Jackson extended the very clan network in which he had been raised. There were some seventeen legal wards and perhaps more.

There are numerous stories that abound from Jackson's youth regarding his feisty personality and penchant for violence. One such account told of the eight-year-old Andy as the butt of other boys' jokes when he was given a musket with a large charge of powder that knocked him off of his feet. Jackson's reaction was instant. Springing to his feet, he announced, "By G-d, if any of you laughs, I'll kill him." One could spend countless hours and pages speculating as to the inner meaning of such an outburst, but it is just as

---

[39] Booraem, *Young Hickory*, 10-13.
[40] Curtis, *Andrew Jackson and the Search for Vindication*, 2-5; Booraem, *Young Hickory*, 17. Booraem also stated, on page 25, "This was the kind of community where the young Andrew Jackson grew up—tightly knit with bonds of kinship and tradition, religion and neighborhood, a settlement where hunting and song, whiskey and doctrine, fighting and feasting were all important."

reasonably to conclude, as Booraem has, that here was a boy who lived in a community in which bravery and toughness were prized, and therefore refused to be ridiculed and played the fool by other boys. Jackson's early toughness was also known from other stories. One former school-mate remembered their wrestling matches: "I could throw him three times out of four, but he would never *stay throwed*. He was dead game, even then, and never *would* give up."[41] Was Jackson's determination pathology or boyish competitiveness?

Certain of Jackson's physical ailments are also favorites of those who analyze his youth for indications of deep-seated problems. The young Jackson was known to have slobbered a bit when speaking, to which Rogin surmised that "slobbering, commonly derive from tensions in the early maternal tie."[42] Jackson also suffered from the "big itch" and Curtis asserted, "He was often cantankerous and extremely defensive. In part this sensitivity had physical origins. He was never robust and early in life suffered from a serious skin disease known as the 'big itch,' which no doubt added to his irascibility." Once again, the problem regarding Curtis' conclusions are two-fold: first, most accounts, the bulk of which are taken from Parton, reveal that Jackson may have been slight for his age, but was quite "robust" and very physically active. Indeed, "He was," according to Parton, "exceedingly fond of running foot-races, of leaping the bar, and jumping; and in such sports he was excelled by no one of his years." Second, the big itch, or scabies as it is known in medical terms, was caused by microscopic insects, and a common affliction among the Ulster Scots at the time.[43] Jackson was hardly singular in his contraction of the ailment and it is therefore simplistic and overdone to attribute itching as a daunting component to be featured in his youthful agony.

Prior to and into the early years of the Revolution, Jackson, just approaching his teens, had been on a promising path. Elizabeth Jackson hoped that her youngest son would become a Presbyterian minister, and she therefore focused more on Andrew's education than she did her older two boys'. After intermittently attending a local school to learn the basics of reading and writing, Jackson was sent in 1776 to live with his uncle, Captain Robert

---

[41] See Parton for the incident. James Parton, *The Life of Andrew Jackson, vol. 1* (New York, Mason Brothers, 1861), 46; Booraem, *Young Hickory*, 17.

[42] Parton, *The Life of Andrew Jackson*, 64; Rogin, *Fathers and Children*, 45; Remini also wrestled with Rogin's interpretation on this matter. See, Remini, *Andrew Jackson: The Course of American Empire*, 10.

[43] Parton, *The Life of Andrew Jackson*, 64; Booraem, *Young Hickory*, 29; Reuben Friedman, *Scabies – Civil and Military: Its Prevalence, Prevention and Treatment* (New York: Froben Press, 1941); James G. Leyburn, *The Scotch-Irish: A Social History* (Chapel Hill, The University of North Carolina Press, 1962), 152-153.

Crawford, still in the Waxhaws, to attend an academy that taught Latin, Greek, and mathematics. This higher level of schooling revealed both a belief in Jackson's abilities as well as expectations for his future. The surviving evidence reveals, as does Jackson's adult life, that he was never enamored of reading the classics. He certainly did not come close to the educational background or broad classical training of other early presidents. He did reveal a talent with words, which is evidenced in a number of later addresses to his military troops, as well as some of his presidential papers. Of one thing, there is no doubt: early on Jackson revealed competitiveness, cleverness, and confidence, as well as a desire to lead that inevitably shaped his adult personality.[44]

It was 1779 that brought the beginning of Jackson's collapsing world. Previously, the Revolution was something that had been discussed and debated among those in the Waxhaws. There existed in the region sympathies for independence as well as loyalty to King George III. During the spring, news of a British attack on Charles Town (now Charleston) arrived and many men of the Waxhaws mounted their horses and rode out in mid-June to aid in the revolutionary cause. Jackson's uncle, Captain Crawford, was among them, as was Andrew's oldest brother, Hugh. The first tragedy came shortly thereafter, when news of Hugh's death arrived. He had apparently engaged in a battle even though sick, and subsequently collapsed from exhaustion and died.[45]

The next year, 1780, things worsened for South Carolina and the Waxhaws. In May, the British arrived en masse and captured Charles Town. Shortly after, the infamous British commander Lieutenant Colonel Banastre Tarleton and his troops rode through the region (Jackson later stated that he saw Tarleton and his dragoons), and proceeded to capture a group of American soldiers, then literally hack them to pieces with swords. The wounded were brought to the Waxhaw meeting house and Jackson witnessed first-hand the reality and violence of war. This was the beginning of his preparation as a soldier. Though too young to fight, he was only thirteen and his mother would allow neither Andrew nor his brother Robert to serve, they nevertheless frequented the local military encampment and learned about drilling and the preparation of soldiers.

Over the next several months Jackson's world continued to be dominated by war and bloodshed. He witnessed, though did not engage in, the August battle at Hanging Rock, and was later forced to flee the Waxhaws with his

---

[44] Booraem, *Young Hickory*, see chapter three, in particular.
[45] Booraem, *Young Hickory,* 47; Remini, *Andrew Jackson: The Course of American Empire,* 15.

relatives and other residents when the British invaded the region. This was surely an unsettling time, and Hendrik Booraem notes that during this period Jackson and his kinfolk disappear from the historical record. The problems of the war were compounded by the fact that it was not simply a matter of revolutionaries versus the British. It was often neighbor against neighbor, which escalated the tensions and lack of security. By the time Jackson and his family returned to the Waxhaws in the late winter-early spring of 1781, the internecine war on the home-front had reached truly dangerous proportions. The defense of their homes had now made the young Jackson and his older brother Robert soldiers in every sense of the word. Both boys found themselves defending neighbors, riding out in skirmishing parties, and ducking Tory and British patrols.[46] It was a dangerous time, and Andrew Jackson's luck was about to run out.

On an evening in April of 1781, Andrew, Robert, and their cousin Tommy Crawford spent the night bedded down in the woods after narrowly escaping capture. The next morning, Tommy rode off to survey the situation. Andrew and Robert were supposed to wait, but soon decided to follow their cousin and learn for themselves what was going on. No sooner had the boys entered the Crawford cabin to have breakfast, than a group of British soldiers led by a Tory neighbor burst upon them. What followed next is a scene that virtually every Jackson biographer has engaged. Ordered to clean a British officer's muddy boots, the young Jackson revealed both his courage and willingness to challenge authority by announcing, "I am a prisoner of war and claim to be treated as such." This impertinence was responded to with a sword blow that narrowly missed cleaving Jackson's head in two, leaving a permanent scar on his hand, which he had used to fend off the strike, as well as on his head. The officer then repeated the order and the sword blow to Robert, who was more seriously wounded than Andrew. The strike was believed to have ultimately resulted in his death. The brothers were then carted off to Camden, where they were thrust into a filthy, smallpox-infested jail. There, the boys languished with other American prisoners. They also witnessed the nearby Battle of Camden from their cell, with the hopes of Continental victory and release. Victory did not come, but release did. A swap was arranged in which several British soldiers were exchanged for the boys from the Waxhaws.

Though Elizabeth Jackson joined the other Waxhaw women to fetch her boys and bring them home, it was immediately apparent that Andrew and

---

[46] Booraem, *Young Hickory*, 49-50, 58, 77; Remini, *Andrew Jackson: The Course of American Empire*, 14-15.

Robert were gravely ill. Robert soon died, and Andrew learned during the drenching rain on the way home that he had contracted smallpox. As he slowly recovered during the month of May, his mother once again engaged her clan duties by riding out to Charles Town to see about the release of other family members from British prison ships. It was not long, July, when Jackson learned that his mother had died from typhus, also known as ship's fever, while aiding sick kinsmen. Young Andrew, though he still had clan ties in the Waxhaws, was alone. His immediate family were all dead.[47]

Here was a true life-altering tragedy that up-ended Jackson's world and forced him to confront insecurity and death. Both of his brothers and his mother, his immediate family, were dead. For historians such as James Curtis and Michael Paul Rogin, Jackson's fate was sealed. He never recovered from the trauma of his family's death and spent the remainder of his days agonizing over this awful event and trying to prove that he was worthy of being the sole Jackson to survive the Revolution. Every subsequent event in his life was dramatically shaped by the trauma. "There were always suitable scapegoats," insisted Curtis, "the Indians, the British, the Bank. Believing himself under attack, Jackson felt exonerated for striking back. The battle enjoined, he could then renew his mission, triumph over the terrible fears that haunted him, and thereby reassert his right to survive."[48] To an extent, one can potentially imagine a reckless, guilt-ridden young man who acted carelessly and achieved little in life; Jackson could have essentially given up.

At the outset, Jackson's sudden adulthood reflected such possibilities. He traveled to Charles Town, gambled, drank, and almost bankrupted himself. Hendrik Booraem even notes that Jackson, like many back country men who had survived the war, engaged "a total fearlessness, a sort of fatalistic feeling that the worst had already happened and that there was nothing left to be terrified of."[49] The issue of how other survivors of the Revolution acted is particularly relevant because many young men had similar experiences to Jacksons. Many lost family members and witnessed the savagery of war. The difficulty with the generalized psychological theories offered by some historians is that most young men with Jackson's life experience should have ended up just like him. Yet the fact is that the personalities of those who engaged in the war were as varied as those who did not. As one reviewer of Rogin's work remarked, "Other children went though the excitements and

---

[47] Parton, *The Life of Andrew Jackson, vol. 1, 89*; Booraem, *Young Hickory*, chapter nine; Remini, *Andrew Jackson: The Course of American Empire*, 20-25.
[48] Curtis, Andrew Jackson and the Search for Vindication, 11.
[49] Booraem, *Young Hickory*, 111.

deprivations of war without imitating Jackson's life. Many teen-age orphans went nowhere, many successful men had surviving parents."[50]

The primary question is, did Jackson overcome the tragedy of his youth? I believe the answer is yes. He did not forget the sacrifices that his family and so many others made during the revolutionary period. Rather, it is entirely reasonable to argue that they instilled in the young Jackson an unquenchable zeal for duty and a fire for safeguarding his immediate community and the Union. He also remembered his mother as a woman who had unselfishly given her life for others and instilled in him a sense of duty and commitment. The Revolution taught Jackson that dangers were ever present and that one way to solve them was through violence. Even James Curtis noted that in Jackson's world "violence and bloodshed became accepted means of resolving conflict." Historian Harry Watson explained, "Personal violence was commonplace on the Carolina frontier, and young Andrew Jackson grew up certain that a well-known willingness to repay violence with more violence was essential to a respected man's reputation."[51] Booraem insisted that Jackson embraced a willingness to take on hazards and potentially death in order to move both himself and the nation forward.

If anything, Jackson was emboldened by the circumstances of his life. He picked himself up, brushed off, and continued a path that an already formidable ambition had directed. After a brief time he determined that the best way to escape the season to season, dirt-laden existence of the Waxhaws was to engage in the study of the law and achieve distinction as a part of the aristocracy.

JACKSON'S PATH TO SUCCESS

It was in the midst of the war that Jackson first experienced a life different from that which he had known in the Waxhaws. In 1781 and 1782, many of the Charles Town social elite were forced to flee the city due to British occupation. As a result, some of these well-to-do resided for a time in and around the Waxhaw region and gave Andrew his first glimpse of refined

---

[50] Lewis Perry, *Review of Fathers and Children: Andrew Jackson and the Subjugation of the American Indian*, by Michael Paul Rogin, *History and Theory 16, no. 2* (May, 1997): 174-195.

[51] Curtis, *Andrew Jackson and the Search for Vindication*, 3; Harry L. Watson, *Andrew Jackson vs. Henry Clay: Democracy and Development in Antebellum America* (New York: Bedford/St. Martin's, 1998), 24.

manners and fashionable gentry. If this was not enough to spark the young Jackson's aspirations, shortly thereafter, in late 1782 or early 1783 at the age of sixteen, he accompanied his uncle Major Robert Crawford to Charles Town, the state's main port. As Booraem noted, "For a boy brought up in the Waxhaws, coming to Charleston meant experiencing a succession of strange sights, sounds, and smells from the time he first arrived at the Town Gate on Charles Town Neck."[52] This was the first of two journeys to the city, the second of which Andrew imparted on by himself about a year later. One of the trips may have had something to do with a modest inheritance. Various stories abound, whether he received money from an Irish grandfather, from the value of his family's meager belongings, or from debts owed to his mother or brothers.[53] Whatever the source, Andrew apparently spent liberally and enjoyed all that Charles Town had to offer. One of his favorite places was the horse racing track, where he mingled with the elite, learned the rituals related to the sport, how to judge fine horses, and, as his early biographer Henry Lee, wrote, observed the "unstudied elegance of air" and "the carriage of polite society."[54] The race track remained a favorite place for Jackson throughout the remainder of his life. He also apparently managed to pay some of his bills through various gambling skills.

Jackson learned other important lessons while visiting Charles Town. One was the social necessity of having a servant. Another was how gentlemen settled disputes. Like horse racing, there were rules and proper ceremony that had to be observed. Jackson weighed his options and settled on the law as the best means of both earning a living and establishing himself as a gentleman. In order to do so, however, he needed to update his rather spotty book learning and, important for studying the law, grasp some basic Latin. He enrolled in a local Waxhaw school for a period of time and shortly thereafter moved from the area where he had been reared, ultimately settling in Guilford County, North Carolina, and later in Salisbury to study with and utilize the library of attorney Spruce Macay. Jackson understood the importance of connections and quickly established friendships with young men such as Charles Bruce and Tom Henderson, both of whom came from good families and were involved in the county government. As Booraem noted, Jackson "gravitated to some degree toward the element in North Carolina whose manners were showier, more formal, and more concerned with rank. These were among his concerns

---

[52] Booraem, *Young Hickory*, 120.
[53] Booraem, *Young Hickory*, 122; Remini, *Andrew Jackson: The Course of American Empire*, 27.
[54] Lee, *Memoirs of the War in the Southern Department of the United States*, 6.

too."[55] About halfway through his study of the law, Jackson changed his tutelage to John Stokes, another well reputed attorney, for reasons that are not entirely clear. Nevertheless, he concluded his training and received a license to practice in September of 1787.[56]

Jackson's years as an aspiring law student were hardly devoted solely to study. Nor was he suddenly a refined gentleman who had separated himself entirely from the more juvenile, rambunctious, and intense nature of his backwoods upbringing. He was after all, only twenty. On one occasion he invited, as a joke, two prostitutes to the Christmas ball. The scandal caused by the prank, surmise some historians, may have been the cause of his departure from Spruce Macay's law tutelage. On another occasion Jackson and his friends literally trashed a room at the tavern where they were drinking. They destroyed all of the glasses, the furniture, and even the bed and sheets, then set the whole pile on fire. Here was hardly the man of society he was attempting to become. The historical interpretations of such events, as with everything related to Jackson, runs to extremes. Robert Remini viewed such incidents as harmless, boyhood humor and indiscretion, insisting of the tavern episode, "Oh, it was a tumultuous night, one that was remembered in the town for decades." James Curtis viewed it with a decidedly different slant: "At times…[Jackson's] debts came from bizarre and violent events." The young Jackson earned a reputation as "wild" and "a roaring, rollicking fellow."[57]

These early years also reveal Jackson's willingness to resort to violence if he felt it necessary. No longer, however, were these the times of wrestling matches among friends. In one instance, a man attempted to pick a fight by stepping on Jackson's toes. Jackson dismissed the action as an accident, but when told by friends that it was intentional, and when the "big bullying fellow" attempted it again, Jackson pulled a rail from a nearby fence and jammed the end directly into the man's stomach. "Sir, it doubled him up," explained Jackson later. "He fell at my feet, and I stamped on him. Shortly the man sat up again, and was about to fly at me like a tiger. The bystanders made as though they would interfere. Says I, Gentlemen, stand back—give me room, and I'll manage him. With that I stood ready with the rail pointed. He gave me one look, Sir, and turned away, frightened, a whipped man and feeling like one."[58]

---

[55] Booraem, *Young Hickory*, 147.
[56] Remini, *Andrew Jackson: The Course of American Empire*, 29.
[57] Remini, *Andrew Jackson: The Course of American Empire*, 29; Curtis, *Andrew Jackson and the Search for Vindication*, 13; Booraem, *Young Hickory*, 159.
[58] Booraem, *Young Hickory*, 151.

Oddly enough, that Jackson chose to use a wooden rail rather than his fists reveals that he was embracing lessons of gentlemanly conduct. Fighting was not prohibited. In fact, settling personal disputes was expected of a gentleman and increased his standing in a community that prized honor and bravery. When confronted with someone of lesser social status, however, it was inappropriate for a man of rank to engage in fisticuffs. Thus Jackson used an object instead. Nor did he ever steer away from utilizing violence if it suited him. This, and his penchant for exploding into tirades, has caused disagreement among historians as to whether Jackson was out of control. Remini insisted in a number of works that Jackson could turn his temper on and off for good effect. It cowed opponents. Curtis, however, believed that Jackson was "always at war with himself" and unable to maintain his composure.

These interpretations, in fact, represent one of the underlying themes in the authors' respective works.[59] The truth most certainly rests somewhere in the middle. There are times in Jackson's life when both he and those around him commented on his ability to fume, extort, and thunder from the heavens in order to intimidate others and win a confrontation. Yet there were other incidents in which Jackson's temper truly got the better of him. He was hardly capable of constant self-control and at times revealed why some considered him little more than a raging madman. Examples of both will be discussed later in the book. Though it does not fully explain Jackson's temper, one must remember that he was raised in and later moved to an area that was to a large extent on the outskirts of society. In such settlements, violence and threats from thieves or Indians was an ever-present concern. It was essential for a man in this society to know how to fight. Jackson did, and he was willing to engage in violence to defend his sense of honor and establish himself as a gentleman. The rough and tumble frontier and the violence that went with it were the context of the times in which Jackson lived.

In the aftermath of gaining his law degree, Jackson, according to Curtis, "drifted" for a time and was "unable to find clients." He deduced that the young Jackson was incapable of competing with the established lawyers of the day and therefore decided to flee over the mountains to the Tennessee territory, which was under North Carolina control. Even in making the decision to go west, insisted Curtis, Jackson was hardly "the envy of the legal

---

[59] Remini addressed this subject in *Andrew Jackson: The Course of American Empire*, 32, but focuses on it more specifically in *Andrew Jackson;* Curtis, *Andrew Jackson and the Search for Vindication*, 14; the premise of Burstein's *The Passions of Andrew Jackson* reveals a similar focus as Curtis, as indicated by the title.

profession. Few established lawyers were willing to give up the security of a settled practice for the uncertainty of the frontier." Booraem provided a decidedly different interpretation. Jackson traveled the two-tier court system in the state with fellow lawyers and watched the court room maneuverings of more experienced men. He opted to get his license in the lower, county court to gain experience and earn some money. He decided to go west when his friend John McNairy was appointed superior court judge of Davidson County, a fairly new North Carolina region in the Cumberland settlements established beyond the Appalachian Mountains, and offered Jackson the position of state's attorney for the district. At the outset, it seems that Jackson was not wedded to the idea of permanent settlement in the region. Yet he had no reason to not take the chance and adventure of trying such an opportunity. He was ambitious, tough minded, and young enough to make something of himself. Indeed, he had been preparing his future for just this type of opportunity. The facts of the case do not support the notion that he was "drifting" or lacked direction. Moreover, Jackson was not yet an established attorney and therefore had nothing to lose in venturing west.[60]

It was also around this time that Jackson became involved with the Masons. The Masonic Order was an important fraternity that brought men together. George Washington and Benjamin Franklin were well known Masons. In this secret society, social ties were formed that often resulted in advantageous alliances. For Jackson, it was an additional way to continue his gentlemanly path and make more contacts within the gentry. His decision to join the organization was calculated. It was yet another example of Jackson's clear mindedness in preparing for his place in life.

Jackson left for the Cumberland region in the spring of 1788, stopping for a time in Jonesborough, in the eastern portion of the North Carolina district, prior to heading further west to Nashville. Up to this point the young Jackson had done well in establishing himself as a gentleman. He had decided upon the law as a way to improve his status, successfully passed his legal examination, and made important connections that resulted in his appointment as a public prosecutor. This, however, was merely the beginning. While in Jonesborough he took two important steps on his road to further status. First was the acquisition of a slave, an eighteen year old female, "a Negro Woman named Nancy," purchased on November 17, 1788.[61] Jackson had traveled the circuit court in North Carolina with attorneys attended by personal servants and

---

[60] Curtis, *Andrew Jackson and the Search for Vindication*, 15; Booraem, *Young Hickory*, 189-91.
[61] Matthew Warshauer, "Andrew Jackson: Chivalric Slave Master" *Tennessee Historical Quarterly, 65* (Fall 2006): 203-229.

understood that it was an important mark of status. He had also learned this fact during his brief sojourns to Charles Town. It was important that he appear in Nashville with all the accoutrements of the upper class. Historians speculate as to why Jackson purchased a female rather than a male slave, as was customary for a personal servant, but there is no clear answer to such a question.

The second step in Jonesborough involved another important aspect of gentlemanliness: honor. Men of status were expected to act honorably towards one another and in doing so uphold their own honor. This was something about which Jackson remained steadfast throughout his life. Moreover, he needed no lessons on becoming a gentleman to understand the importance of respect. Early on, he had not wanted to lose face when other boys tricked him with an over-charged musket, and his mother had specifically counseled him on the importance of defending his honor. Becoming a gentleman simply solidified a lesson already ingrained in his personality.

Defending one's honor often entailed settling disputes, and for gentlemen this was done through the formal, ritualized code of the duel. Jackson's first duel was surely more about seizing an opportunity to further establish himself as a notable gentleman than it was any great desire to risk his life. While in Jonesborough he represented a number of cases in the court and on one occasion was embarrassed by a more senior attorney, Waightstill Avery. Ironically, or perhaps as an additional source of animosity, Jackson had approached Avery to serve as a potential law teacher but was turned away because Avery had no openings. What initiated the Jonesborough dispute in court is unknown, but Avery, the more seasoned attorney, ultimately embarrassed Jackson in front of the court. The treatment was enough to offend the young man's sense of propriety and cause a formal, written challenge. Jackson wrote:

> "My charector you have injured; and further you have Insulted me in the presence of a court and larg audienc. I therefore call upon you as a gentleman to give me satisfaction for the Same…it is consistent with the character of a gentleman when he Injures a man to make a spedy reparation."[62]

Avery had little choice but to accept. Refusing a formal challenge could brand a man a coward, and Avery had no intention of throwing away his

---

[62] Andrew Jackson to Waightstill Avery, August 12, 1788, in Sam B. Smith and Harriet Chappell Owsley, eds., *The Papers of Andrew Jackson, vol. 1* (Knoxville: University of Tennessee Press, 1980), 12.

reputation. Yet he was also no fool and had no intention of throwing away his life. As was often the case in duels, friends arranged a solution and when the two men met outside of town they merely completed the long established code of the duel. Neither man planned on killing or even injuring the other. They fired their shots into the air, shook hands, and proclaimed satisfaction. Such were the actions of gentlemen. The duel was another advance in Jackson's aristocratic ambitions. As Remini wrote, "When all was said and done, Jackson assured himself that his actions had been totally appropriate and proper and that he proved himself a man of honor and character."[63]

After a number of months, Jackson's westward group joined with others to make the almost 200 mile trek from Jonesborough to Nashville. Traveling in numbers was a matter of safety, and it was on this first jaunt westward that Jackson had his first potential run-in with hostile Indians. After encamping for the night and while the majority of the party slept, Jackson remained awake smoking a corn-cob pipe. At about 10 p.m. he was aroused by the too natural sounds of owls hooting in the distance. Jackson rallied his fellow travelers, broke camp, and moved off from the area as quickly as possible. They learned later that a group of hunters settled in the abandoned camp and were attacked by Indians. Only one of the hunters survived. A year later, Jackson's friend, Judge McNairy, camped in the same vicinity, this time without Jackson, and suffered an Indian attack that killed several in his party.[64] This may very well have been Jackson's lesson that Indians made the western frontier a dangerous place and imparted in him a determination to safeguard his community from such attacks.

THE MEANING OF JACKSON'S YOUTH

Jackson's arrival in Nashville on October 26, 1788 marked both an end and a beginning. It was the end of his boyish youth. He had been forced to grow up quickly. War has such an effect. He faced tragedy, but it did not own him. Everything points to the fact that he raised himself up, made clear decisions about his future, and fulfilled those decisions. Was he a perfect specimen of gentlemanly conduct, coolness, and consideration? Surely not. Jackson always remained rough around the edges, supremely confident to the point of vanity, and something of a tyrant. Hendrik Booraem correctly

---

[63] Remini, *Andrew Jackson: The Course of American Empire*, 38-9.
[64] Parton, *The Life of Andrew Jackson*, 122-4.

surmised, "Two serious weaknesses marred his character: his thirst for risk, which led him into needlessly dangerous enterprises, and his need to control any situation he was in, which made him an unnerving companion, because he was always calculating, and which sometimes found expression in bullying, feigned anger, and unnecessary enmities."[65]

What Jackson was not, however, was the psychologically impaired mess theorized by James Curtis, Michael Paul Rogin, and Andrew Burstein. The evidence simply fails to support such speculations. If the tragedy of the Revolution taught Jackson anything, it was not that he needed to continually prove his right to survive. Rather, it was that there existed friends and enemies. There was no in between. Jackson spent the rest of his life with this stark reality before him. It was a conviction for both his own personal dealings and for the future security of his immediate community and the larger nation. As he grew in age and stature, Jackson achieved positions that allowed him to turn this conviction into action.

---

[65] Booraem, *Young Hickory*, 199.

Chapter 2

THE NASHVILLE FRONTIER AND BUILDING A REPUTATION

Jackson's decision to travel over the Appalachian Mountains and see what the West had to offer is a clear indication of his ambition and desire to rise beyond his Waxhaw beginnings. He had been raised among frontier people and understood the challenges that existed. Indeed, the lessons of the Revolution had for the most part left him with little fear of the future. Really, what did he have to lose? This is a rationale that he carried with him for the remainder of his days and often influenced his decision making. Nor was it merely a rash, reactionary sort of thought. Jackson was more calculating than that. Still, even in accepting this, one can also recognize that he was hardly a man who aspired to be a rational product of Enlightenment thought, like so many of the nation's early leaders. Rather, Jackson was rough around the edges and surely more interested in action than espousing philosophy, even though he did have distinct and growing beliefs about the Union and the frontier's place in it.

The importance of recognizing such points is in understanding that Jackson's views were largely representative of many who lived on the frontier. This is why he ultimately came to be a symbol of America's restless energy, desire for expansion, and the corresponding economic and political power that came with both. What set Jackson apart was his gargantuan ambition and willingness to challenge others for power. Such traits inevitably led to conflict, and Jackson's penchant for settling potential challenges with a quick, decisive act of violence if he deemed it necessary, has caused some to view him as little more than a blood thirsty lunatic, or worse, a victim of psychological trauma.

Other aspects of his life, however, show him to be more complex, careful, and thought provoking than such singular explanations offer.

ARRIVAL, THE LAW, AND SOCIAL CONNECTIONS

In 1788, the Nashville area was little more than a frontier settlement that boasted only a few hundred occupants. Yet it was a region on the rise and this was the very reason that Jackson and his friends opted to check out what the West had to offer. And it offered a great deal. Jackson's friend, John McNairy, now the superior court judge of the region, appointed Jackson as attorney for the Mero District, which comprised Davidson, Sumner, and Tennessee counties. Unfortunately, the position came without pay until Jackson petitioned the North Carolina legislature and received a salary of forty dollars. When the region was ceded to the federal government and set up officially as a federal territory in 1790, the new governor, William Blount, reappointed Jackson, then just twenty-three, as attorney general. In that position he prosecuted eighty-nine criminal cases for the North Carolina and territorial governments. Most were for assault and battery, some for larceny, perjury and horse stealing. On one day in April of 1793 he engaged in eight jury trials and won five of them, though this was hardly a typical schedule.

The real allure of the attorney general position was the status and other opportunities it afforded Jackson, including helping his law practice. One of the great problems in the territory was the failure of debtors to pay property claims. Jackson therefore became an important resource for creditors who wanted to collect what was owed to them. Within two months of his arrival Jackson had a legitimate and busy legal practice. In one month alone he served some seventy writs to those who owed creditors. Davidson County court records reveal that during his first few years in Nashville, Jackson represented between one-fourth and one-half of all the civil court cases. In a single 1789 court session he presented thirteen suits, most related to debt. He also traveled the some 270 miles between Jonesborough and Nashville twenty-two times in order to serve in various cases.[66] Jackson was serious about establishing himself as a lawyer of repute. He was an enterprising, untiring man on the make.

---

[66] The best source for Jackson's legal career is James W. Ely, Jr. and Theodore Brown, Jr., eds., *The Legal Papers of Andrew Jackson* (Knoxville: The University of Tennessee Press, 1987). See in particular the introduction. See also, Remini, *Andrew Jackson: The Course of American Empire*, 45.

Jackson also understood the importance of connections. Upon arrival in Nashville he boarded with one of the well-established families in the territory, the Donelsons. Colonel John Donelson had moved his family to the area and was subsequently killed in 1785. His widow, Rachel Stockley Donelson, continued living in Nashville with a large family that was both respected and connected. Jackson quickly became forever entwined in the Donelson clan. The key reason was his marriage to the widow Donelson's daughter, Rachel. The story of Rachel Donelson Robards and Andrew Jackson is tumultuous and controversial.

According to the account of their courtship provided by Jackson's presidential campaign in the 1820s, upon Jackson's arrival Rachel was already married to Lewis Robards of Kentucky. The two had a stormy relationship in which Robards fumed and exploded at Rachel's alleged flirtations and he supposedly banished her from his Kentucky home. He later asked for forgiveness and journeyed to Nashville to convince her to take him back. Robards had purchased property in the Nashville area and this may be an indication that he had not actually separated from Rachel. By the time Robards did arrive, however, Jackson had entered the picture and, though he insisted that his intentions were honorable and that he had never behaved inappropriately towards Rachel, Robards was suspicious and accusatory. Robards himself had a rather rocky reputation. Not only did his alleged treatment of Rachel indicate his personality, but he was reputed to have been a rather unrepentant adulterer, frequently associating with negro women. He was apparently hyper-jealous, and Jackson's overly confident manner certainly did not help matters. The quarrel grew to the point where Jackson threatened to do Robards bodily harm should he persist in making unsubstantiated claims. A duel was suggested, but never occurred.

Jackson subsequently left the Donelson home for the sake of propriety, and Robards followed suit, insisting that he was done with Rachel for good. He returned to Kentucky with the announced intent of requesting a divorce from the North Carolina legislature, which was required for any divorce proceeding at the time. When news came in the fall of 1790 that Robards was intent on coming back to Nashville and forcing Rachel to return to Kentucky, she opted to escape to Natchez in the Spanish controlled Mississippi territory. Colonel Robert Stark, an old friend of the Donelson family was to escort her. The ultimate difficulty came when Jackson decided to join them. As Robert Remini properly noted, there were plenty of Donelson sons who could have accompanied their sister. There was no need for Jackson to do so. As a result, surmised Remini, "Jackson's decision to accompany the Stark party to

Natchez was either absolute folly or absolute calculation." He should have, or did know, that such an action would push and provide grounds for Robards to sue for divorce. The rub, however, is that Jackson and Rachel allegedly believed that Robards had already received a divorce. With this belief in mind, they supposedly wed in Spanish territory.

The problem with this story is that there exists no record of a marriage in Catholic controlled Mississippi, where records were well kept and marriage proceedings quite strict. Moreover, the timing is off. Jackson and Rachel later claimed that they had returned to Natchez in 1791 and married then. This, however, is a fiction created years later, in 1827, when Jackson ran for the presidency and needed to erase any possibility of an improper relationship with Rachel. At that later time, one of Jackson's very good Tennessee friends, John Overton, whom he had met while both boarded with the Donelson's, rewrote the history of the couple's relationship.

No matter the timing, the two later learned in December of 1793 that Robards had never received a divorce. Rachel was technically an adulteress and the Jacksons were not legally married. They remedied the situation immediately by remarrying. By this time Robards had actually gotten a divorce. Yet the sting of the whole affair followed them both and at one point resulted in a duel between Jackson and a man who dared mention the issue.

There is no simple way to explain away Jackson and Rachel's conduct. As recent research by Ann Toplovich reveals, spousal abandonment was frowned upon even though divorces were extremely difficult to obtain, and was further complicated by questions of jurisdiction and legislation as new states were carved out of what had previously been Virginia and North Carolina territories. To some extent, social guidelines were slightly more relaxed on the frontier and the ultimate approval of a self-imposed divorce and remarriage was dictated by community acceptance. Nonetheless, legislation was moving away from such social customs. What seems certain is that Jackson and Rachel knew what they were doing. Jackson, as an aspiring gentleman and especially as an attorney, should have known better than to supposedly believe that Robards had already received a divorce. Yet there most likely would have never been a major problem with the episode had Jackson not run for the presidency years later. Only then did it become necessary for the matter to be "managed" by John Overton. There is, of course, the question of why Jackson would potentially threaten his future. Possible answers are that he and Rachel were truly in love and, as history can attest, love causes people to act impetuously. There is also the colder notion that Jackson weighed his options and calculated that marriage into the Donelson clan had more benefits than negatives. Perhaps it was a mixture of these motivations. Historians will never really know.

What historians have concluded with certainty is that Jackson and Overton later played with the dates of the marriage for political effect. Andrew Burstein recently insisted that he discovered new information regarding the subject, but the reality is that Robert Remini had uncovered the truth nearly thirty years earlier. What is truly new about the episode is Ann Toplovich's belief that Jackson and Rachel may have eloped to Natchez a year earlier than Remini assumed, and, significantly, that Lewis Robards also remarried before actually obtaining a divorce. He wed Hannah Winn in December of 1792, then remarried her a year later after the divorce was final.[67] The core of the marriage controversy, however, continues to revolve around that fact that the Jacksons married illegally and most certainly knew it.

POLITICAL POWER, APPOINTMENTS, AND PROFIT

Marriage complications aside, Jackson continued to prosper on the Tennessee frontier. He aligned himself with the territorial governor, William Blount, and as a result continually moved forward in prestige and power. In 1796, with the requisite population necessary for statehood, delegates from the various counties met in Knoxville and created a constitution so that Tennessee could apply to the U.S. Congress for statehood. Jackson was one of the delegates and his involvement revealed a commitment to representative government by his arguing that residency, rather than substantive property holding, should be enough for any man to have voting rights. He had not yet fully embraced his later arguments when serving as president that any man should be able to hold political office. Rather, for Tennessee he supported property requirements to serve in the legislature or as governor. Jackson also steadfastly supported freedom from religious requirements by opposing a resolution that representatives must vow to a profession of faith. It was not that Jackson opposed religion. He had been raised a Presbyterian and his papers

---

[67] Virtually every Jackson biographer has discussed the marriage debacle. A good source is Remini, *Andrew Jackson: The Course of American Empire*, chapter 5. For Burstein's argument see *The Passions of Andrew Jackson*, appendix. For a comparison of Remini and Burstein's findings, see Matthew Warshauer, "The Passions of Andrew Burstein: A Review of The Passions of Andrew Jackson," *Tennessee Historical Quarterly* 38, no 4 (Winter 2003): 366-373. For Robards' marriage and the newest information on the subject, see Ann Toplovich, "Marriage, Mayhem, and Presidential Politics: The Robards-Jackson Backcountry Scandal," *Ohio Valley History 5, no. 4* (Winter 2005): 3-22.

reveal a devotion to God. He simply did not believe that one should be bound by ideas of faith when it came to serving the government. Jackson's involvement in the convention revealed not only his growing stature in Tennessee, but some thought on the nature of a republic. His reward for serving in the convention, as well as his political connections, was being chosen as the new state's first and sole congressman to the U.S. House of Representatives. At only twenty-nine, Jackson had come a long way since his backwoods Waxhaw existence.

Still, the question of Jackson's suitability as a federal representative is another source of dispute among historians. Remini believed that Jackson was hardly enthralled with the position, but nonetheless performed his duty and, as a congressman, managed to convince Congress to reimburse the new state just over $20,000 for the 1794 Nickajack Expedition against Indians in southeast Tennessee. Overall, Jackson served on five committees, chaired one, presented two petitions, introduced one resolution, made five speeches, and voted twenty-four times with the majority out of a total of thirty-nine votes. Jackson also, significantly, was one of only a handful of men who refused to vote in favor of a resolution honoring the outgoing President Washington because Jackson opposed the president's support of the infamous 1795 Jay Treaty, which many believed favored Great Britain too greatly in matters of trade. The act, if not politically wise, was nonetheless bold. James Curtis considered the event merely a "symbolic protest," and insisted that Jackson "did not distinguish himself in federal politics....The young congressman was more angry than eloquent." Curtis thought little of Jackson's success in obtaining federal reimbursement for the Nickajack Expedition, even though it was an important political victory considering that the federal government had insisted the military expedition was illegal. For Andrew Burstein's part, he successively informs readers that "Jackson introduced no legislation," he was a "passive legislator," and "he was outshone on Capitol Hill."[68]

After only a year of serving as a congressman, Jackson moved up to the Senate to replace William Blount, who was the first senator ever dismissed for improper conduct, having disclosed in a letter his involvement in a plan to invade Spanish West Florida. Jackson never liked serving in the upper chamber, in part because he was experiencing financial difficulties that distracted him, and also because he was inexperienced and surrounded by much more seasoned men. Here, historians like Remini and Curtis are in

---

[68] Remini, *Andrew Jackson: The Course of American Empire*, 100; Curtis, *Andrew Jackson and the Search for Vindication*, 30-1; Burstein, *The Passions of Andrew Jackson*, 153-4.

agreement. Both surmised that Jackson was unsuited for the Senate. He served only one term, requested a leave of absence, then returned home and resigned his position.

While east in Philadelphia serving in the legislature, and during travels a year earlier in 1795, Jackson continued his man on the make ways. Land was the great source of wealth in the West and in return for his legal services Jackson sometimes received land in lieu of cash payments. The leading men of Tennessee speculated in land. William Blount certainly did. It therefore seemed clear to Jackson that amassing land, selling and trading, was another way to make a fortune. While in Philadelphia, one of his goals was to unload more than fifty thousand acres. The difficulty is that he fell in with David Allison, a fairly well-known, but, as it turned out, bankrupt speculator. Jackson accepted three promissory notes for the value of the land and then used the notes, much like signing over a personal check to another individual, as payment for supplies to stock a store that he had opened in Tennessee. When the notes turned out to be no good, Jackson was stuck with a sizable bill for the supplies. It was this financial debacle that weighed on Jackson during his sole term in the Senate. He tried for several years to get his money from Allison, who ultimately landed in debtor's prison.

The episode was a hard lesson, but it did not stop Jackson from continuing in land speculation. Risk is always a part of capitalism and Jackson was always a risk taker. Yet in James Curtis' assessment, Jackson's actions take on a deeper, psychological meaning: "Jackson abhorred debt and fought to avoid being victimized by forces beyond his control. But some inner compulsion drove him to make further investment."[69] The question that must be asked is, was this "inner compulsion" some sort of psychological defect, or merely Jackson's towering ambition? Was it simply his desire to excel and establish himself as a part of the landed, wealthy gentry of the West? There is also the issue of Jackson's penchant for gambling. He was always willing to take risks if there might be reward.

Upon resigning from the Senate, Jackson was presented with another opportunity. In fact, his resignation may have had something to do with the possibility of receiving a judgeship on the state supreme court. It was a prestigious position and carried a sizable, $600 per year salary. Jackson was elected to the position by the Tennessee state legislature in 1798 and served until 1804. It was while serving as a judge that another of the legendary

---

[69] Remini, *Andrew Jackson: The Course of American Empire*, 86-90; Curtis, *Andrew Jackson and the Search for Vindication*, 34.

episodes involving Jackson comes down through history. One Russell Bean had been indicted for cutting the ears off of his child and, when appearing in court, ridiculed everyone in the court room before walking out. Jackson ordered the sheriff to arrest Bean, only to be told it was impossible. The judge therefore took it upon himself, pistols in hand, to apprehend Bean. Jackson adjourned the court for ten minutes, approached Bean, and announced, "Surrender you infernal villain, this very instant, or I'll blow you through!" Bean surrendered immediately and when asked several days later why he succumbed to Jackson and not the sheriff or others, responded, "when he came up, I looked him in the eye, and saw shoot, and there wasn't shoot in nary other eye in the crowd; and so I says to myself, says I, hoss, it's about time to sing small, and so I did."[70]

Such an episode lends to the seriousness of Jackson's disposition. He was without question a man of intensity and conviction. It may also help to support Hendrik Booraem's conclusion that after facing death during the Revolution, there was little more that Jackson feared. His ability to stand in the face of fear is one of the things that made him a formidable opponent and, later, a remarkably successful military commander.

If Jackson was resolute and fearsome in confronting potential enemies, he revealed remarkable tenderness in his personal life. Writing to Rachel in 1796, he began his letter, "My Dearest Heart, It is with the greatest pleasure I sit down to write you. Tho I am absent My heart rests with you. With what pleasing hopes I view the future period when I shall be restored to your arms there to spend My days in Domestic Sweetness with you the Dear Companion of my life, never to be separated from you again during this Transitory and fluctuating life."[71] Here was most certainly James Parton's man of contradictions.

It was also during these years that Jackson continued his gentlemanly and aristocratic path by expanding his slave holdings. Being a slaveholder in this age of the republic was a mark of status and wealth. Jackson knew this and wanted to build his land holdings and agricultural profits. This could be done only through the acquisition of slaves. By 1798 tax records indicate that he owned fifteen slaves, which placed him in the upper percentile of slave owners in Tennessee. Even by the 1850s the largest group of slave masters in the state

---

[70] Parton, *The Life of Andrew Jackson, vol. 1*, 228-9; Remini, *Andrew Jackson: The Course of American Empire*, 115.

[71] Andrew Jackson to Rachel Jackson, May 9, 1796, in Samuel B. Smith and Harriet Chappell Owsley, eds., *The Papers of Andrew Jackson, vol. 1* (Knoxville: The University of Tennessee Press, 1980), 91.

held four or less slaves, and just less than seventy percent owned fewer than ten. Jackson had not yet achieved the status of "planter," which, according to one Tennessee historian, required thirty or more slaves, but only time held him from that classification.[72]

Steadily moving up the political and legal ladder of Tennessee politics, marrying into an established family in the Cumberland, and expanding his slave holdings were all tangible ways of improving his standing in the state. An additional path was through military service. Jackson had never had formal military training – only what he gleaned from his Revolutionary War experience – but during this time of the republic becoming an officer was more a matter of popularity and standing among the community than military renown. Militias elected officers and Jackson eyed the much respected position of major general in the Tennessee militia. He made his first attempt in December of 1796. Remini noted that such a position could "advance his name, reputation, and political ambitions throughout the state, for there was no surer way of gaining popularity with Tennesseans than military success—particularly against the Indians." Remini concluded, "Jackson's decision to seek the post of major general—the highest military rank in the state—when he was not yet thirty years of age indicates the gargantuan size of his ambition."[73]

Though Jackson was unsuccessful in his first bid for major general, it was merely a matter of time, 1802, before he achieved that goal. Even in gaining victory, however, the major generalship came with political feuding. The election resulted in a tie between Jackson and John Sevier, who was both the former governor and the former major general. Having already served in the position and possessing military experience, Sevier dismissed Jackson's pretension of lobbying for the generalship. He could not, however, dismiss Jackson's political connections, and when the tie was broken by the new governor and Jackson's political ally, Spencer Roane, Sevier was outraged. The two had always been in different political camps. Sevier headed one group and William Blount the other. When Blount died in 1800, Jackson became the undisputed political leader of the faction, which also solidified the antagonism with Sevier.

In this era of the republic, political factions had far more to do with devotion to a particular man or set of men, than a wider, national political party affiliation. Personal loyalty was everything. This is a political reality that

---

[72] Warshauer, "Andrew Jackson: Chivalric Slave Master," 204; Chase C. Mooney, *Slavery in Tennessee* (Bloomington: Indiana University Press, 1957), 87.
[73] Remini, *Andrew Jackson: The Course of American Empire*, 100-1.

Jackson carried with him for the remainder of his life. Even when the nature of party politics began to change with the advent of the Second American Party System, Jackson still viewed politics in very personal terms. In many respects, he had one foot in the old and one in the new political world.

Disputes, Duels and Violence

Historians have often debated whether or not Jackson was out of control. Did he lash out in unthinking and rash explosions of fury? Was he calculating in his acts of violence? One answer lay in the politics of the period and the concomitant quest for power. Jackson's rise as a burgeoning political leader set the stage for a battle with Sevier. It came in 1801 when Sevier again ran for the governorship and Jackson released documents from his days as prosecutor that implicated Sevier in land fraud. The event not only revealed that Jackson was adept in the game of politics, but that he was willing to challenge an older and well respected man for power. In truth, Jackson had never had difficulties in challenging anyone if he deemed doing so in his interest or in defense of his honor. This is one of the issues that has caused historians to debate whether or not Jackson was out of control. James Curtis and Andrew Burstein viewed such conduct as prime examples of Jackson's insecurities and his pathological need to prove himself. Though there were certainly times when Jackson fumed and exploded, they cannot all be categorized as reckless. More often than not he calculated what would achieve success and power. It did not always work out as planned, but Jackson did consider strategies for securing his future. The major generalship, he surmised, would increase his stature and provide him with a steady salary. Destroying Sevier would also remove his most formidable political challenger in the state.

Sevier was hardly willing to go without a fight. A newspaper battle ensued and when the two men happened upon one another in Knoxville, sharp words were exchanged and Sevier ultimately blasted Jackson for stealing another man's wife. This was a tender spot and one that could unleash Jackson's worst traits. He demanded satisfaction of his honor and a duel was arranged that turned into a fiasco. Both men were enraged and when they spotted each other on horseback near the dueling ground each man charged forward. Pistols were drawn, then a sword; soon Sevier's son drew his pistol, then Jackson's second his. Cooler heads among the men who accompanied the duelists finally prevailed and the matter was ended without bloodshed or even going through with the duel. The two men continued to loath one another, but never attempted to duel again. Moreover, Sevier won the governorship anyway, revealing that he still possessed considerable political power and that Jackson, perhaps, had overestimated his own.[74]

The battle with the famous and popular Governor Sevier no doubt hurt Jackson's standing in Tennessee. It was also followed by another affair of honor that, coming so close to the Sevier fiasco, along with the fact that it resulted in a man's death, unleashed widespread animosity towards Jackson. The 1806 Jackson-Dickinson duel is a legendary affair and stands as the only conflict of honor in which Jackson actually killed a man. The origin of the dispute stemmed from a race between Jackson's prized horse, Truxton, and Joseph Ervin's horse, Plowboy. When Ervin's stallion went lame just before the race, he was required to forfeit a portion of the bet to Jackson. A disagreement arose over the type of notes agreed upon for payment and in the next several months, because of gossip and harsh words, the matter expanded so that it included a number of men, one of whom was Ervin's son-in-law, Charles Dickinson, as well as one Thomas Swann. At one point, Dickinson made remarks about Rachel Jackson and when Jackson demanded to know what he had said, Dickinson apologized and noted that he had been drunk. Jackson accepted the younger man's explanation and the matter seemed settled.

Yet the disagreement over the notes continued to fester and Thomas Swann was pulled into the matter over rumors and alleged statements. This time Jackson became the target, receiving a challenge from Swann. He refused, viewing Swann as ungentlemanly and therefore deserving of a beating rather than a duel. Jackson was true to his word. When he happened upon Swann in a Nashville tavern, Jackson struck him with a cane. From there, the matter continued to escalate and even drew other men, Jackson's friend John Coffee, and a political enemy, Nathaniel McNairy, onto the dueling ground. When Dickinson learned of the Jackson-Swann incident, he stepped back into the fray by publishing a letter in which he called Jackson a "worthless scoundrel a poltroon and a coward." Jackson's friend Thomas Overton immediately notified Jackson of the letter, informing him, "It's a piece that can't be passed over....General Jackson, you must challenge him." The use of such terms, "scoundrel," "poltroon," and "coward," were far more than mere name-calling. They were well-understood code words in the world of honor that demanded a formal response. As historian Joanne Freeman noted, they

---

[74] Parton, *The Life of Andrew Jackson, vol. 1*, 232-5; Remini, *Andrew Jackson: The Course of American Empire*, 119-23.

"were fighting words, and anyone who hurled them at an opponent was risking his life."[75]

Overton fully understood the implications of Dickinson's words. He was a man of standing in the community and to avoid the matter would have placed Jackson in exactly the same position in which Waightstill Avery had found himself years earlier when Jackson was the young man. Honor and reputation were serious matters and dueling was an accepted, even sacred, method of settling such disputes. To contemporary sensibilities dueling may seem like little more than glorified violence, but historians have repeatedly explained the importance and tradition of the code. Historian Bertram Wyatt-Brown noted of Jackson that he "channeled his emotions in conventional, conservative rituals." Freeman insisted, "Far more than directives for negotiating a duel, the code of honor was a way of life....Honor was the core of a man's identity, his sense of self, his manhood."[76]

Dickinson and Jackson met on the dueling ground in Kentucky, just over the Tennessee border. They stood a mere twenty-four feet apart with pistols at the ready. Dickinson was reputed to be the best shot in Tennessee and Jackson therefore decided upon a risky, yet perhaps his only viable, strategy: allow Dickinson to fire first. Jackson simply believed he could not beat Dickinson in terms of speed, thus it was better to hope he missed and then make the return shot really count. Jackson therefore waited and promptly received a bullet in his left chest. Nevertheless, he stood his ground, much to Dickinson's amazement. Jackson then raised his pistol and cut his opponent down. He later uttered what have become infamous words: "I should have hit him if he had shot me through the brain."

Jackson defended his honor and won the duel, but it came at a heavy price. He carried a bullet in his chest for the remainder of his life and often suffered from near incapacitating pain. Moreover, he was not accorded the sense of honor and right that he expected. Dickinson was a popular man with many friends and rather than ending the affair, his death merely enraged many in the community, especially those who were already politically opposed to Jackson. James Parton noted, "It is certain that at no time between the years 1806 and 1812, could General Jackson have been elected to any office in Tennessee that

---

[75] Remini, *Andrew Jackson: The Course of American Empire*, 139-140; Joanne B. Freeman, *Affairs of Honor: National Politics in the New Republic* (New Haven: Yale University Press, 2001), xvi.

[76] Bertram Wyatt-Brown, *Southern Honor: Ethics and Behavior in the Old South* (New York: Oxford University Press, 1982); Bertram Wyatt-Brown, *The Shaping of Southern Culture: Honor, Grace, and War, 1760s-1880s* (Chapel Hill: University of North Carolina Press, 2001), 74; Freeman, *Affairs of Honor*, xv.

required a majority of the voters of the whole State." In the weeks following Dickinson's death a newspaper battle ensued in which Jackson's enemies abused him for killing Dickinson in cold blood, while the General wrote in defense of his conduct. The newspaper battle, too, was a formalized and expected part of the code, especially when the duel involved a political chieftain like Jackson.[77]

The Dickinson duel has been fodder for historians who want to portray Jackson as blood-thirsty and murderous. It is easy to do so. Yet the context of the time and the events themselves are important. Had Jackson been the only man in the region or nation to utilize duels for settling conflicts, or had he been the only person in the whole affair to press the matter and escalate the tension, perhaps he could be legitimately labeled as an unrepentant killer. The truth, however, is that Jackson had walked away from Dickinson once before and it was Dickinson who later forced the challenge. Was Jackson blameless? Was he calm and collected throughout the entirety of the dispute? Certainly not. Yet he was also not the sole participant who had instigated and exacerbated the matter. Dickinson meant to kill Jackson. Should Jackson have merely taken a bullet to the chest with no response? Dickinson's death was hardly out of the ordinary when it came to dueling. Jackson was without question willing to resort to violence, but the reality is that the early republic was a violent place with very real threats. Some of these threats involved honor, which to many was more sacred than life itself.

Still, some historians take Jackson's killing of Dickinson to extremes, imparting psychological demons that have Jackson symbolically killing himself. Writing of Jackson's "insecurity and confusion," James Curtis theorized that "Jackson probably saw something of himself in his young opponent—some unpleasant reminder of the insecure past. Jackson felt no guilt in punishing Dickinson's insolence, not when it stemmed from the very defects of character that Jackson had vowed to uproot."[78]

There is also the matter of the extent to which Jackson engaged in violence to settle disputes. The fact is that he fought only one duel, with Dickinson, that ended in violence. Still, he did reveal a willingness to resort to violence in other instances. One such episode was with Silas Dinsmore, a U.S. Indian agent, who had been in the habit of requiring every person crossing into or out of Indian territory with slaves to show documentation or he would place

---

[77] For the particulars of the duel and the events that led up to it, see Parton, *The Life of Andrew Jackson, vol. 1*, ch. 23 through ch. 27. For the quote by Parton, see p. 305; Remini, *Andrew Jackson: The Course of American Empire*, ch. 9; Freeman, *Affairs of Honor*.

[78] Curtis, *Andrew Jackson and the Search for Vindication*, 37-8.

the slaves in custody. The action outraged many in the region and Jackson took it upon himself to teach Dinsmore a lesson by purposely traveling with undocumented slaves, and even arming two of his more trusted slaves. Fortunately, Dinsmore was not present and nothing ensued, though he was later removed from his position because so many people had complained. Jackson was one of them, insisting that Dinsmore's actions were outrageous and questioning whether the people of the area were themselves free or slaves. He was also particularly irked that Dinsmore had exacted his self-proclaimed powers on a woman who had traveled past the agent's home, and whom Jackson in a letter referred to as a "helpless and unprotected female."[79]

Many in Nashville applauded Jackson's actions, but it nonetheless revealed his willingness to confront those he believed were acting improperly or affronting his sense of propriety and correctness. There is no doubt that Jackson was arrogant to a fault. Yet was he motivated by inner demons, as James Curtis would have readers believe? Writing of the incident, Curtis insisted that Jackson "could never forget that the last war had taken another 'helpless and unprotected female' [his mother] and left him an orphan, tormented by ambivalent feelings about his own mortality. Since then, he had struggled to give meaning to that sacrifice, to conquer the secret fears." Thus for Curtis, even an event like the Dinsmore episode revealed Jackson's constant need for vindication. At the core of everything was the great tragedy.

Historian Lorman Ratner offers a far more logical and contextual explanation of the Dinsmore confrontation. Jackson's sense of honor was rooted in his clan and gentry culture. "Because women provided a means for men to establish their right to be called honorable, their attitude may be better viewed as cultural rather than a psychological phenomenon. It is reasonable to argue that if action worthy of the description 'honorable gentleman' was the single most important force shaping Jackson's life, then action in defense of women's physical well-being and social standing ranked just behind defense of country as means by which he could achieve the reputation he so earnestly sought."[80] It was, therefore, more a matter of Jackson's, and his community's, sense of honor that motivated his actions towards Dinsmore than a traumatic childhood.

Still, the reality of an honor culture does not explain away all that Jackson did when it came to confrontations. Certainly the most famous and bizarre example of Jackson's often violent nature was with the Benton brothers, Jesse

---

[79] Parton, *Andrew Jackson, vol. 1*, 357.
[80] Curtis, *Andrew Jackson and the Search for Vindication*, 46; Ratner, *Andrew Jackson and His Tennessee Lieutenants*, 28-9.

and Thomas Hart. Jesse Benton had argued with one of Jackson's officers, William Carroll, and the matter escalated to a duel in which Jackson was asked to serve as Carroll's second. When Carroll and Benton met on the dueling ground, they were back to back and required to wheel and fire at one another. Both men did so and Benton got off the first shot, hitting Carroll in the thumb. In doing so, however, Benton had bent over while firing, a clear violation of the rules. Carroll subsequently fired and grazed Benton across both butt cheeks. It was an embarrassing occurrence and one that quickly spread across the state.

Thomas Hart Benton learned of the episode and engaged in a heated exchange of letters with Jackson. News of the dispute echoed around Tennessee, each time escalating in nature and rumor to the extent that confrontation was virtually inevitable. When in September of 1813 Jackson, John Coffee, and Rachel Jackson's nephew Stockley Hays arrived in Nashville while the Bentons were there at the same time, the stage was set. Jackson was clearly looking for trouble. He walked with Coffee to retrieve his mail, then journeyed past the City Hotel where the Bentons were staying and standing in the entry way. Jackson lunged at Thomas Hart Benton and a general melee ensued. Jesse shot Jackson in the shoulder and arm, while John Coffee backed Thomas down a flight of stairs. Stockley Hays then entered the hotel and dove on Jesse, stabbing him several times in the arms with a knife. It was a western brawl in the streets of Nashville and without question solidified Jackson's reputation for violence. It also left Jackson bloodied and bed-ridden while his shoulder healed.[81]

The Benton episode reveals Jackson's worst trait: vengeance. He had grown up in a society in which violence was common and accepted. He then experienced the blood letting of the American Revolution and came away with an understanding that violence was a ready and quick way to settle disputes. It had also caused him to place people in the camps of friends or enemies. Thomas Hart Benton had been a friend and young protégé, but no longer. Jackson could be a hothead, but then so too could other men. The Bentons certainly were, and the mixture of egos and anger fueled a dispute that could only have caused further criticism of Jackson's reputation in the state.

The question remains, however, whether Jackson's penchant for settling disputes was an indication that he was out of control? Was it some sort of inner compulsion fueled by the need to prove his right to survive? James

---

[81] Parton, *The Life of Andrew Jackson*, 386-95; Remini, *Andrew Jackson: The Course of American Empire*, 181-6.

Curtis offers that Jackson considered the attack on Benton a "settlement of accounts, a proof of courage." Remini did not view it with such psychological motivations; rather, it was merely an example of Jackson's ability to be petty, to be too quick to resort to violence, and that the episode, like all of Jackson's disputes, diminished him. It also threw in question the honor he sought. For gentlemen did not brawl in the streets.[82]

THE DOMESTIC JACKSON

Disputes were not the only things that Jackson engaged during the early 1800s. He also focused on stabilizing his economic circumstances and expanding his land holdings. The Allison debacle in which Jackson had accepted bad promissory notes had severely damaged his financial situation. One of the very reasons that certain government positions, such as the judgeship, appealed to him was because they came with a steady salary.

Sometime in 1794, after his marriage to Rachel, Jackson purchased a home and small plantation called Poplar Grove on the Cumberland River. Two years later he sold it and purchased Hunter's Hill, which had actually been owned at one point by Lewis Robards, Rachel's first husband. Jackson later sold the property, in part because of debt, and by 1804 acquired a 420 acre parcel of land with two log houses. He named his new home the "Hermitage" and slowly added property until it reached some 1200 acres, on which he built a new mansion in 1819. The plantation was a sprawling place, and Jackson eventually owned upwards of 150 slaves to work it. With his love of fine horses Jackson had a considerable stable. The main market crop on the plantation was cotton, though the Hermitage produced some eighteen additional crops. Most farms at this time were meant to be primarily self-sufficient enterprises. The crops and livestock provided, with some supplement through purchasing and hunting, for both the white and black families.[83]

It was in his domestic life that Jackson revealed his greatest tenderness. His letters to Rachel are evidence of this. Jackson also appears to have been something of a romantic. He aided a number of young couples in eloping, often to the dismay and ridicule of their parents. Perhaps this is an indication

---

[82] Curtis, *Andrew Jackson and the Search for Vindication*, 48; Remini, *Andrew Jackson: The Course of American Empire*, 186.

[83] The operations of the plantation and acquisition of land are discussed in Warshauer, "Andrew Jackson: Chivalric Slave Master."

of his passion and love for Rachel when they too ran off to marry. Jackson's commitment to family was also quite clear. The Jacksons never had any children of their own. Some historians speculate that Rachel was unable to bear children, noting that she had none with Lewis Robards either. Yet Jackson loved children and readily served as a guardian for many. Some instances were the result of death. Jackson's friends and Rachel's family, aware of the very real dangers that existed on the frontier, often asked that he look after their children should anything occur. In all, Jackson took responsibility for some seventeen children and formally adopted one of the twin sons of Severn and Elizabeth Rucker Donelson (Rachel Jackson's brother), naming him Andrew, Jr.[84] With the many children, including the nephews and nieces who were a constant fixture, the Hermitage was a bustling place. The Jacksons entertained frequently and with inns sparsely located on the frontier, the home was often frequented by house guests.

THE BURR CONSPIRACY AND THE QUESTION OF JUDGMENT

Certainly the most famous, or infamous, of Hermitage guests in the early years was none other than Aaron Burr, former vice-president of the United States and the man who had killed the Federalist Alexander Hamilton in a fateful duel in 1804. Burr first visited the west in 1805 and enjoyed widespread popularity, especially with Jackson and the social elite of Nashville. Burr was a beguiling character. The grandson of the famous theologian Jonathan Edwards, Burr served admirably in the Revolution and was known for his eloquence and charm. He spoke of the problems related to Spain's influence in the Southwest, something that had rankled westerners for years, and confided with some whom he met, including Jackson, that he was preparing a secret mission to travel down the Mississippi River and engage in a campaign to push the Spanish away from American territory. It was a plan that any good westerner could support.

The difficulty in what became known as the Burr Conspiracy is that Burr told a different story to everyone he met. After being jettisoned from the Republican Party and by Thomas Jefferson after the famous tie in the 1800 presidential election – Jefferson believed that Burr had attempted to steal the presidency and therefore never trusted him again – he in turn loathed Jefferson

---

[84] Remini, *Andrew Jackson: The Course of American Empire*, 160-1.

and decided to embark on a scheme to separate the newly acquired Louisiana territory, in particular New Orleans, from the United States. The story has all the trappings of a good Hollywood movie: conspiracy, intrigue, secret agents. Burr had actually approached both the English and Spanish ambassadors in Washington, D.C., to employ their aid in the scheme. Neither agreed. He also traveled throughout the West, enlisting the help of men like Jackson, even declaring that he was on a secret mission on behalf of the president to descend on New Orleans and meet up with American forces to push the Spanish from the region. If all of this was not enough, one of Burr's co-conspirators was none other than General James Wilkinson, commander of U.S. forces in New Orleans, and also, unbeknownst to Burr, Spanish agent number thirteen, on the payroll of Spain! The level of duplicity and scheming was mammoth. Jackson and many other men were easily sucked into the plan. Burr paid Jackson to build boats and amass supplies for the expedition and when it ultimately left for New Orleans Jackson even had his nephew Stockley Hays accompany Burr.

When word of a treasonous plot against the government reached the West in 1806, Burr was brought before a grand jury in Lexington, Kentucky, to determine what exactly was going on. Henry Clay, an aspiring young attorney who later became a critical force in American politics, defended Burr and gained his release because no proof of a plot against the United States could be shown. Jefferson did not give up so easily, and requested that Congress suspend the writ of habeas corpus so that Burr and his accomplices could be arrested and detained indefinitely. Congress refused because not enough evidence existed to warrant such a momentous action.

When news of possible treachery reached Jackson he immediately wrote to the president and to the governor of Louisiana, W.C.C. Claiborne, warning them of a possible plot. In his letter to Claiborne, Jackson revealed his commitment to the Union: "I love my country and Government, I hate the Dons [the Spanish] —I would delight to see Mexico reduced, but I will die in the last ditch before I would yield a part to the Dons, or see the Union disunited." He also had the opportunity to meet up once again with Burr, who professed his innocence of any movement against the U.S. government. Jackson was seemingly satisfied, but remained suspicious and told his nephew Hays that if he learned treason was involved to immediately go to Governor Claiborne. Shortly thereafter, in December of 1806, Burr left with a small flotilla, which he subsequently abandoned after learning that federal authorities were pursuing him. He was later arrested, transported to Virginia, and stood trial for treason against the United States. The trial was overseen by

Chief Justice of the Supreme Court John Marshall, who served as judge of the federal district court. Thomas Jefferson, who loathed Burr, became heavily involved in the trial, to the point of interference, revealing that the president too could hate with a passion. Burr was ultimately acquitted because no one was able to tell the same story and the prosecution was therefore unable to satisfy the federal treason statute.[85]

The importance of this episode as it relates to Jackson is many-fold. It revealed his expansionist sentiments. He, like most westerners, never liked Spain being so close to American territory and would have been happy to force them out militarily and in doing so broaden U.S. holdings. He also coveted the possibility of a military action in which he would have the opportunity to command. He showed his strict devotion to the Union, revealing what he did many times later when insisting that he would never allow it to be separated. There are also larger questions about Jackson's character. Citics have insisted that the Burr Conspiracy reveals Jackson's deeper insecurities and lack of judgment. James Curtis argued that Jackson desired any military glory he could get: "He desperately wanted to be on the march—against Spain, against Burr, against someone. The longer he remained inactive, the more vulnerable he felt." Michael Paul Rogin offered that "the Burr conspiracy further isolated him," insinuating that the whole affair was some sort of grand inner rage. Andrew Burstein fixated more specifically on Jackson's indiscretion, titling a chapter, "Judging Character: Burr." Yet Burstein added little if anything that Burr Conspiracy historians as well as Burr and Jackson biographers have already discussed. Still, the implication is that in being duped by the wily Burr, Jackson was somehow foolish and unthinking. Burstein opined, "To the zealot from Tennessee, there was no excuse for misjudgment of a man's character."[86]

The problem in these interpretations is that Burr engaged half-truths with literally everyone involved in the affair. This was one reason that no one could testify to the same story and thus convict Burr of treason. That Jackson too

---

[85] Andrew Jackson to W.C.C. Claiborne, November 12, 1806, in Harold D. Moser, et al, eds., *The Papers of Andrew Jackson, 1804-1813, vol. 2*, (Knoxville: University of Tennessee Press, 1984), 116-7; hereafter referred to as *Jackson Papers, vol. 2*; for Jackson's involvement with Burr, see Parton, *The Life of Andrew Jackson*, chs. 23-30; Remini, *Andrew Jackson: The Course of American Empire,* ch. 10; for a wider treatment of the Burr Conspiracy and Jefferson's involvement, see Melton F. Buckler, *Aaron Burr: Conspiracy to Treason* (New York: Wiley, 2002); Leonard W. Levy, *Jefferson and Civil Liberties: The Darker Side* (Chicago: Ivan R. Dee, 1989); Thomas Perkins Abernathy, *The Burr Conspiracy* (New York: Oxford University Press, 1954).

[86] Curtis, *Andrew Jackson and the Search for Vindication*, 43; Rogin, *Fathers & Children*, 139; Burstein, *The Passions of Andrew Jackson*, 83.

was duped is of no great surprise. One could argue that Henry Clay was in a worse position than Jackson. The Kentucky lawyer had successfully defended Burr in Frankfort. These same historians revel in charging that Jackson was consumed with a fear of conspiracies. The key problem here is one of context. The fact is that in these early days of the republic conspiracies did in fact exist. Jackson's experience with Burr and with politics in general taught him this very real lesson. That Jackson, like most westerners, welcomed an opportunity to oust the Spanish from the region, whether doing so was sanctioned by the U.S. government or not, was of no great surprise at the time. Thus Jackson listened to and even worked with Burr.

Conclusion: A Man of Standing in Tennessee

In 1788, Jackson arrived in Tennessee with little more than the horse he road in on. Yet in only a few years he was established as an enterprising attorney, connected himself to one of the founding families, became an important part of one of the leading political cliques, and subsequently rose politically. He also engaged in numerous land and business transactions, not all of which were successful. Jackson desired wealth and prestige. He had always been tremendously ambitious. It was what made him successful in virtually everything that he did. It also made him headstrong. As a rising force in Tennessee, there were inevitable disputes. Jackson's penchant for settling matters with quick, violent solutions made him a man to fear. Indeed, he most certainly embraced such a reputation. The frontier was an unsettled and dangerous place and Jackson had learned early on that friends and enemies existed. Those who were friends could be trusted and accorded limitless devotion. Enemies were treated as such. Once someone fell into that category, Jackson did not waste time with subtleties. His experience from the Revolution was that death came quickly. Better to face it and triumph. It was not a matter of weakness or insecurity. It was a matter of understanding, conviction, and resolution.

At the same time, this ferocious Jackson – a man who brooked no insult – could reveal tremendous compassion and tenderness. There was nothing that required Jackson to fill his home with children, or to take care of those from fallen friends and relatives. Part of it was surely the traditional clan nature of Ulster Scots society in which he had been raised. It may also have come from the fact that he himself had been taken in by family. Whatever the reason, his devotion to friends, family, and their children provides historians with something of a counter balance to the dueling, violence driven Jackson. He was, without question, James Parton's complex man.

Chapter 3

THE MILITARY JACKSON: THE CREEK WAR

Andrew Jackson's quest to become Tennessee's elected militia general was not based on any vast military experience. He had served in a limited capacity during the American Revolution, but certainly received no formal training as a soldier or commander. His generalship, then, was based on political power and popularity. Nonetheless, Jackson's 1802 victory to become general ultimately marked a turning point in his life that eventually led to the presidency. His success in fighting the Creek Indians on the southern frontier during the War of 1812 led to his appointment as a major general in the regular army, in charge of the seventh military district, which comprised the southern United States, including the Gulf Coast. In 1815 he devastated a formidable British army determined to capture New Orleans. That victory, the greatest in American history up to that point, made Jackson an overnight hero. It was only a matter of time before enterprising men looked to Jackson as a potential presidential candidate. His ambition was certainly up to the task.

THE NATURE OF A MILITARY CHIEFTAIN

The great debate over Jackson's role as military leader parallels the other disputes in his life. Was he merely a violent-minded, blood-thirsty monster who unleashed his fury on anyone in his path? His defeat of the Creeks and punishing confiscation of their land in the 1814 Treaty of Fort Jackson, the strict treatment of his own soldiers (to the extent of charging and executing a number of soldiers for mutiny), his imposition of martial law in New Orleans (which was the first time that the writ of habeas corpus was ever suspended and civil liberties curtailed by the military) – all of these items and more allows one to view Jackson as nothing more than a tyrant, the ultimate danger to a liberty-bound republic. Was he merely lashing out at everyone in an impotent attempt to control his inner demons? Such interpretations are certainly the representation made by historians such as James Curtis, Michael Paul Rogin, and Andrew Burstein, among others.

Context, however, matters. Jackson was certainly no saint. His treatment of Native Americans was brutal and quite effective. The battle for Indian lands had begun long before Jackson was born and continued long after he died. Yet Jackson unquestionably played a major role in dispossessing Indians. In modern terms, he engaged in ethnic cleansing, yet not to the extent that he wanted to eradicate all Indians, to engage in genocide. He, as did most white Americans, wanted Indian land and one way was through removal. This was the cleansing in which Jackson engaged. It was also a policy that began with the earliest of American administrations and expanded considerably as whites began pouring over the Appalachian Mountains. Continued conflict was inevitable.

Jackson's first trek to Tennessee taught him that Indians represented a dire threat to white settlers. He had awoken fellow travelers just in time to avoid an attack, and knew this most certainly when virtually everyone in the hunting party that followed was killed. Once in Nashville, Jackson learned that settlers had to band together to survive the Indian "menace." The frontier was a dangerous place and settlers viewed Native Americans as the greatest security threat. It was a daily concern. The French and Indian War, 1756-1763, revealed the extent to which Indian tribes could be encouraged to attack frontier settlements. The same was true in the years leading up to and during the War of 1812, the second war with Great Britain. This issue of frontier security is an incredibly important contextual issue when considering Jacksonian Indian policy.

The reality, of course, is that the land belonged to Native Americans long before white, European and Euro-Americans ever had claim to it. The very notion of a king in some far away land granting charters that provided title to colonists is rather bizarre in this day. Yet it was a fact in these times and settlers flocked to the new world, laying claim to land that was not theirs to take. Nothing changed after independence. Americans were just as land-hungry as their colonial forebears and viewed natives as the key obstacle to expansion. They were savages who failed to use the land properly, for purely agricultural pursuits. Nor did they have "proper," European conceptions of ownership. These alone were license enough to take the land. That Indians failed to have the military power to defend themselves, inevitably resulted in "might makes right" for the newly established settlers. Jackson did not invent such an attitude, nor did he originate such a governmental policy. His beliefs were those of his western neighbors: Indians were inferior, savage, and a threat. Such views were racist, intolerant, and greedy. They were also wholly American.[87]

The treatment of Native Americans in the United States is one of the great black marks in the history of the republic. Yet one must not interpret the history of this period out of context. Today many romanticize Native American culture, but it is primarily in the aftermath of the 1960s and 70s Civil Rights Era that most Americans have come to embrace diversity and multi-culturalism. These are largely contemporary understandings. It is amazingly difficult to fully grasp the racial predilections of an earlier generation. We find it hard to understand Jackson's treatment of Indians and therefore gasp at the inhumane nature of conquest. Yet the expansion of America, and Jackson was a diehard expansionist, was predicated on the corralling and containment of Native Americans. There is simply no other conclusion, no matter the discomfort with which Americans view it today. Racism and subordination, in part, built the United States.

Such facts do not mean that Jackson was genocidal. His desire was not to destroy all Indians and wipe them off the face of the earth. That he changed their culture by forcing them to cede significant portions of land, there is no doubt. For some, this is definition enough for genocide. Generations of Americans preceded Jackson in this. Yet Jackson's adoption of Indian children, most significantly Lyncoya, is one indication that genocide was not his aim. He also revealed respect for particular Indians. Moreover, his later actions as president when he removed the Cherokee from Georgia, which will be discussed in a later chapter, was focused primarily on claiming their lands and allowing them to maintain their culture as best they could away from white settlers. It was brutal and unfair, but there was a degree of logic to it. Jackson realized that white settlement could not be contained and Indians living in close proximity to whites could not be protected. The mood of America would not stand for it, and historians who argue otherwise do so in distinct opposition to the racial realities of early America. To southerners and westerners, Jackson was a savior who helped make the frontier safe. He did it well.

---

[87] For a further explanation of such an outlook, see John Buchanan, *Jackson's Way: Andrew Jackson and the People of the Western Waters* (New York: John Wiley & Sons, 2001); Robert V. Remini, *Andrew Jackson's Indian Wars* (New York: Viking Books, 2001).

His other less shining military exploits, such as executing militia men and imposing martial law on New Orleans, must also be viewed in context. The army had always been plagued by the problems of an inefficient, unprofessional, and undisciplined militia. George Washington loathed the militia for this very reason and he too dealt with military discipline which resulted in the execution of soldiers. Jackson simply refused to lose the Creek War because the militia would not serve. Enacting harsh discipline and punishment forged a real army that extinguished the Creek Indian threat on the southern frontier. This is a fact that cannot be disputed.

Who, then, was Andrew Jackson the military chieftain? He was, in James Parton's words, "a patriot and a traitor. He was one of the greatest of generals, and wholly ignorant in the art of war….A most law-defying, law-obeying citizen….A democratic autocrat. An urbane savage. An atrocious saint."[88]

THE PATH TO MILITARY GLORY

Like many Americans, Jackson welcomed the announcement of war with England in the summer of 1812. Many had grown increasingly disgusted with the continual violation of neutral trading rights, the English and French blockades of Europe that had so defined the Napoleonic Wars, as well as the use of English impressment in which American sailors were high-jacked from their own vessels and forced to serve on board British war ships. If this was not enough, the English incited Indian attacks on the western frontier.[89] War was warranted and Jackson coveted the opportunity to distinguish himself, defend American sovereignty, and expand U.S. holdings. The start of the war, however, provided the Tennessee general with little more than a nickname.

Prior to the June 18th declaration of war, Congress authorized the enlistment of 50,000 volunteers. Jackson responded with alacrity, issuing a proclamation from the Hermitage in March of 1812 lauding America's freedoms: "Volunteers to arms!….we are the freeborn sons of America; the citizens of the only republik now existing in the world; and the only people on earth who possess rights, liberties, and property which they dare call their own." The published address was laden with patriotic declarations, retribution against those who violated American rights, and the belief that no true

---

[88] Parton, *The Life of Andrew Jackson, vol. 1*, vii.
[89] For more on the causes of the War of 1812, see Donald R. Hickey, *The War of 1812: A Forgotten Conflict* (Urbana: University of Illinois Press, 1989).

American would shrink from the duty of being called to arms. It also revealed some of Jackson's less sterling qualities and, perhaps, his more personal sentiments: "Your impatience is no longer restrained," he announced. "The hour of national vengeance is now at hand."[90] Even in recognizing that Jackson's statements betrayed his own impatience and vengeance, one must admit that these were traits that existed among many in the nation, especially in the West. How else could Aaron Burr have enticed so many to dream of forcing the Spanish out of the region. Americans thirsted for a sense of justice. The War of 1812 was about making a statement that the nation was no longer a British colony. Hence the reason that it was often referred to as the Second War of Independence.

The Tennessee militia readied itself for military exploits. Yet the call for service from the federal government did not come immediately. Jackson waited for his opportunity even as news of military failures in Canada and along the northern U.S. border poured in. The war began miserably for America and worsened as time went on. Finally, in October of 1812, the governor of Tennessee received orders to provide 1,500 troops in support of General James Wilkinson's defense of New Orleans. Governor Willie Blount, William Blount's half-brother, chose Jackson as the commander of the expedition and he subsequently issued orders for the militia to meet in Nashville on December 10, 1812 in preparation for a march south.[91] Winter is not an appealing time to prepare troops for war, but Jackson went about the task with precision, leaving Nashville in early January of 1813. The trek to Natchez took just over a month. Upon arrival, Jackson was greeted with disturbing news: stay in Natchez until further orders. Do not descend to New Orleans. If these orders were bad news, those that followed were devastating. Secretary of War John Armstrong directed Jackson to dismiss his troops and turn over all public property to Wilkinson.

Jackson was understandably upset. He also had no intention of dismissing Tennessee troops so far from home and told Armstrong so in a letter dated March 15, 1813: "If it was intended by this order that we should be dismissed eight hundred miles from home, deprived of arms, tents, and supplies for the sick…it appears that these brave men, who certainly deserve better fate and return from their government was intended by this order to be sacrificed—Those that could escape from the insalubrious climate, are to be deprived of the necessary support and meet death by famine The remaining few to be

---

[90] Andrew Jackson to the 2nd Division, March 7, 1812, *Jackson Papers, vol. 2*, 290-3.
[91] Andrew Jackson to the Tennessee Volunteers, November 24, 1812, *Jackson Papers, vol. 2*, 342-3.

deprived of their arms pass through the savage land, where our women children and defenceless citizans are daily murdered....I mean to commence my march to Nashville."[92]

Jackson was true to his word. He also disobeyed his superior by marching the troops home. He did not care. Like so many times in his life, Jackson did what he thought correct. Only a few days later, on March 16th, he issued a general order to his troops informing them of Armstrong's orders and his intention to march home: "The Major Genl, Having pledged himself that he never would abandon one of his men, and that he would act the part of a father to them—has to repeat that he will not leave one of the sick nor one of the detachment behind, that he has lead you here he will lead you back again to your country and your friends."[93] Here was Jackson at his best: forceful, loyal, self-assured; a real leader of men. And his troops knew it. On the long journey home they witnessed for themselves the fortitude that had made Jackson a success on the western frontier; it was the same fortitude that allowed him to stand and face Charles Dickinson's bullet. Hence the contrasting characteristics of Jackson's personality. In this instance, he was a hero to his men, and they accordingly nicknamed him "Old Hickory," the toughest thing in the forest. He ordered officers to turn over their horses to the sick and did the same.[94]

For his efforts in getting the militia back to Tennessee, the *Nashville Whig* announced, "Long will their General live in the memory of the volunteers of West Tennessee...for his benevolence, humane, and fatherly treatment to his soldiers; if gratitude and love can reward him, General Jackson has them."[95] The endeavor south had not resulted in Jackson's desire for military action, but he had proven his ability to lead. No one doubted him on that score and he was universally lauded as a hero. Secretary of War Armstrong did nothing to reprimand the General for disobeying orders.

Still, the blemishes of Jackson's personality, and hence the complexity, was never far from the surface. Shortly after returning he engaged in the ugly conduct that led to the Benton brawl, revealing that his judgment was at times questionable and his willingness to resort to violence too ready. Even worse, Thomas Hart Benton had been one of Jackson's commanders on the trip and proven himself quite able. The later feud was distressing for both men. Benton

---

[92] Andrew Jackson to John Armstrong, March 15, 1812, *Jackson Papers, vol. 2,* 383-5.
[93] Andrew Jackson to the Tennessee Volunteers, March 16, 1812, *Jackson Papers, vol. 2,* 391-2.
[94] For a good account of the march home, see Remini, *Andrew Jackson: The Course of American Empire,* 178-80.
[95] Parton, *The Life of Andrew Jackson, vol. 1,* 384.

ultimately left the state to start a new career in Missouri because there were too many pro-Jackson men in Tennessee. Jackson was left with a badly wounded arm that carried a bullet for years to come.

THE CREEK WAR

Jackson's recuperation ended suddenly when news arrived in Nashville of the Creek Indian massacre at Fort Mims in Alabama. On August 30, 1813, 1,000 Creek warriors, known as Red Sticks because of the red painted clubs they carried, poured into the fort and descended on the roughly 275 to 300 white, Muscogee Indian, black, and mixed race inhabitants. The brutality of the attack was particularly horrendous. Only a few survived; the rest were slaughtered. Some were burned alive when they barricaded themselves in buildings. Others were scalped. Pregnant women had their unborn children cut from their bellies. Children were swung by the ankles so that their heads dashed on the stockade fencing and their brains spewed upon the ground.[96] Here was the hostility and ferocity of the Indians that Jackson and other settlers had come to know. To be sure, white settlers were equally guilty of horrific depredations against Native Americans and the Creeks who attacked Fort Mims undoubtedly felt justified in attempting to rid settlers from what was viewed as Indian land. This is what happened when two competing cultures vied for the same territory.

It was only a few short years earlier, in 1810, that the Indian Prophet Tecumseh had traveled throughout the northwest territory of the Ohio region and into the South in an attempt to create a multi-tribe Indian confederation to wipe out white settlers. He preached total destruction; the exact kind that had taken place at Fort Mims: "Let the white race perish! They seize your land. They corrupt your women. They trample on the bones of your dead! Back whence they came, upon a trail of blood, they must be driven! Back—aye, back to the great water whose accursed waves brought them to our shores! Burn their dwellings—destroy their stock—slay their wives and children that their very breed may perish! War now! War always! War on the living! War

---

[96] For good accounts of the Fort Mims attack, see Frank L. Owsley, Jr., *Struggle for the Gulf Borderlands: The Creek War and the Battle of New Orleans, 1812-1815* (Gainesville: University of Florida Press, 1981); Sean Michael O'Brien, *In Bitterness and Tears: Andrew Jackson's Destruction of the Creeks and Seminoles* (Westport: Praeger, 2003).

on the dead!"[97] This was the Indian threat that Jackson and other frontier settlers confronted. Bloodshed was inevitable.

Governor Blount quickly issued orders for Tennessee troops. Jackson took command on October 7, 1813, and shortly thereafter headed south into Creek country. Not all members of the Creek tribe had decided on warfare. A split that eventually led to civil war had been brewing for sometime over traditional Creek ways versus the degree of contact tribal members had with whites. Some Creeks who wanted to avoid war with the United States aided Jackson in his push to punish those responsible for the attacks. His first opportunity came at Tallushatchee, a Red Stick village in northeast Alabama. Jackson ordered General John Coffee's cavalry to attack the village and the resulting battle was an overwhelming success for the Americans. Jackson wrote to Rachel in the aftermath, informing her that Coffee had killed some 200 warriors and captured seventy-four. The vengeance of the attack mirrored that displayed by the Red Sticks at Fort Mims. Lieutenant Richard Keith Call recorded in his journal that the slaughter had sickened him. David Crocket noted, "We shot them like dogs." Such was the nature of Indian/white warfare. Neither side was restrained. Newspapers from across the nation heralded the victory, announcing in their headlines, "Good News. Victory Over the Creek Indians." Articles printed letters from Jackson to Governor Blount, quoting, "We have retaliated for the destruction at Fort Mimms."[98]

In the midst of the killing there were also moments of strange humanity. After the Tallushatchee battle, a baby was found in the arms of his dead mother and when surviving Indians refused to take the child, Jackson sent him back to the Hermitage and informed Rachel in the same letter telling her of the battle. It was the characteristic, uncharacteristic nature of Andrew Jackson. He reveled in defeating the Red Sticks and exacting what he believed was due vengeance for the murder of whites, but he did not hate all Indians and certainly did not blame a child for the actions of adults. Jackson already had at least one Indian boy at the Hermitage when he sent Lyncoya, the Tallushatchee survivor, home. He subsequently wrote Rachel to "Keep Lyncoya in the house—he is a savage [but one] that fortune has thrown in my

---

[97] Quoted in Robert V. Hine and John Mack Faragher, *The American West: A New Interpretive History* (New Haven: Yale University Press, 2000), 127.

[98] Andrew Jackson to Rachel Jackson, November 4, 1813, *Jackson Papers, vol. 2, 444*; Herbert J. Doherty, Jr., *Richard Keith Call: Southern Unionist* (Gainesville: University of Florida Press, 1961), 6; Davy Crockett, *A Narrative of the Life of Davy Crockett, by Himself* (reprint, Lincoln: University of Nebraska Press, 1987), xi; "Good News. Victory Over the Creek Indians," *Boston Daily Advertiser*, November 29, 1813; "Victory Over the Creeks," *Nashville Clarion*, November 30, 1813.

h[ands when] his own female matrons wanted to k[ill him] because the whole race & family of his [blood] was destroyed—I therefore want him well taken care of, he may have been given to me for some Valuable purpose—in fact when I reflect that he as to his relations is so much like myself I feel an unusual sympathy for him."[99]

Some historians have viewed Jackson's adoption of Lyncoya as anything but humanity. Rather, they judge it as merely an example of Jacksonian paternalism towards those who were considered inferior. Jackson believed himself to be a superior, father figure to slaves and Indians. Taking in Lyncoya was simply another matter of domination for Jackson. James Curtis referred to the treatment of Lyncoya as "coercive paternalism," blasting Jackson for attempting to raise the boy by white societal standards that "denied the boy's cultural heritage." Curtis also went a step further by injecting the great tragedy, offering that Jackson's sympathy was not "so unusual…not to a man who desperately needed proof that he too had been saved for 'some valuable purpose'."[100] That Jackson embraced the idea of paternalism there is no doubt. It was a common concept of the period and viewed as proper in terms of social interactions among those who were unequal. Jackson took on the same paternal tone when dealing with his soldiers, often speaking of his fatherly concern for their well being. As one historian noted of the period, "this paternalistic role was a critical feature of gentry life."[101] Also remember the language of the period, those who had helped forge the young republic were founding "fathers."

That Jackson did not embrace Lyncoya's cultural heritage is also of no great surprise and should not have been to Curtis. One of the overarching themes of white and Indian relations was that if they were to survive, Indians would have to be "civilized" by embracing white society. This was hardly unique to Andrew Jackson. Thomas Jefferson advocated this belief. Moreover, in the aftermath of the American Civil War the government removed young Indian boys from their tribes, enrolled them in schools to learn white, civilized ways, cut their hair and forbade the speaking of their native languages.[102] This

---

[99] Andrew Jackson to Rachel Jackson, December 29, 1813, *Jackson Papers, vol. 2*, 515-16. For another Indian boy named Theodore, see *ibid*, p. 444, note 5. Bracketed insertions by the Jackson Papers editors.

[100] Curtis, *Andrew Jackson and the Search for Vindication*, 54, 72-3; for Jackson's paternalism, see Rogin, *Fathers & Children*, 189; Burstein, *The Passions of Andrew Jackson*, 175.

[101] Ratner, *Andrew Jackson and His Tennessee Lieutenants*, 13.

[102] For Jefferson's view, see the quote in the introduction of this work; David Wallace Adams, *Education for Extinction: American Indians and the Boarding School Experience, 1875-*

was cultural hegemony at its worst. Jackson believed, for good or not, that he was helping Lyncoya by raising him as white. He also believed that his paternalism was genuine and caring. That it was also racist and discriminatory is wholly American in the nineteenth century and beyond.

Having sent Lyncoya off to the Hermitage, Jackson prepared for the next battle in the Creek War. On November 9, 1813, the American army advanced on the Indian town of Talladega, which had decided to abandon the war in the aftermath of the Tallushatchee loss. Enemy Red Sticks prepared to attack the village for withdrawing from the war and Jackson meant to stop them. He directed his infantry to march directly into the center of 1,000 Creek warriors, hoping to draw in and then encircle them with his cavalry. The strategy nearly worked, but the Indians found a hole in the American line and some 700 escaped. Still, Jackson's troops managed to kill 300 warriors and put the Creeks on the defensive for the remainder of the campaign. Again, newspapers lauded the Tennessee general's success. The *Rhode Island Republican* announced, "ANOTHER VICTORY OVER THE CREEK INDIANS!" The *True Republican* of New York reported, "Another Brilliant Victory Over The CREEK INDIANS."[103]

The hostile Creeks, however, were not Jackson's only worry. In the midst of the conflict, militiamen, hungry from lack of food, petitioned Jackson to abandon the campaign and return home. He experienced continual problems with supplies and attempted to ensure the men that supplies were on the way. Jackson wrote of the problem to Governor Blount, noting, "petition on petition has been handed from the officers of the different Brigade's containing statements of their privations & sufferings & requesting me to return into the settlements with my Division." At one point the militia attempted to leave camp and Jackson managed to turn them around with entreaties to wait just a little longer. He asked for two days. The last thing Jackson wanted was to abandon the campaign. He knew that complete victory over the Creeks was within sight. "A retrograde motion is dangerous in an Army," he lamented, "& becomes fatal when accompanied with hunger."[104] When the two days came and went, Jackson decided, on November 17th, to split his forces, leaving 150 at Fort Strother, where they had been encamped, and march the rest to Fort

---

1928 (Lawrence: University Press of Kansas, 1995); Michael C. Coleman, *American Indian Children at School, 1850-1930* (Jackson: University Press of Mississippi, 1993).

[103] Andrew Jackson to Rachel Jackson, November 12, 1813, *Jackson Papers, vol. 2*, 448-9; "Another Victory Over the Creek Indians," *Rhode Island Republican*, March 3, 1814; "Another Brilliant Victory Over The Creek Indians," *True American*, April 27, 1814.

[104] Andrew Jackson to Willie Blount, November 14, 1813, and Andrew Jackson to John Cocke, November 16, 1813, *Jackson Papers, vol. 2*, 453-4; 454.

Deposit to check on supplies. Fortunately, only twelve miles into the march they ran into a supply train and Jackson allowed the men to feast. They were then ordered to return to Fort Strother.[105]

Much to the General's lament, some of the soldiers had a different idea and a company of men turned back towards Tennessee. This was desertion in the midst of a military campaign. Jackson had not personally given the order to return and when hearing of the mutiny he appeared on his horse ahead of the men with General John Coffee and some of his cavalry alongside. As James Parton related the story, "On coming up, the homesick gentlemen gave one glance at the fiery general and the opposing force, and fled precipitately to their stations." But the mutiny was not over. Jackson turned his horse around and found an entire brigade marching home. Mere words would not do. The General dismounted and laid a musket across the saddle of his horse, promising that the first man to take a step forward would be shot. As it turned out, the musket did not even work, though it is unclear if Jackson knew that.[106] In the end, the force of the threat was enough to derail the mutiny and Jackson averted a movement that might have ended the Creek campaign. This was the fortitude that had carried Jackson through his life. He refused to give up, and refused to let his men do so either.

In the days after the mutiny he penned a letter that expressed his concern and conviction: "I left Tennessee with the bravest army, I believed, that any general ever commanded. I have seen them in battle; & my opinion of their bravery is not changed. But their fortitude—upon this too I relyed, but it has been too severly [tes]ted. You know not the privations we have suffered, nor do I like to describe them. Perhaps I was wrong in belie[ving that] nothing but death could conquer the spirits of brave men. I am *sure* I was, for my men, I know, *are* brave. Yet privations have rendered them discontented: that is enough. The Campaign must nevertheless be prosecuted; & brought to a successful termination."[107]

The very day after Jackson wrote this letter, on December 4, he received a polite and imploring communiqué from one of his officers, William Martin, informing the General of an even more dire situation. Many of the volunteers had signed on for a one year tour of duty and believed that the clock had begun when they first mustered in Nashville for the march to New Orleans the previous December. Even though that campaign was abandoned and Jackson had marched the men back to Tennessee and allowed them to return home,

---

[105] Andrew Jackson to John Cocke, November 18, 1813, *Jackson Papers, vol. 2*, 457-8.
[106] Parton, *The Life of Andrew Jackson, vol. 1*, 463.
[107] Andrew Jackson to Gideon Blackburn, December 3, 1813, *Jackson Papers, vol. 2*, 464-5.

they believed that the year of duty was still underway. Martin explained to Jackson that the volunteers planned on departing for home in six days.[108] Here was a disaster. Jackson was within reach of a complete victory over the Creeks. It was more than merely his own need to vanquish a foe. He realized that if the Creeks were not stopped when the opportunity existed, they would merely regroup and in a few months or a year bloodshed would reign once again and the army forced to retake the field. Jackson was determined to not let that happen.

Writing to Martin, Jackson insisted that the men's tour of duty was not up and that they had not fulfilled their obligation to the nation. The letter was filled with legalisms about times of enlistment, who could properly authorize a discharge, and the difference between dismissal and discharge. Jackson also pleaded and threatened: "I still cherish the hope that the evil has been magnified, & will be dissipated by the exercise of reflection. I cling to the belief, as I would to the last hold on life, that when the hour of trial comes the 'Volunteers of Tennessee'—a name ever dear to fame, will not disgrace themselves, & a country which they have honoured, by abandoning its standard as Mutineers & deserters. But should I be disappointed, & compelled to resign this 'last, best hope,' one thing I will not resign—my duty. Mutiny & desertion *shall* be put down, so long as I retain the power of quelling them; & when deprived of this, I shall in the last extremity, be still found in the discharge of my duty."[109]

Jackson was true to his word. On December 10th, he faced down the militia with artillery at the ready to show the depth of his conviction. No one moved. This was the same general who had sprung to his horse only weeks after being shot in the arm by the Bentons; the same general who had marched them back to Tennessee from the Mississippi wilderness; the same general who had stared them down in an earlier act of mutiny. If Jackson was anything, he was steadfast. He would not budge. Would they? No. The mutiny did not go forward and two days later, on the 12th, General John Cocke arrived with 1500 men. Jackson subsequently released those who wanted to return home, but not before delivering an address that once again urged the men to see the campaign through. Not surprisingly, he lashed them with the belief that they were shrinking from duty: "The Volunteers of Tennessee. That very name calls back to his heart a thousand endearing recollections, which he can never forget. Yet these men—these Volunteers of Tennessee have become

---

[108] William Martin to Andrew Jackson, December 4, 1813, *Jackson Papers, vol. 2*, 467-9.
[109] Andrew Jackson to William Martin, December 6, 1813, *Jackson Papers, vol. 2*, 470-4.

MUTINEERS!...Yes fellow Soldiers, you who were once so brave, & to whom honour was once so dear; you shall be permitted to return to your homes if you desire it. But with what language, when you arrive there will you address your families & y[our] late associates in arms, within fifty miles of an assemblage of a savage enemy, that as much delights in sheding the blood of the innocent female & her sleeping babe as that of the warrior contending in battle?"[110]

Jackson's entreaty and bullying were to no avail. The troops turned homeward much to their general's chagrin. Moreover, the problems with enlistments did not cease. General Cocke's men were also due to be released, as were General Coffee's cavalry. Jackson confided his concerns in a December 19th letter to Rachel, noting, "Should it [the campaign] stop here I feel for the Scenes that will be transacted on our frontier—The creeks, conquered and beaten, on a retrograde of our forces, will give them new vigor, and full confidence in their prophets [Indian holy men who advocated war] and we will have to fight them on our frontier."

Jackson understood what the future held. The history of Indian warfare was not that complicated. Either end the threat by total victory, or expect more bloodshed in the future. Nonetheless, on the 22nd, Jackson received a letter from Governor Blount in which he sided with the troops on the enlistment issue and advised Jackson to return from Fort Strother.[111] The enemy was within his grasp, yet it seemed that everyone wanted to abandon the field. Jackson refused.

On the 26th at 10 p.m., he penned a forceful, frank letter to the governor. "I am wearied with dating letters at this place," began Jackson, "every exertion that was within my power has been made, to progress with the campaign and save the State from disgrace—still insurmountable difficulties present themselves, and it appears, that I am to be left alone struggling to obtain the object." The General then entreated Blount to issue a call for more troops, as was authorized by state law. "Here Sir, permit me to be plain, is a greater responsibility upon you; in not ordering, than to order," for, Jackson explained, to not order more troops was shrinking both from duty and from the federal government's decree to have soldiers in the field. Jackson advised Blount that the British were on the Gulf Coast waiting for the opportunity to re-supply the Creeks "and reanimate their sinking spirits." He closed the letter with Jacksonian fortitude: "I have given you mine [opinion] with the frankness

---

[110] Andrew Jackson to the 1st Brigade, Tennessee Volunteer Infantry, December 13, 1813, *Jackson Papers, vol. 2*, 482-4.

[111] Andrew Jackson to Rachel Jackson, December 19, 1813, and Willie Blount to Andrew Jackson, December 22, 1813, *Jackson Papers, vol. 2*, 494; 498-500.

of a friend, in the present disagreeable situation of our country—I believe you have the power, I believe every patriot, will Justify your exercising of it, and the publick good requires that you should promptly exercise it."[112] The force of Jackson's letter was clear, and this time the entreaty worked. Governor Blount ordered 2,500 new troops. The campaign was saved.

    What does one say about Jackson's refusal to quit? Was it mere stubbornness? Was it his own fear of failure? Was he merely attempting to prove his own right to survive? Did he believe in his professions about patriotism and the future destruction that the Creeks would inflict on the frontier? Was his letter to Blount a sign of determination or weakness? James Curtis interpreted Jackson's difficulties in particularly personal terms. "Jackson suddenly seemed powerless." "Unable to understand why 'his children' had disobeyed authority, Jackson cast about for scapegoats." "To Jackson the war was not a matter of contracts, terms of service, or dates of discharge, but a campaign to vindicate national honor and to prove his personal worth by triumphing over the enemy's wickedness." Curtis' conclusions are not entirely wrong, but they stem from the wider defects of his overall work: that Jackson was consumed by his own selfish need for success and to prove himself. Surely, Jackson viewed the struggle in personal terms, at least to the extent that he did not want to leave the campaign unfinished. What commander wants to fail? Yet such facts should not impart some sort of extra-psychological motivation. Jackson's concerns over the Creek threat were logical and his desire for national vindication realistic in the face of the War of 1812's causes and colossal failures. That he wanted to believe the best of his men and was ultimately disappointed that they would leave the field of battle is also no great mystery. It is a disappointment that any commander would feel. Yet not just any commander would refuse to give up. It was Jackson who made the last ditch effort in his letter to Governor Blount. And that letter proved successful. It would seem, then, that Robert Remini's conclusions about Jackson and the letter are more telling and accurate than Curtis': "It was a powerful letter, one very typical of Jackson. It throbbed with determination and resolution to save the frontier and the nation. It contained many Jacksonian sentiments: the relentless patriotism; the energy to face down adversity; the will to prevail. The language hit hard—and tellingly. With all his faults—and they were legion—he was a tenacious, courageous, formidable

---

[112] Andrew Jackson to Willie Blount, December 26, 1813, *Jackson Papers, vol. 2*, 504-7.

man."[113] Such traits are what won the first two campaigns against the Creeks, and what ultimately proved successful in the final major battle.

Jackson wasted no time in preparing another blow against the Indians. The main body of troops had not yet arrived, but some 800 new recruits entered Fort Strother in early January 1814, and on the 21st Jackson marched them to Emuckfaw Creek, just three miles from a formidable breastwork created by the Creeks at a site known as Horseshoe Bend. The area was located in a broad loop of the Tallapoosa River, which made the only possible entry point a direct assault on the breastwork at the bend's neck. The troops camped and the very next morning the Indians attacked. Jackson's men, few in numbers and experience, barely held off the assault. When Jackson ordered a retreat, another attack ensued, this time while crossing Enotachopco Creek and some of Jackson's men momentarily fled. They ultimately regrouped, held on, and then retreated to Fort Strother until additional troops arrived. Neither of the encounters were victories for Jackson, but they were not losses either. Jackson's men had withstood the attacks and his abilities as a commander were now garnering attention. Major General Thomas Pinckney, a regular, rather than a militia, officer in charge of the southern military district, wrote to Secretary of War Armstrong on February 6th, lauding Jackson's determination and success: "I take the liberty," wrote Pinckney, "of drawing your attention to the present and former communications of General Jackson. Without the personal firmness, popularity, and exertions of that officer, the Indian war, on the part of Tennessee, would have been abandoned, at least for a time....If government think it advisable to elevate to the rank of general other persons than those now in the army, I have heard of none whose military operations so well entitle him to that distinction."[114] Pinckney was correct; no other army commander had been as successful as Jackson.

As new troops arrived in the next few weeks, Jackson focused on two goals: discipline and a final assault on Horseshoe Bend. Discipline was always a problem in the militia, but the recent mutinies and the new troops that had briefly fled at Enotachopco Creek taught him that victory would only come with a better trained army. He expressed this view in a letter to one of his officers, William Carroll, noting, "The disorder that prevailed amongst officers

---

[113] Curtis, *Andrew Jackson and the Search for Vindication*, 53-4; Remini, *Andrew Jackson: The Course of American Empire*, 204.

[114] For a description of the battle, see Andrew Jackson to Rachel Jackson, January 28, 1814, in Harold D. Moser, et al., eds., *The Papers of Andrew Jackson, vol. 3*, 1814-1815 (Knoxville: University of Tennessee Press, 1991), 17-21; hereafter referred to as *Jackson Papers, vol. 3*. Thomas Pinckney to Alexander Armstrong, February 6, 1814, in Parton, *The Life of Andrew Jackson*, 498.

& men in our late excursion, was a striking example, and a sufficient warning never to enter the country of our enemy with troops not reduced to some kind of obedience & order—I have barely to add, that you must have every disobedience of order, religiously punished, and repitition will not be made."[115] Jackson was, as always, true to his word. When General Isaac Roberts and four officers from his brigade began complaining about terms of service, Jackson had the lot arrested and court martialed. Around the same time, a young, eighteen year old militiaman named John Woods engaged in a dispute with one of his officers, leveled a gun, and accusations of mutiny rang out. When news of the incident reached Jackson, he immediately had Woods arrested and tried.[116] On March 12th the young man was found guilty and two days later executed in front of the army. It was brutal, unforgiving, and quite effective. It was war. "Out of the pain," observed Robert Remini, "Jackson forged an army. Now he could get on with the war."[117]

Little was made of the execution at the time, but it became a rallying cry against Jackson when he ran in the 1828 presidential election. One of the dirtiest campaigns in American history, it should come as no surprise that a great deal was made of Woods' death. Historians, too, have taken issue with the incident. Andrew Burstein referred to Woods as "Jackson's scapegoat," insisting that he was "a martyr, and the enduring symbol of Jacksonian ruthlessness." Michael Paul Rogin attempted to compare Jackson's refusal to follow a British officer's order to clean his boots during the Revolution to Woods refusal to obey orders. Rogin then noted that Jackson was particularly "short-tempered" because he was suffering from "A severe attacke of the Bowell complaint." It was only after drawing such conclusions that Rogin refocused and offered his standard paternalistic suppositions: "Jackson had failed to instill 'discipline and subordination' in his ranks and weld his troops into 'engines of destruction' under his paternal control. The sacrifice of Woods would demonstrate his authority."[118] Rogin's final determination is correct. It did demonstrate Jackson's authority and determination. Without such severe determination, Jackson would have quit the field in December of 1813. Was the execution of a soldier in wartime worth instilling obedience in such a notoriously disobedient body as the militia?

---

[115] Andrew Jackson to William Carroll, February 17, 1814, *Jackson Papers, vol. 3*, 30-2.

[116] For the problem with the officers, see Andrew Jackson to John Coffee, February 17, 1814, and Andrew Jackson to John Wood, March 14, 1814, *Jackson Papers, vol. 3*, 32-3, 48-9.

[117] Remini, *Andrew Jackson: The Course of American Empire*, 212.

[118] Burstein, *The Passions of Andrew Jackson*, 167,105; Rogin, *Fathers & Children*, 154.

James Parton, certainly not an uncritical biographer, noted, "The effect of the execution upon the army is said to have been salutary. A promptness of obedience and a regularity of discipline, before unknown among western militia, are declared to have marked the conduct of the troops during the remainder, the brief and brilliant remainder, of the campaign." Parton also concluded that no American militia general other than Jackson would have gone to such extremes as executing a soldier. "It is equally certain," he continued, "that no militia general that was then in service, except General Jackson, could, in the face of such difficulties as those which he encountered and mastered, have saved the campaign, protected the frontiers, subdued the Creeks, and gained every object proposed to be gained by the war."[119]

On the very day that John Woods was executed, Jackson led his army out of Fort Strother in preparation to finish the work he had attempted at Horseshoe Bend earlier in the year. This time he arrived with a sizable, well-trained, well-disciplined army. On March 27 the attack began and lasted well into the early hours of the evening. By the end, Jackson's men counted some 900 dead warriors. It was a devastating defeat for the Creeks and secured the southern frontier. The Creeks never posed another serious threat. Matters might have been quite different had the campaign ended in late 1813 and the British arrived to re-supply the Indians. Overall, the Creek War must be viewed in a larger geopolitical context regarding the balance of power, not only among the United States and the Indians, but among European nations as well. The English and French were still attempting to control American trade. This was one of the reasons for the War of 1812. The Spanish also represented a particularly troubling danger on the southern frontier, and both they and the English were fond of utilizing Indians to harass and endanger American settlers. Jackson's defeat of the Creeks, therefore, was an important message to Indian tribes that the United States was capable of bringing destruction to their doorsteps. His goal was to end the Creek ability to wage war. He was successful.

After the victory at Horseshoe Bend, Jackson led his army to an old French fort at the confluence of the Coosa and Tallapoosa Rivers, which he renamed Fort Jackson. There he continued operations to capture or kill the remaining Creek chiefs and warriors who were still at large. The one that Jackson wanted in particular was Red Eagle, or William Weatherford, 1/8 Creek whose father was White and mother of Creek-White lineage. He was also one of the chiefs responsible for the Fort Mims attack, though he had

---

[119] Parton, *Andrew Jackson*, 511-2.

attempted in vain to stop the ensuing slaughter. In mid-April Weatherford rode into Jackson's camp and approached the General's tent, announcing, "General Jackson, I am not afraid of you. I fear no man, for a I am a Creek warrior." He then acknowledged that Jackson's army had defeated his nation and he requested that the starving Creek women and children be escorted to the camp and fed. Weatherford offered his own death as payment, and many soldiers who heard of his arrival chanted, "Kill him!" Jackson instead invited Weatherford into his tent, shared a glass of brandy, and discussed the situation.

Weatherford agreed to total capitulation, though announced that if he still had warriors he would continue the war: "Once I could animate my warriors to battle; but I can not animate the dead." "You will exact no terms of a conquered people," he continued, "but such as they should accede to: whatever they may be, it would now be madness and folly to oppose." Jackson was impressed with Weatherford's bravery and allowed him to stay in camp several days and then leave of his own volition. There was no arrest. No execution. Jackson respected Weatherford and abided by their deal. The Creek survivors were led to the camp and fed for the next five months. There was no genocide; no murderous Jackson intent on killing every Indian that appeared. In later years Weatherford visited Jackson on occasion at the Hermitage.[120]

That Jackson did not hate every Indian he met did not mean he trusted them, considered them equal, or that it was safe to leave them in even relative proximity to American settlers. He therefore planned a gathering of all Creek tribes, both those who had been his enemy and ally, at Fort Jackson in July of 1814. In the interim, Jackson marched his victorious army home. News of his arrival in Nashville reached across the nation. The *True American* reported, "This distinguished and accomplished officer" has "returned from the Creek War – 'a war more honorable for our country, or more bloody and disastrous to the enemy the annals of Indian Warfare does not furnish an example'." It was also at this time that Jackson received a commission in the regular army, further elevating his status and reputation. The *Connecticut Journal* announced, "We are much pleased to learn that the military conduct, combining skill and courage of General Jackson, has attracted the attention of the Executive."[121]

---

[120] Parton, *Andrew Jackson*, 533-4; see also, Andrew Jackson to Willie Blount, April 18, 1814, *Jackson Papers, vol. 3*, 64; For Weatherford's visiting Jackson, see Remini, *Andrew Jackson: The Course of American Empire*, 219; and Angie Debo, *The Road to Disappearance* (Norman: University of Oklahoma Press, 1967), 82.

[121] "General Andrew Jackson," *True American*, June 15, 1814; "Andrew Jackson of Tennessee Appointed a Major General in the army of the United States," *Connecticut Journal*, June 6, 1814.

When Jackson ultimately returned and conducted the Treaty of Fort Jackson he exacted a heavy, brutal price for the Creek War. The irony, or perhaps horror, is that he exacted the price on both friendly and hostile Creeks. They were forced to give up some twenty-three million acres, nearly half of their domain, which comprised three-fifths of present-day Alabama and one-fifth of Georgia. Jackson's rationale was to break entirely the Creeks' ability to wage war, to stop any potential British and Spanish influence from Florida, and to serve as an example to other tribes that considered warfare against the United States. It was also a tremendous land grab for westerners, fueled by greed, which was an essential ingredient in the origins of Indian-White conflict. In the immediate aftermath of the treaty, Jackson wrote to John Coffee, explaining precisely his goals: "This you will observe secures the U.S. a free settlement from Georgia to Mobile and cuts (as soon as settled) all foreign influence from the Indians, and gives to the U.S. perfect security added to this in my oppinion the best unsettled country in america." An article in the *Essex Register* of Savannah, Georgia, understood, in part, Jackson's strategy, noting that the Indians "are cut off from all communication with the Spanish Government, which will prevent future Indian Wars." Jefferson, too, had recognized such a necessity, when he wrote the Senate in 1808 that "It is now, perhaps, become as interesting to obtain footing for a strong settlement of militias, along our southern frontier, eastward of the Mississippi, as on the west of that river....The consolidation of the Mississippi Territory, and the establishment of a barrier of separation between the Indians and our southern neighbors [the Spanish and English], are also important subjects."[122]

CONCLUSION

There was certainly nothing fair about the Treaty of Fort Jackson, but it was nonetheless effective in achieving all of the aims that Jackson determined were necessary to safeguard and build the Union. Historians may not like Jackson's methods or his results, but it is impossible to ignore or deny that he intended to make the frontier more secure for white Americans, or that he did so. The notion that Jackson was merely lashing out at his own inner demons – and that Indians were therefore essentially scapegoats – defies the realities of

---

[122] Andrew Jackson to John Coffee, August 10, 1814, in *Jackson Papers, vol. 3*, 112-13; Remini, *Andrew Jackson: The Course of American Empire*, 226; Essex Register, August 23, 1814; Jefferson quoted in *Kennedy, Burr, Hamilton, and Jefferson*, 361.

Indian warfare and the seriousness with which Jackson confronted those realities. Such notions also defy the expansionist beliefs that Jackson held. These ideals secured the future of America as much as did the later 1848 Mexican War land grab that filled out the remainder of the continental United States. That too was inspired by land greed. It too was unfair to those who owned the land previously. Yet it was also the nature of European and American conquest in this period of history. Conquest had allowed European powers to enter the new world. Conquest had allowed England to take all of Canada from the French in 1763. Conquest, or revolution, had allowed thirteen British colonies to take control of their own destiny. Conquest and its corresponding commitment to the Union drove Andrew Jackson to foster the security and growth of the still fledgling republic by forcing "savage" tribes away from white settlements.

One might question the extent to which America has ceased in such activities. The expansion of the Jacksonian and Manifest Destiny Era (Texas and the Mexican War), as well as the 1898 Spanish-American War, have given way to sometimes less overt acts of expansion in the twentieth and twenty-first centuries, but the drive to increase the availability of resources and markets has continued to shape American foreign policy, as has the desire to safeguard the nation. Jackson's sensibilities of "America first" have not changed considerably. His dispossession of Native Americans from their land was a necessary, albeit brutal and unjust, fact of building the Union. To expect otherwise is not in keeping within the context of this turbulent era of history.

Jackson's treatment of his own soldiers was also harsh, but effective. The execution of John Woods resulted in the creation of a real army, one that was capable of defeating the Creeks and of establishing enough supremacy that the Treaty of Fort Jackson was possible. James Curtis noted that if Jackson had any flaw as a tactician it was "excessive boldness."[123] In reality, it was Jackson's boldness in all that he did which made him successful. His boldness laid waste to the Red Sticks and maintained the campaign when his soldiers wanted to go home. His boldness convinced Governor Blount to send more troops when everything seemed lost. Jacksonian boldness was the essential ingredient in both Jackson's heroism and his despotism.

---

[123] Curtis, *Andrew Jackson and the Search For Vindication*, 51.

Chapter 4

THE MILITARY JACKSON: FLORIDA, NEW ORLEANS, FLORIDA

Andrew Jackson's defeat of the Creek Indians and punishing retribution in the Treaty of Fort Jackson was a clear message to other Indian tribes that might consider war against the United States. In this respect, it was critical to the continuing war on the southern frontier. One of Jackson's concerns was the British and Spanish presence in Florida and their ability to incite Indians to attack Americans. He also believed, correctly, that the British were in Florida and working to convince Indians to engage in warfare against America. Jackson's defeat of the Creeks gave pause to other tribes. To make that lesson even clearer, the iron General prepared for an offensive against Spanish Florida to force the British out and make another clear statement that the United States would defend itself against foreign nations. He launched such a mission late in 1814.

Nor was this the only time that Jackson entered Spanish soil. In 1818 he crossed the border again, this time to stop Seminole attacks against Georgia settlers. In this instance Jackson arrested, tried, and executed two British citizens. In doing so he disobeyed orders, violated the Constitution by engaging in an act of war without congressional approval, and sparked an international incident. Jackson's actions in his second Florida campaign represented an all too familiar pattern of rogue, lawless behavior.

His first example of running roughshod over the Constitution had come only three years earlier while defending New Orleans from British attack. In saving the city, Jackson also became the first American general – or any American for that matter – to suspend the writ of habeas corpus and impose martial law. The writ was and remains one of the most important safeguards against potentially abusive power by allowing a judge to require a holding authority – a police department or the military – to bring a prisoner before the court to show that there is just cause to continue imprisonment. Habeas corpus translates from Latin to "provide the body." The Constitution allows suspension of the writ, but an 1807 Supreme Court decision, *Ex Parte Bollman Swartwout*, which grew out of the Burr Conspiracy, determined that only Congress possessed such an authority.

The inclusion of martial law was a different issue altogether. The Constitution makes no mention of it whatsoever and virtually every state constitution from the founding of the nation well into the 1840s stated that the military shall remain subordinate to civil authority. Moreover, every legal and military treatise, and every court decision in the United States denied the legality of martial law as an extraordinary measure applicable to civilians. Martial law, for all of these sources, was considered synonymous with military law, which was a code of conduct for the armed forces. Thus Jackson not only overstepped the Constitution in declaring martial law, he also tread upon new ground in terms of emergency powers in times of national crisis. The difficulty is that without martial law, New Orleans would likely have been lost. Certainly, the benefits of Jackson's actions weighed heavily in favor of the United States. That weight, however, was a chain around the Constitution and the principle of law.

Jackson's illegal and unprecedented actions resulted in victory at New Orleans and ended the War of 1812 with a surge of nationalism the likes of which the young American republic had never witnessed. It was the greatest military victory in U.S. history up to that point and Jackson became an overnight sensation. The defeat of Britain's greatest army, the Peninsular War veterans who had vanquished Napoleon, turned what had been a miserable war that witnessed few successes into a source of national pride and vindication. Jackson could not have been more popular and it was easy for both the General and those who surrounded him to see that such popularity made him attractive politically.[124]

What, then, does one say about the lawless hero, Andrew Jackson? He believed that all of his actions were warranted because of national self-defense. He never wavered in this belief. There is no denying that Jackson's methods were effective. His first invasion of Florida was an important additional warning to southern tribes that they should not ally themselves with the British. This was apparent when Jackson's army forced British troops to

---

[124] Warshauer, *Andrew Jackson and the Politics of Martial Law*.

flee Pensacola. The second Florida invasion furthered Jackson's expansionist goals when Secretary of State John Quincy Adams convinced the Spanish, already in negotiation to settle the western boundary of the Louisiana Purchase territory, that they could not effectively control Florida and should therefore sell it to the United States for a mere five million dollars. That occurred in the 1819 Transcontinental Treaty. Adams insisted, and he was the only member of James Monroe's presidential cabinet to defend Jackson, that the General's invasion was a matter of national self-defense.

Here again is the complexity of Andrew Jackson. For one cannot simply conclude that he was lashing out with no clear conception of what he was doing. These instances were not surrogate attempts to prove his own right to survive. They were obvious, palpable actions meant to secure the nation from outside attacks. Jackson argued, as did his followers in ensuing years that in times of dire emergency paramount necessity authorized extreme, sometimes extra-constitutional measures. This is a doctrine that remains controversial to this day. Jackson was also shrewd enough to understand that military success shielded him from potential backlash. He was correct. Though there were certainly critics who challenged his illegal acts, the general from Tennessee was so popular, his nationalism so potent, that he could ride a wave of support right past his detractors and into the White House. Jackson understood his popularity and used it effectively.

FLORIDA PART 1

During the War of 1812 Vice Admiral Sir Alexander Cochrane commanded the British Navy in North America and intended to utilize southern Indians in concert with the Spanish to push Americans from the Gulf coast and back into the interior of the South. British officers had already been in contact with Indian chiefs in the region and Cochrane had sent Major Edward Nichols of the Royal Marines to Spanish Pensacola to arm the Indians and prepare for a broader invasion of U.S. territory. The plan was to take Mobile, join the hostile Creeks, and then spearhead towards the Mississippi River.[125] The idea was to hem the Americans in and deny them access to the Gulf.

---

[125] Frank L. Owsley, Jr., "Role of the South in the British Grand Strategy in the War of 1812," *Tennessee Historical Quarterly 31* (Spring, 1972): 22-38; Robin Reilly, *The British at the Gates: The New Orleans Campaign in the War of 1812* (New York: Putnam, 1974), 130-1, 170; John K. Mahon, "British Command Decisions Relative to the Battle of New Orleans,"

The plan was doomed for three reasons. First, Jackson had crushed the Creeks and in doing so made an important statement to other tribes. Second, he swiftly moved his army from Fort Jackson to Mobile, arriving there on August 22, 1814, thereby robbing Cochrane of his initial invasion point and forcing him to shift the operation to New Orleans. Third, Jackson then invaded Pensacola and the British troops there were forced to flee, providing a very clear lesson to their Indian allies of who exactly was in charge of the region. His strategy was flawless.

The British arrived at Mobile on September 12th with four ships. Jackson had directed his troops to repair Fort Bowyer in anticipation of the invasion. On the 15th the British attacked, but were unable to take the fort and thus their plans to invade Mobile were foiled. Still, Jackson anticipated a continued attempt to invade the region and he therefore stayed in Mobile, planning to move on Pensacola. On August 25th, he wrote a forceful letter to Secretary of War John Armstrong. There was no question of what Jackson wanted to do:

> "How long will the government of the united States tamely submit to disgrace and open insult from Spain. It is alone by a manly dignified course of conduct that we insure respect from other nations and peace to our own. Temporising will not do. Captain Woodbine of the British Marines is now and has been for a considerable time in Pensacola, drilling and organizing the hostile fugitive creeks under the Eye of the Governor, exercising all the hostile as well as the friendly Indians....I can but regret that permission had not been given by the government to have seized Pensacola, had this been done the american Eagle would now have soared above the fangs of the British Lyon."[126]

In the midst of his preparations, Jackson once again received news that militiamen were engaged in mutiny, this time at forts Strother, Williams, and Jackson. A private named David Hunt was arrested in late August, then forcibly freed by some of his fellow soldiers in early September. They subsequently raided the commissary and stole supplies for their unapproved march back to Tennessee. Over the next few weeks some of the soldiers returned to duty and some were arrested. Jackson approved courts martial. Two officers were dismissed from service. Five privates and a sergeant who were believed to be leaders of the mutiny were sentenced to execution.

Louisiana History 6 (Winter, 1965): 53-76; Remini, *Andrew Jackson: The Course of American Empire*, 235-6.

[126] Andrew Jackson to John Armstrong, August 25, 1814, Harold D. Moser, et al., eds., *The Papers of Jackson Papers*, vol. 3, (Knoxville: University of Tennessee Press, 1991), 122-3; hereafter referred to as the *Jackson Papers, vol. 3*.

Jackson approved the court's decree and the men were shot on February 21, 1814.[127] Once again, Jackson's treatment of soldiers was brutal and very effective.

Jackson also received other startling news during the late summer and early fall.

The British had landed in the Chesapeake Bay region and, on August 24-25th, invaded and burned the nation's capitol. The news steeled Jackson's conviction that extraordinary measures were warranted to stop a similar British victory in the South. On October 10th, the General wrote to John Rhea, a representative from Tennessee, commenting on the invasion and burning of Washington, D.C. The letter is a consummate representation of Jackson's views concerning the reality of war and the belief, as he put it, that *"necessary means"* are required to win. "I regret to learn the distruction of our capital and the national disgrace, but whilst I feel regret on the one hand, I rejoice that it will produce unanimity of feeling throughout the united states, and unity of action in the deliberative councils of the nation, and without counting the cost we will be viewed in the midst of *war*, that requires the whole energies of the nation, and the means of carrying on this war, to an honourable termination, will be sought better without calculating the *expense of the necessary means.*"[128] Jackson's comments revealed his wider justification for invading Pensacola, executing militia men who engaged in mutiny and thereby threatened the campaign, as well as in declaring martial law in New Orleans to ensure victory.

Shortly thereafter, on October 26th, Jackson wrote to the new secretary of war, James Monroe, explaining his intentions to invade Pensacola and the rationale for doing so: "I have been induced to determine to drive the British and Indian force from that place, possess myself of the [Fort] Barancas, (which I expect to find occupied by the former) and all other points that may be calculated to prevent a British fleet from entering Pensacola Bay. This will put an end to the Indian war in the South, as it will cut off all foreign influence." Jackson continued, "As I act without orders of government, I deem it proper to state my reasons for it." The presence of the British in Florida with the tacit approval of the Spanish governor, the British preparation for an assault against the United States, inciting the Indians to war, all justified, in Jackson's opinion, the invasion of Pensacola. He never wavered on the question of necessity and even acknowledged the potential consequences of his actions:

---

[127] See editor's notes, *Jackson Papers, vol. 3*, 133-5.
[128] Andrew Jackson to John Rhea, October 10, 1814, *Jackson Papers, vol. 3*, 156-7.

these acts "will be a sufficient justification in the eyes of my government, for having undertaken this expedition. Should it not, I shall have on consolation; a consciousness of having done the only thing which I can, under present circumstances, give security to this section and put down an Indian war; and the salvation of my country will be sufficient reward for the loss of my commission."[129] In his clearly unauthorized action Jackson stood on the principle of his convictions. He was nothing, if not steadfast. He was also smart enough to realize that success would shield him from potential governmental harm.

Fortunately for Jackson, and perhaps unfortunately for Monroe, a letter the secretary had written on October 21st had not yet arrived. Had it, Jackson's invasion may have been canceled. Monroe was quite clear: "you should at present take no measures, which would involve this Government in a contest with Spain."[130] On the 29th, Jackson left Mobile and on November 7th he captured Pensacola and watched as the British blew up Fort Barancas and fled the area on board their ships. Their Indian allies saw it too. Jackson's strategy was correct. The Indian war ended then and there.

NEW ORLEANS

New Orleans was still in danger. Jackson had received continual reports that the British were planning a major invasion of the city. His goal in occupying Mobile was to cut off any possibility of the British coming overland and descending on New Orleans. Even after capturing Mobile and invading Pensacola, he still worried that the British would return and make another assault on Fort Bowyer after the main part of his army had left for New Orleans. He therefore fortified the fort and determined to have John Coffee's cavalry encamp in Baton Rouge and be prepared to ride in either direction once the enemy's intentions became clear.

For months prior to his arrival in New Orleans, Jackson received urgent pleas from Governor William C.C. Claiborne and others to take military control of the city. Through its history, New Orleans had bounced around from French to Spanish control, then back to French, and ultimately became a part of the United States when Jefferson approved the Louisiana Purchase in 1803. Louisiana became a state in 1811. Still, the population was significantly

---

[129] Andrew Jackson to James Monroe, October 26, 1814, *Jackson Papers, vol. 3*, 173-4.
[130] James Monroe to Andrew Jackson, October 21, 1814, *Jackson Papers, vol. 3*, 170-1.

mixed, made up of every nationality that had ever controlled the region. To top it off, the notorious pirate Jean Laffite operated with virtual impunity, preying on ships in the Gulf region. This multi-ethnic element, combined with the natural geographic inroads of the Mississippi River, lakes Bourgne and Ponchartrain, and the countless bayous and inlets from the lakes, made defending New Orleans a virtual nightmare.[131]

"On the native Americans and a vast majority of the Creoles of the country, I place much confidence," wrote the governor in August of 1814, "but there are others much devoted to the Interest of Spain, and whose partiality for the English, is not less observable than their dislike to the American Government."[132] Claiborne complained that the state legislature had in the past failed to respond to potential threats of rumored British invasions and when he attempted to prepare the city, members of the legislature thwarted his plans. The governor subsequently wrote Jackson in September: "there is in this City a much *greater spirit of Disaffection* than I had anticipated." Others wrote the General that Claiborne was the problem: "the total want of Confidence by all Classes of people, in the Chief Magistrate of the State, puts it in a truely [sic] alarming Situation." The repeated and conflicting warnings served to prejudice Jackson's view of the inhabitants of New Orleans, especially the foreign population. "We have more to dread from Spies, and traitors, than from open enemies," wrote the General to Claiborne, "Vigilance and Energy is only wanting and all is safe."[133]

Jackson arrived in the city on December 1, 1814, and immediately prepared for a British invasion. For two weeks he inspected the various routes into the city, judged their defensibility and dispatched troops to warn of the

---

[131] For a broad background of the region, see Warshauer, *Andrew Jackson and the Politics of Martial Law*.

[132] William C.C. Claiborne to Andrew Jackson, August 12, 1814, *Jackson Papers, vol. 3*, 115-116. See also, Claiborne to Jackson, August 21, 1814, in which Claiborne states, I "strongly suspect, that some Spanish or English agent has made injurious impressions on the minds of these people." Claiborne's concerns were also expressed in a letter dated August 8, 4; for both letters, see John Spencer Bassett, ed., *The Correspondence of Andrew Jackson, vol. 6* (Washington, D.C.: Carnegie Institution, 1933), 437, 434; hereafter referred to as *Correspondence*. For an excellent account of foreign discontent, see Tom Kanon, "The Other Battle of New Orleans: Andrew Jackson and the Louisianans," *Gulf South Historical Review 2d ser., 17* (Spring 2002): 41-61.

[133] William C.C. Claiborne to Andrew Jackson, September 8, 1814, *Correspondence, vol. 6*, 438. For complaints against Claiborne, see Colonel Samuel Fulton to Andrew Jackson, September 20, 1814, *Correspondence*, 56; For additional complaints of disaffection, see Committee of Safety to Jackson, September 18, 1814, *Correspondence, vol. 6*, 51-54; Edward Livingston to Andrew Jackson, November 5, 1814, *Correspondence, vol. 6*, 90-91; on "vigilance," see Andrew Jackson to William C.C. Claiborne, August 30, 1814, *Jackson Papers, vol. 3*, 126.

enemy's arrival. He also contemplated the best course of action to control the disaffection reported by the governor. On December 10th the General wrote Claiborne, requesting him to "obtain the sence [sic] of the Legislature how far they will aid in erecting the works for the defence of the State." The request was not solely about money, for he added, "should I be disappointed in the laudable feelings, that I am induced to believe pervades your whole Legislature, it is necessary that I should know it, that I may employ what means I have in my power for the best defence of this Section of the District that is intrusted for my care."[134]

Claiborne must have engaged in a persuasive session with the legislature. On December 14th a joint resolution passed both houses appropriating $20,000 to be expended under the governor's orders. Still, both Claiborne and Jackson remained suspicious, perhaps in part because the legislature refused to suspend the writ of habeas corpus in order to allow the impressment of seamen for duty on the American ships *Louisiana* and *Carolina*. The governor therefore requested the legislature to adjourn for two to three weeks. They refused, insisting that many reasons existed for continuing the session, not the least of which was that it would cost more to travel to their homes than remain within the city.

The legislature's refusal to suspend its session, combined with distressing reports about spies, did little to allay the General's concerns over the loyalty of those in the city. Compounding Jackson's anxiety was news that the British had arrived below New Orleans and approached the pirate Jean Lafitte to enlist his aid in capturing the city. Lafitte had stalled the British and informed members of the Louisiana legislature of the enemy's plan. He also joined Jackson's forces, supplying the General with much needed cannons, gun powder, and flints. On December 15th Jackson published an address to the citizens: "The Major-General commanding has with astonishment and regret learned that great consternation and alarm pervade your city....The General with still greater astonishment, has heard that British emissaries have been permitted to propagate sedi[t]ious reports amongst you." He subsequently announced that all citizens were expected to engage in the country's defense, declaring, "should the general be disappointed in this expectation he will separate our enemies from our friends. Those who are not for us are against us, and will be dealt with accordingly."[135]

---

[134] Andrew Jackson to William C. C. Claiborne, December 10, 1814, *Jackson Papers, vol. 3*, 202-203.

[135] Thomas L. Butler, Aid de Camp to New Orleans Citizens and Soldiers, December 15, 1814, *Jackson Papers, vol. 3*, 204-205.

This ominous warning foreshadowed the proclamation of martial law. Prior to publishing his address, Jackson contemplated imposing military rule and requested the legal opinions of two leading New Orleans attorneys, both of whom acted as aides to the General. Jackson's advisors, Edward Livingston and Abner Duncan, concluded that martial law suspended all civil functions and placed every citizen under military control. The lawyers disagreed, however, on the legality of the proclamation. Livingston believed that it was "unknown to the Constitution or Laws of the U.S." and thus "justified only by the necissity [sic] of the Case and that therefore the General proclaims it at his own risque [sic] and under his responsibility." Taking a decidedly different view, Duncan insisted that the constitutional provision authorizing suspension of the writ of habeas corpus impliedly permitted the operation of martial law and that it was the "guardian of the Public safety" who is "to judge of those cases provided for by the Constitution."[136] The question of martial law's legality was important considering that a key provision was suspension of the writ of habeas corpus. Though the Constitution allowed suspension, and the Supreme Court's 1807 decree in *Ex parte Bollman & Swartwout* ruled that only the national legislature had that authority to implement such an act, even that decision failed to define or authorize the use of martial law as implemented by Jackson. American law simply had no precedent for such an action.

Jackson did not quibble over the question of constitutionality presented by Livingston and Duncan. The General was satisfied that martial law canceled all civilian authority and placed the city under military control. On December 16th he issued the proclamation. All who entered or exited the city were required to report to the adjutant-general's office. Failure to do so resulted in arrest and interrogation. All vessels, boats or other crafts desiring to leave the city required a passport either from the General, his staff, or Commodore Daniel T. Patterson. All street lamps were ordered extinguished at nine p.m. and anyone found after that hour without a pass was arrested and held as a spy. New Orleans was officially an armed camp and General Jackson the only authority.[137] For the next two weeks Jackson's army hurriedly prepared the city's defenses. There was no time to waste. On December 23rd a report arrived announcing that the British had surprised an outlying post and entered the

---

[136] Livingston and Duncan opinions were provided orally to Jackson and were subsequently issued as written opinions in March of 1815. See *Correspondence, vol. 2*, 197-199.

[137] Declaration of Martial Law, December 16, 1814, in Harold D. Moser, *The Papers of Andrew Jackson: A Microfilm Supplement*. Also in James Parton, *The Life of Andrew Jackson, vol. 2* (New York: Mason Brothers, 1860), 60-61.

country with a large force through Bayou Bienvenue, which offered a direct route to the city. Jackson learned of this news in the afternoon and immediately prepared an offensive. His decision to engage in a night attack on the British advance force was bold, potentially fool-hardy, and most certainly saved New Orleans. Night battles were fairly rare because it was difficult to survey what exactly was occurring in the midst of an engagement. The actual battle resulted in no clear victory for either side, but the British general in temporary command, John Keane, assumed wrongly that Jackson must have had a significant reserve force if he was willing to endanger his troops with a risky night attack. This assumption caused Keane to stay where he was and await reinforcements rather than march towards the city. The delay provided Jackson with critical time to prepare his defenses. Had Keane set out for the city immediately, there was little that could have stopped his better equipped and more disciplined force. Jackson had gotten strategically lucky with his night battle, but it was his boldness that made such a battle possible in the first place.

The Tennessee general was also lucky that the same geographic nightmare that made New Orleans' defense so difficult to defend did the same for the British tactical position. Keane had led his men into an untenable situation, with the Mississippi River on one side and a virtually impenetrable cypress swamp on the other. There was no possibility of flanking Jackson's army, which had used the valuable time of the British stall to erect a massive breastwork stretching from the river to the swamp. When the main commander of the British forces, Lieutenant General Sir Edward Michael Pakenham, arrived, he momentarily considered withdrawing his forces and attacking the city from some other vantage point. Had he done so the battle would likely have turned out far differently.

On December 28th the British launched a probing attack to gauge the American position, and on January 1, 1815, the two armies engaged in an artillery duel that shook the country for miles around. In each encounter the British were unable to overcome Jackson's defenses. They had not, however, thrown everything they had at the Americans. That came on the morning of January 8th. What ensued was a battle of horrific proportions. As the British marched towards Jackson's line under cover of a thick fog, the weather shifted and the fog lifted, revealing a sea of red coats flooding toward the barricade. Jackson's well-directed cannons and muskets rained down a deafening, destructive fire on the invaders. They were decimated. Some 2,200 British soldiers were killed and wounded. The entire British high command was killed, including General Pakenham, who was later packed in a keg of rum to preserve his body and shipped back to England. A mere six Americans were killed, with another seven wounded. The victory was astounding. The battle was the final British attempt on New Orleans.[138]

On January 18th the British silently and quickly slipped back to their awaiting fleet. The next day Jackson investigated the abandoned camp, then quickly penned a letter to James Monroe: "there is but little doubt that his [the British army's] last exertions have been made in this quarter, at any rate, for the present season." "I hope, however," continued the General, "I need not assure you that wherever I command, such a belief shall never occasion any relaxation in the measures for resistance." Jackson, always fervent about duty, remained true to his word. For the next two months New Orleans prepared for a battle that never came. The General increased fortifications, ordered further obstruction of the bayous, and, to the regret of many, continued martial law. Jackson apparently had real concerns that the British would attempt another assault upon the city. In a letter to Claiborne the General reported the capture of a British sailor who told of a fleet expected to arrive with reinforcements numbering 15,000 and a plan to attack New Orleans by land.[139]

Jackson also continued to have concerns over the loyalty of those within the city, and he therefore kept an especially tight rein. Those without passes were quickly arrested and delivered to the guardhouse at the city hotel. Within ten days of declaring martial law so many individuals, both soldiers and citizens, had been arrested that Mayor Girod wrote to Jackson complaining "before two days the Guard House shall be full." Some citizens gained release by signing up for immediate militia duty, while others were freed after brief interrogations.[140] In a number of cases, however, citizens languished in jail for weeks. No longer perceiving a threat to their city following the January 8th victory, the citizens of New Orleans desired a return to their former lifestyles. The rigors as well as diseases of camp life did not appeal to a citizenry motivated only by imminent invasion. Just as important, the spring planting season had arrived and fields needed tending. Even more ominous was the fear of possible slave insurrections while so many plantation owners served in the

---

[138] For excellent accounts of the battles, see Reilly, *The British at the Gates*, and Robert Remini, *The Battle of New Orleans: Andrew Jackson and America's First Military Victory* (New York: Viking, 1999).

[139] Andrew Jackson to James Monroe, January 19, 1815, *Jackson Papers, vol. 3*, 250-251; for Jackson's concerns of another attack, see Andrew Jackson to William C.C. Claiborne, January 21, 1815, *Jackson Papers*, Library of Congress microfilm edition.

[140] Nicholas Girod to Andrew Jackson, December 25, 1814, *Jackson Papers*, Library of Congress microfilm edition.

militia. Desertion and mutiny among American troops became rampant and prompted even more arrests.

Equally distressing were rumors that a peace treaty had been reached, but that no official word had arrived from Washington. Jackson still believed that a hostile and far larger British army intended another assault on New Orleans. With that belief in mind, he refused to relax his defenses. A showdown between the General and certain citizens in New Orleans was underway. Jackson's attempt to rally the citizens of New Orleans was met with open defiance on March 3rd when an article appeared in the *Louisiana Courier*. "A Citizen of Louisiana of French Origin," declared,

> "It is high time the laws should resume their empire; that the citizens of this State should return to the full enjoyment of their rights; that, in acknowledging that we are indebted to General Jackson for the preservation of our city and the defeat of the British, we do not feel much inclined, through gratitude, to sacrifice any of our privileges, and, less than any other, that of expressing our opinion of the acts of his administration; that it is time the citizens accused of any crime should be rendered to their natural judges, and cease to be brought before special or military tribunals, a kind of institution held in abhorrence, even in absolute governments; that, after having done enough for glory, the moment of moderation has arrived; and, finally, that the acts of authority which the invasion of our country and our safety may have rendered necessary are, since the evacuation of it by the enemy, no longer compatible with our dignity and our oath of making the Constitution respected."[141]

Here was a direct challenge to General Jackson's authority. He thought carefully about his next course of action and after ascertaining the author's identity from the newspaper's editor, waited two days before issuing arrest orders for state senator Louis Louaillier. Moreover, believing that Louaillier was merely one actor in a larger conspiracy, the General prepared for a move by the local magistrate, including in the orders, "should any person attempt serving a writ of Habeas corpus to arrest the prisoner Louaillier from confinement immediately confine the person making such attempt." Having decided to arrest Louaillier, Jackson wanted to ensure that no judge could release the senator. The second order showed the General's shrewd foresight. For on the very day of Louaillier's arrest, attorney Pierre Louis Morel, a witness to the arrest, petitioned Federal District Judge Dominick Augustin

---

[141] "A Citizen of Louisiana of French Origin," *Louisiana Courier*, March 3, 1815, in Parton, *The Life of Andrew Jackson, vol. 2*, 309-11.

Hall for a writ of habeas corpus. Upon learning of Hall's action on the evening of the 5th, Jackson wasted no time in arresting him for "aiding and abetting and exciting mutiny within my camp."

To head off further plots the General issued a proclamation to the people and repeated his belief in a conspiracy:

> "The commanding general is responsible for the safety of this section of the union; and it *shall* be protected against every design of the enemy, in what manner soever he may shape his attack, whether it be made by the known and declared foe, or by the pretended and deceitful friend....The lurking traitor is now laboring to feed fresh fuel, a spirit of discontent, disobedience and mutiny, too long secretely [sic] fomenting."[142]

While Louaillier and Hall languished in the same jail cell, Jackson was faced with more distressing news. Daily expecting word of the peace treaty from Washington, the General suffered only disappointment on March 6th when a post rider arrived and, because of an unexplained mix-up, carried only orders to raise two more regiments of volunteers. Yet the rider also bore a letter from the postmaster general directing all on the post route to aid the rider because he carried news of peace.[143] Refusing to accept such an unofficial communication, Jackson continued martial law.

Within a week, on March 13, 1815, the peace treaty arrived and the steely General lifted martial law, but not before he had Louaillier face a court martial and even after acquittal continued to hold the senator in a jail cell. Jackson also banished Judge Hall from the city. The return of peace brought the return of Hall, who was bent on exacting retribution. The ensuing case, *The United States vs. Major-General Andrew Jackson,* allowed the judge to vindicate both his judicial station and his injured pride. Jackson was ultimately hauled before the court and, after Hall refused to hear Jackson's defense and then Jackson refused to answer Hall's questions, the General was fined $1000 for contempt of court. Jackson paid the fine, and delivered an impromptu speech in front of the court house in which he lauded the supremacy of the civilian government over that of the military. With the threat to the nation and New Orleans passed, so too had Jackson's need for extraordinary military measures. Though Secretary of War Alexander Dallas had written Jackson in April 1815 on

---

[142] Andrew Jackson to Lieutenant Colonel Mathew Arbuckle, March 5, 1815, *Correspondence, vol. 2,* 183; "Andrew Jackson and Judge D.A. Hall, Report of the Committee of the Senate (Of The State of Louisiana, 1843)," *Louisiana Historical Quarterly* 5 (1922): 509-570.

[143] Andrew Jackson to James Monroe, March 6, 1815, *Jackson Papers,* Library of Congress microfilm edition.

behalf of President Madison, and expressed concern at the reports of martial law, neither the secretary nor the chief executive followed up on the matter.

With New Orleans there is hardly a better example of Jackson as hero and despot.

The degree of the General's success was amazing. Yet the victory came with a price: American civil liberties. In the immediate aftermath of the battle, however, Americans focused solely on the amazing success in which it had been won. Everyone had expected New Orleans to be lost. Washington, D.C., had been invaded and burned. Little more was expected of the Crescent City. The victory not only astonished the nation, but created a wave of nationalism the likes of which Americans had never seen.[144] As one scholar noted, "The American people were vicariously purged of shame and frustration. At a moment of disillusionment, Andrew Jackson reaffirmed the young nation's self-belief; he restored its sense of national prowess and destiny."[145] Next to George Washington, no general stood in higher esteem than Jackson. It seemed that nothing was beyond the extraordinary abilities of this backwoods Tennessean. And with victory, Jackson had been shielded from any real criticism of martial law.

FLORIDA PART II

The ability of the New Orleans victory to protect Jackson from political harm was sorely tested in 1819 when Congress debated his second foray into Florida. It was a mere year earlier, in 1818, that the iron General rode across the Georgia border into Spanish Florida and once again took control of Pensacola, as well as St. Marks. This time the United States was not at war and there were no British troops to force from the area. Rather, Jackson had been ordered to take command and follow the orders sent to General Edmund Gaines to pursue Seminole Indians who crossed into American territory and attacked settlements there. The Spanish were required by treaty to control the Seminoles, but failed to do so. Jackson relished the idea of forcing the Spanish from all of Florida and claiming it. Doing so not only fit within his expansionist vision but his concerns about frontier security. Southerners and

---

[144] For a detailed account of New Orleans under martial law and the nationalism that followed the victory, see, Warshauer, *Andrew Jackson and the Politics of Martial Law*.

[145] Ward, *Andrew Jackson: Symbol For An Age*, 5.

westerners had always hated the Spanish, or any foreign presence in such close proximity to the United States.

With this belief in mind, Jackson wrote to President Monroe in January of 1818, insisting that the orders were too limited because they did not allow him to pursue the Indians if they "shelter themselves under a Spanish port." Jackson believed that this is exactly what the Indians would do and thereby effectively thwart the military operation. Yet the General also understood Monroe's concern that any official act on the part of the American government could potentially cause a war and he therefore offered the president a decidedly more surreptitious way to solve the problem: "the whole of East Florida [should be] seized & held as an indemnity for the outrages of Spain upon the property of our citizens…this can be done without implicating the Government; let it be signifyed to me through any channel, (say [Tennessee representative] Mr. J. Rhea) that the possession of the Floridas would be desirable to the United States, & in sixty days it will be accomplished."[146]

What occurred next is the stuff of politics and disputed history. Monroe apparently received Jackson's letter, but claimed to be ill at the time and handed it off to Secretary of War John C. Calhoun. The president later stated that he never actually looked at the letter until a year later, after Jackson had acted in Florida. This is remarkable given Jackson's rather astonishing proposition and past actions. For his part, the General claimed that he did in fact receive word through John Rhea approving of the scheme to invade Florida, but that he had burned the letter in 1819 at Monroe's request. Rhea later vacilated between supporting the president and the General. Much of this came to light years later, in the 1830s, when a controversy erupted between Jackson and Calhoun, then president and vice-president, over what had become known as the Seminole Affair. Historians have attempted to clarify what exactly occurred and their judgments have generally concluded that Rhea had not actually given Jackson any such clandestine approval, though the two had been discussing a completely different matter involving the president, one related to military orders, and that this was the alleged approval Jackson received.

Depending on an historian's overall view of Jackson, the reality of the Rhea letter either becomes a Jacksonian act of total dishonesty or a mere mistake on the General's part. Michael Paul Rogin and James Curtis, for example, believe the Jackson had wantonly fabricated the entire episode, and

---

[146] Andrew Jackson to James Monroe, January 6, 1818, in Harold D. Moser, ed., *The Papers of Andrew Jackson, vol. 4* (Knoxville: University of Tennessee Press, 1994), 166-7; hereafter referred to as *Jackson Papers, vol. 4*.

David and Jeanne Heidler stated bluntly that Jackson "lied."[147] Robert Remini is more forgiving in his appraisal, insisting that Jackson had indeed invented the Rhea letter, but "did not realize he was fabricating."[148] Rather, he was remembering in the 1830s what had occurred years before and made a mistake about what Rhea was approving. Remini supplements this determination by adding that Jackson certainly did not misunderstand Monroe's long-term interests, one of which was the acquisition of Florida. In a letter Monroe wrote to Jackson on December 28, 1817, only days before Jackson tendered his provocative offer, the president noted, "this days mail will convey to you an order to repair to the command of the troops now acting against the Seminoles, a tribe which has long violated our rights, & insulted our national character. The mov'ment will bring you, on a theatre, when possibly you may have other services to perform."[149]

Jackson's temperament, his zeal for expansion, and his hatred of the Spanish were no mystery to Monroe. Nor was the fact that Jackson had invaded Florida in 1814 without so much as a worry over how it might violate his military authority or an international treaty. It was enough for him to believe that necessity demanded such an action. The same had been true of his martial law declaration. Thus how could the president have possibly believed that the indomitable Jackson would use restraint in pursuing enemy Seminoles into Spanish territory? This is certainly the understanding that Remini deduced, writing, "Great interests meant the Spanish presence in Florida, and the President of the United States was instructing his General not to cease activity until the danger of that presence was settled permanently." Even Andrew Burstein, no admirer of Jackson, concluded, "Monroe knew what to expect of Jackson and could not have been entirely surprised by the aggressive posture the general assumed."[150] One must also remember that when president, James Monroe had secretly authorized an insurrection in East Florida and ultimately claimed that territory from the Spanish as part of the Louisiana Purchase. Thus the American desire for the region was hardly a mystery, as

---

[147] Rogin, *Fathers & Children*, 200-2; Curtis, *Andrew Jackson and the Search for Vindication*, 69; Heidler and Heidler, *Old Hickory's War*, 119-121; see also, Richard R. Stenberg, "Jackson's 'Rhea Letter' Hoax," *The Journal of Southern History 2, No. 4*, (November, 1936): 480-496.

[148] Remini, *Andrew Jackson: The Course of American Empire*, 348.

[149] Remini, *Andrew Jackson: The Course of American Empire*, 348-9.

[150] Remini, *Andrew Jackson: The Course of American Empire*, 348-9; Burstein, *The Passions of Andrew Jackson, 129*; see also, Remini, *Andrew Jackson and His Indian Wars, 138*; Buchanan, *Jackson's Way*, 366.

Thomas Jefferson noted in an 1803 letter in which he announced, "we shall certainly obtain the Floridas, and all in good time."[151]

Whether Jackson, knowingly or not, fabricated the Rhea letter will continue to be a point of dispute. What he did not fabricate, however, was Monroe's or southern and western Americans' desire for Florida and their animosity towards the Spanish. Still, such a conclusion shines no great light on Jackson's willingness to do whatever he thought proper to secure benefits to the nation, legal or otherwise. Equally, if not more problematic is the way in which Jackson went about achieving those benefits. For the Seminole Affair became far more than a mere fabrication or disregard of military orders. In the process of pursuing the Seminoles into Florida, Jackson sent an abusive and disrespectful letter, the tone of which even Robert Remini described as "lordly arrogance," to Spanish Governor José Masot. Next, the General invaded both St. Marks and Pensacola, and in the process arrested two British citizens, turned them over to a court martial, and approved their executions for crimes against the United States by inciting and aiding an Indian war. Such actions were not only a wanton breach of his official orders, but an act of war against Spain and potentially against Great Britain.

The letter to Masot, in which Jackson announced, "I wish to be distinctly understood," and followed with, "any attempt to interrupt the passage of my transports cannot be received in any other light than as a hostile act on your part," was sent on March 25, 1818.[152] On April 6th, he seized St. Marks and raised the American flag in the Spanish fort. It was at this time that U.S. forces captured the Englishman Alexander Arbuthnot, who Jackson described in a letter to Secretary of War John C. Calhoun, as "a Scotch man and suspected as one of the Instigators of this savage and cruel war....He is in confinement untill evidences of his guilt can be collected." In the same letter, Jackson reported that his troops had invaded a Seminole village and though the hostile Indians had escaped earlier, "more than fifty fresh scalps were found." He explained, "The old red Stick's standard, a *red pole*, was erected, crowned with scalps recognised by the hair, as torn from the heads of the unfortunate

---

[151] Stephen F. Knott, *Secret and Sanctioned Covert Operations and the American Presidency* (New York: Oxford University Press, 1996). Jefferson quoted on 88.

[152] Remini, *Andrew Jackson: The Course of American Empire*, 353. For a good account of the Seminole Affair, one can begin with Remini, and also see the various works listed in notes 24 and 27. For the specifics of Jackson's trial and execution of British citizens, see Deborah A. Rosen, "Wartime Prisoners and the Rule of Law: Andrew Jackson's Military Tribunals during the First Seminole War," *Journal of the Early Republic 28, no. 4* (Winter, 2008): 559-595.

companions of Scott."[153] Scott had been attacked by Seminoles in mid-November of 1817 while in a boat on the Apalachicola River. Only five people survived the slaughter, in which the children's brains were bashed out by swinging their heads into the side of the boat. In finding the scalps and remembering the slaughter of children, there is little wonder why Jackson's troops put some three hundred Indian homes to the torch and confiscated the Seminoles' food stocks. Jackson also hanged two Creek chiefs, both of whom were engaged in hostilities against Americans.

While in the Indian town Jackson also had the good fortune to capture Robert Ambrister, a former British Marine who entered the Indian village without knowing that Americans had taken it over. The arrest of two Englishmen, both of whom Jackson believed to be inciting the Indians, confirmed the General's constant belief that it was the close proximity of European nations to the U.S. that posed the greatest danger to the frontier. He explained his beliefs in a letter to Calhoun: "On the commencement of my operations I was strongly impressed with a belief that this Indian War had been excited by some unprincipled Foreign or private Agents—The Outlaws of the old red stick party had been too severely convinced, and the Seminoles were too weak in numbers to believe, that they could possibly alone maintain a war with even partial success against the United States." Jackson believed that the Spanish, and the English in the form of Arbuthnot and Ambrister, were culpable. This belief justified not only the invasion and seizure of Spanish territory, but the trial and execution of the two Englishmen. Jackson informed Secretary of War Calhoun, "These individuals were tried under my orders by a Special Court of Select officers—legally convicted as exciters of this Savage and Negro War, legally condemned, and most justly punished for their iniquities." On April 29th, Arbuthnot was hanged from the yardarm of his own ship and Ambrister was shot.

As he had during the Creek War in 1813-14, Jackson, in the same letter to Calhoun, clearly defined the problem in the South and the need for a strong American presence there, insisting, "no security can be given to our Southern frontier without occupying a cordon of Posts along the Sea Shore—The Moment the American Army retires from Florida, The War hatchet will be again raised, & the same scenes of indiscriminate murder with which our frontier setlers have been visited, will be repeated."[154] This rationale, in Jackson's mind and that of many Americans, justified his first invasion of

---

[153] Andrew Jackson to John Caldwell Calhoun, April 8, 1818, *Jackson Papers, vol. 4*, 190.
[154] Andrew Jackson to John C. Calhoun, May 5, 1818, *Jackson Papers, vol. 4*, 197-200.

Florida, his harsh terms in the Treaty of Fort Jackson, and his second invasion of Spanish territory.

In the aftermath of the executions Jackson turned his army towards Pensacola, entering and taking control of the city on May 24, 1818. Just prior to his arrival, Jackson and Masot exchanged heated letters, the governor opposing Jackson's entry into the city and promising "I will repulse you force to force." The General responded with a long letter in which he chastised Masot and the Spanish, exclaiming, "This is the third time that the American Troops have been compelled to enter Pensaco[la] from the same causes—Twice had the enemy been expelled & the place left in quiet possession of those who had permitted the irregular occupancy—This time it must be held until Spain has the power or will to maintain her neutrality....If the peacable surrender be refused, I shall enter Pensacola by violence and assume the Government—until the transaction can be amicably adjusted by the Two Governments."[155]

Jackson spent only a few days in Pensacola before leaving a military force to maintain control of the city and departing for Tennessee, where he was lauded in celebration after celebration. On June 2nd he penned a letter to Rachel, announcing, "I trust I have put an end to indian hostilities for the future, The Just Vengeance of heaven—having vissitted and punished with death, the exciters of the Indian war, and horrid massacre of our innocent weomen & children on the Southern frontier. I have destroyed the Babylon of the South, the hot bed of the Indian war & depredations on our frontier by taking St Marks & Pensacola." The very same day he wrote to President Monroe, echoing the sentiments about protecting the frontier and insisting, as he always did, that his actions were patriotic: "I have consulted publick good & the safety & security of our southern frontier. I have established peace & safety, and hope the government will never yield it, should my acts meet your approbation it will be a source of great consolation to me, should it be disapproved, I have this consolation, that I exercised my best exertions & Judgt. and that sound national Policy will dictate holding Possession as long as we are a republick."[156]

Jackson was not alone in arriving at such conclusions. Hezekiah Niles, the well known editor of *Niles Weekly Register* based in Maryland, announced,

---

[155] José Masot to Andrew Jackson, May 23, 1818, and Andrew Jackson to José Masot, May 23, 1818, *Jackson Papers, vol. 4*, 205; 206-9.

[156] Andrew Jackson to Rachel Jackson, June 2, 1818, and Andrew Jackson to James Monroe, June 2, 1818, *Jackson Papers, vol. 4*, 212-13; 213-15.

"ninety nine hundreths of the people believe that general Jackson acted on every occasion for the good of the country."[157]

THE AFTERMATH OF FLORIDA

The Indians called Jackson, "Sharp Knife." The Spanish, "Caudillo," which translated to "the Napoleon of the woods." Most Americans referred to him as "Old Hickory," or the "Hero of New Orleans." In the aftermath of the Seminole Affair, he garnered a new name: "military chieftain," which symbolized for its originator Henry Clay all that was dangerous to a young republic. In reality, all of these names were apt for the fiery and indomitable general from Tennessee. It merely depended on whether or not one was injured by or benefited from Jackson's patently aggressive and often-times illegal tactics. Yet, however one labeled or labels Jackson – foolish, stupid, blindly lashing out with no vision – none of these suppositions accurately depict the man. He made his move into Florida with very clear intentions, legal or not, and understood two distinct truths: First, many in the nation would applaud his actions. Second, he was the most popular hero in America since George Washington and it would be difficult and potentially dangerous for any politician to chastise him too harshly.

It was exactly such issues that roiled throughout the nation's capitol from mid-July 1818 into the early winter of 1819. Monroe's presidential cabinet was thrown into disarray, with virtually all of the members, including John Calhoun (who Jackson believed had supported him), calling for an investigation and possible censure of the General's conduct. Only Secretary of State John Quincy Adams defended Jackson, arguing that he acted out of national self-defense and therefore his conduct was sanctioned by the law of nations. Indeed, this is what Jackson himself had insisted in letters to Calhoun and Monroe. Adams also had ulterior motives, realizing that Jackson's invasion of Spanish territory could aid the secretary in his contentious negotiations with Spain over the western boundary of the Louisiana Territory.[158]

The House and Senate were also concerned about Jackson's conduct. Both houses of Congress appointed committees that ultimately issued reports

---

[157] Niles, *Weekly Register*, March 13, 1819.
[158] Lynn Hudson Parsons, *John Quincy Adams* (Madison: Madison House, 1998), 140-144; Philip Coolidge Brooks, *Diplomacy in the Borderlands: The Adams-Onis Treaty of 1819* (University of California, 1939; reprint: New York: Octagon Books, 1970), 148-150.

critical of the General. In the House, representatives spent several weeks debating whether to sanction the negative report from the Committee on Military Affairs, and ultimately voted against it. The Senate, however, issued a critical report.

In the midst of the legislative battle virtually every representative, even those who objected to Jackson's actions, realized the importance of treading carefully when it came to the Hero of New Orleans. The General's supporters, abundantly aware of Jackson's nationalist appeal, lauded his unparalleled services and chastised those who attempted to cast a shadow over his fame. "A nation should preserve its glory," warned Alexander Smyth of Virginia, "and, as the glory of a nation is composed of the aggregate of the fame of individuals, to tarnish the character of the most distinguished hero of the United States, of the present age, is to tarnish the glory of the nation." He added, "Let me assure you that the American people will not be pleased to see their great defender, their great avenger, sacrificed."[159] The General's critics took such admonitions seriously, never forgetting to give Jackson the proper respect due America's hero. Speaking for the House Military Affairs Committee, Thomas Nelson noted, "Your committee must here, in justice to their own feelings, express their extreme regret, that it has become their duty to disapprove the conduct of one who has, on a former occasion, so eminently contributed to the honor and defence of the nation, as had Major General Jackson." Nelson also noted gingerly, that the committee engaged in a "temperate expression" on the subject.[160]

Henry Clay of Kentucky seemed to be one of the few legislators willing to go, as it were, toe to toe with Jackson, delivering a fiery speech in which he chastised the General as a dangerous "military chieftain." Yet the degree of Clay's ardor was in part fueled by the threat Jackson posed in future presidential elections.[161] Clay was an ambitious man and wanted to be the first president from the West. Thus mixed motives caused him to lay siege on the General. I hope gentlemen will "deliberately survey the awful position on which we stand," warned Clay. "They may bear down all opposition; they may even vote the general public thanks; they may even carry him triumphantly through this house. But, if they do, in my humble judgment, it will be a

---

[159] House of Representatives, Congressman Smyth of Virginia on the Seminole War, 15th Cong., 2nd Sess., *Annals of Congress*, (January 21, 1819), 700, 703. Similar sentiments abound throughout many speeches on the Seminole War.

[160] House of Representatives, Congressman Nelson of Virginia on the Seminole War, 15th Cong., 2nd Sess., *Annals of Congress*, (January 12, 1819), 518.

[161] Remini, *Andrew Jackson: The Course of American Empire*, 370; see also, Robert Remini, *Henry Clay: Statesman for the Union* (New York: W.W. Norton, 1991), 162.

triumph of the principle of insubordination—a triumph of the military over the civil authority—a triumph over the powers of this house—a triumph over the constitution of this land. And he prayed most devoutly to Heaven, that it might not prove, in its ultimate effects and consequences, a triumph over the liberties of the people."[162]

Clay was in dangerous territory, as one of his friends warned after the House speech: "Your late speech on the Seminole war, in which you condemn the conduct of Genl. Jackson, is disapproved of by some—and some of your friends are apprehensive that you may lose friends as a consequence."[163] Attacking Andrew Jackson's military exploits was serious business, even for a politician of Henry Clay's stature. Yet the "disapproval" expressed by some of Clay's friends was also helped along by Jackson, who, revealing that he too could wage political warfare, mailed copies of the speech to friends in the West and encouraged publication in local newspapers: "I hope the western people will appreciate his conduct accordingly," wrote the General. "You will see him skinned here, & I hope you will roast him in the West."[164]

Though Jackson surely felt some degree of satisfaction over skinning Clay, he nevertheless remained angry that some in Washington and other parts of the nation questioned his actions in Florida. President Monroe ultimately returned the captured territory to Spain and stated that Jackson had attacked the forts on his own responsibility. Doing so allowed the president to skirt a potential war with Spain, but in reality the former colonial power was in dire straits throughout the western hemisphere and certainly in no position to wage a war. More importantly, John Quincy Adams was indeed able to use the Seminole Affair and Spain's continued fear of Jackson to push the sale of Florida to the United States, along with the settlement of the western boundary of the Louisiana Purchase. This was done in the Transcontinental Treaty of 1819. Nor did England make a great fuss over the execution of two British citizens. The end of the War of 1812 had ushered in a wave of positive trade

---

[162] House of Representatives, Congressman Clay of Kentucky on the Seminole War, 15th Cong., 2nd Sess., *Annals of Congress*, (20 January 1819), 631-55; other congressmen also made statements about the protection of liberty and sanctity of the Constitution. See for example, House of Representatives, Congressman Cobb of Georgia on the Seminole War, 15th Cong., 2nd Sess., *Annals of Congress*, (18 January 1819), 589, 597; Senate, Senator Lacock on Report on the Seminole War, 15th Cong., 2nd Sess., *Annals of Congress*, (24 February 1819), 263. For more on Clay's speech and the nationalism of the debates, see Warshauer, *Andrew Jackson and the Politics of Martial Law*.

[163] James Morrison to Henry Clay, 17 February 1819, Hargreaves and Hopkins, eds., *The Papers of Henry Clay, vol. 2* (Lexington: University of Kentucky Press, 1973), 671.

[164] Quoted in Robert Remini, *Andrew Jackson*, 85.

between the two nations and neither side wanted to risk profit over two rather itinerant Englishmen who aided Indians.

Jackson had achieved all that he hoped for – national expansion, removal of the Spanish, security on the frontier, a further weakening of the Indians – and all of it had been done without too much damage to his larger popularity. This, even though he had very clearly violated his orders and the Constitution by waging war without congressional sanction, as well as acting despotically by executing Arbuthnot and Ambrister with a special court. The General's conduct reeked of autocracy.

CONCLUSION: HERO OR DESPOT

Was General Andrew Jackson out of control? Was he a mad man? Or did he plainly see the dangers to a young republic and commit himself to eradicating those dangers? The acknowledgment of the latter question does not condone or legalize Jackson's actions, but it does help to explain them. In both his first and second invasions of Florida, Jackson believed that there was only one way to stop what he and many others living on the frontier viewed as an Indian menace exacerbated by foreign influence. Keeping in mind that white encroachment on Indians' lands was the original source of conflict and had existed for more than a hundred years prior to Jackson's involvement, it was not unreasonable for the General and his fellow settlers to react angrily and vindictively to the Indian massacre at Fort Mims or the cross-border raids in Georgia. Both sides engaged in atrocities and, as is so often the case, military might ultimately won out and cries of self-defense were justification for slaughter. Thus for most of the South and West, Jackson was incredibly popular and seen as a savior.

In between the two Florida campaigns was New Orleans. The victory in that famous battle was accompanied by and made possible because of Jackson's imposition of martial law. Such a decree and the ensuing suspensions of civil liberties were patently unconstitutional. Like the second Florida invasion, Jackson and his many supporters insisted that national self-defense justified his actions and exonerated him of wrong doing or evil intent. The argument was as controversial in Jackson's day as it remains in our own. Americans continue to debate the balance between a proper regard for civil liberties and the need to keep the United States safe.

Ultimately, one's conclusion on such matters often revolves around issues of trust in government and the power of nationalism in the midst of a struggle.

And it is, perhaps, the second of these that best revealed Jackson's sometimes twisted genius. Though he had risen up from his rather lowly beginnings and achieved gentry status, he never lost touch with what settlers on the frontier desired and reacted to. Nationalism is a powerful force, and Jackson understood that. It became a shield that defended him throughout his life and allowed him to engage in what was sometimes considered rogue behavior. Yet that behavior, at least in terms of territorial expansion and national security, always benefited more than it harmed the United States. One can still debate the morality of such actions, but it is difficult to deny their effectiveness. It is also impossible to argue that Andrew Jackson lacked vision or the ability to achieve that vision.

Andrew Jackson / painted by D.M. Carter ; engraved by A.H. Ritchie.
Published by New York: Ritchie & Co., c1860.

REPRODUCTION NUMBER: LC-DIG-pga-02501 (digital file from original print)
LC-USZ62-5099 (b&w film copy neg.)

Reproduced with permission of the Library of Congress.

Chapter 5

JACKSON'S MARCH TO THE WHITE HOUSE

In the immediate aftermath of the Seminole Affair, Andrew Jackson was at the height of his national popularity and controversy. The Creek Wars of 1813-14 had brought notice, and New Orleans had rocketed him to stardom. It was the 1818 invasion of Florida, however, that caused some to pause. Henry Clay attempted to make exactly such a point in his riveting House speech in which he warned of a military chieftain. On the local front in his home state of Tennessee, Jackson had always been controversial, partially because of the struggle for political power there, but also because he killed Charles Dickinson in an 1806 duel. Nonetheless, the amazing success of New Orleans and the sense of many that Jackson had done what was necessary in regard to Spain, that he had made the southern frontier safe, continued his almost overwhelming popularity among the people. If politicians like Clay, and even President Monroe, were wary of Jackson's aggressiveness, many Americans, the frontier stock from which Jackson himself had been raised, saw only a man of action who did not play political games or engage in diplomatic dances with foreign nations. Jackson said what he meant and did what he thought was in the best interest of the nation, whether it was legal or not. His gut, and his political savvy, told him that success and the resounding nationalism that followed would shield him from harm. Is it any wonder that those who surrounded the General, and his own over-powering ambition, directed him towards the steps of the White House?

The road to Washington, however, was still several years in the making. In the interim Jackson served as governor of Florida, where he once again clashed with the Spanish. He also, with the help of supporters, prepared for the 1824 presidential contest, even briefly serving once again as Tennessee's senator, and in the process building and mending political fences in the nation's capitol. And though Jackson was successful in amassing support and even winning the popular vote in 1824, he failed to obtain the requisite number of electoral votes, and for only the second time in the nation's history (the first was in 1800), the election devolved to the House of Representatives. It was there that Henry Clay, Jackson's old nemesis, played a major role in the General's defeat by John Quincy Adams. When Clay was subsequently appointed secretary of state, the General and his followers cried foul, insisting that a "Corrupt Bargain" had been made and that the key issue facing the nation was conspiracy and corruption in government. Such issues became the basis of Jackson's outlook and fueled his ideas about majoritarian democracy.

From that point on, the battle for the 1828 presidential election began in earnest, and this time Jackson soared to victory with voters heralding a man who had come from the common folk. Jackson's inauguration embodied this connection with the people. Thousands turned out to celebrate the General's victory over Adams and what they perceived – due in large part to Jackson's campaign team – as corruption and aristocracy in government. There was, of course, another side to the victory. Many of the well-to-do, the aristocracy, observed the inauguration and recoiled at the newly arrived reign of "mobocracy." A new era was dawning in America and Andrew Jackson both symbolized and led it into existence.

In the process Jackson revealed a political savvy and organization that allowed his victory to be possible. This reality stands in stark contrast to the arguments put forth by historians who have wrongly insisted that Jackson bumbled his way into power with no vision for the nation's future, and that all of his actions were a mere lashing out, an attempt to overcome the demons of his tragic youth.

The truth is that Jackson's successes since the frontier days in the Waxhaws had steeled his determination that anything was possible, and though he often wrote of his desire to retire in solitude to the Hermitage with his wife Rachel, he really coveted the power and prestige of politics. He always had. His successes had also fueled a forever powerful vanity that infused him with an arrogance and single-mindedness about always being right. This, combined with his military achievements and the nationalism that followed, allowed him to do pretty much whatever he wanted: martial law in New Orleans and two invasions of Florida. Jackson's haughty conviction was also a recipe for continued controversy once he became president. These factors caused some to see Jackson as little more than a despot, a decided threat to the republic.

FLORIDA...AGAIN

It was now 1819 and Jackson, at age fifty-two, returned to Tennessee. He was both lauded by his fellow statesmen and physically wrecked. The General was never a particularly healthy man. He frequently suffered from dysentery while on march, sometimes hacked up blood, and continued to carry two bullets in his body, one from Dickinson and one from the Benton brawl. The Florida swamps did little to help such a fragile physical constitution. Yet it was only the physical that was weak. Jackson's drive and determination were unquenchable, and he continued to pay homage to an adoring public. And though the president publicly questioned Jackson's actions in Florida, even returning the territory that had been confiscated and stating that the General acted on his own responsibility, Monroe was no political novice and realized that a break with Jackson was potentially foolhardy, especially with re-election on the horizon in 1820. Thus the president arrived at Jackson's Hermitage in June and the two traveled in both Tennessee and Kentucky, even visiting Henry Clay.

Jackson also kept his eye on the security of the southern frontier by supervising the building of a road through Alabama. Additionally, in the fall of 1820 he continued his expansionist zeal by dispossessing the Choctaw Indians of a huge tract of land in western Mississippi along the great river. Jackson's negotiations in the Doak's Stand Treaty were aggressive, unfair, and wholly American, opening thousands of acres to hungry settlers and avaricious speculators. Robert Remini surmised, "In terms of acquisition, it is not too farfetched to say that the physical shape of the United States today looks pretty much like it does largely because of the intentions and efforts of Andrew Jackson."[165] One might counter that Thomas Jefferson's purchase of the Louisiana Territory was equally if not more significant, but there is no denying Jackson's tremendous impact on an expanding America.

The spring of 1821 promised Jackson's return to Florida. This time, however, he was not a general and not at the head of an invading force. Rather, President Monroe had commissioned Jackson to officially receive Florida from the Spanish and serve as the new territory's first governor. How could observers see this as anything but an endorsement of the iron General's actions in 1818? This is certainly how Jackson interpreted the appointment, even though he initially declined the position and only changed his mind at the urging of political friends, especially John Henry Eaton, Jackson's former

---

[165] Remini, *Andrew Jackson: The Course of American Empire*, 348.

military aide, now a senator from Tennessee, and rapidly becoming one of the General's key political advisors and proponents. Jackson explained his change of decision in a letter to his friend and former military comrade, General John Coffee, noting, "that the change of this my determination was brought about by the solicitations of the President, the secretary of war, and many of my friends in Congress, and many others." Jackson added in a later letter that the president's desire that "I should accept the appointment arose from feelings of friendship, and a desire to give evidence to the world that he fully approved my course in the Seminole campaign."[166]

The president's "solicitations" were also motivated by very real political circumstances generated by Congress' determination to reduce the size of the army and in doing so leave a position for only one major general, rather than two. Monroe was in the delicate situation of deciding between Jackson and Jacob Brown, who was senior to Jackson, but no where near as popular. The Florida governorship provided Monroe with an out, and as John Quincy Adams noted, would "save the nation from the disgrace of even appearing to discard without compunction a man to whom they were so deeply indebted."[167] When it came to Jackson, one always had to consider the nationalism that swirled about him.

Jackson's plan in becoming governor was simple: take possession of the territory from Spain, get the government up and running, then resign and go home to Tennessee. Indeed, this is what he did, but, in part due to Jackson's dislike of and impatience towards the Spanish, and in part because the Spanish themselves were obstinate and troublesome, things did not go smoothly. Jackson and the Spanish Governor José Callava entered into their relationship with animosity, disagreeing over protocol as to who should visit first and present credentials. They then argued over which country owned the cannons in the forts, and each exploded over the possession of certain land records, with Jackson having Callava marched to the new governor's office under armed guard.[168] After a long summer in Pensacola, Jackson wrote to Monroe in October explaining, "Having organised the Government of the Floridas, and it

---

[166] Andrew Jackson to John Coffee, April 11, 1821, and Andrew Jackson to John Coffee, May 11, 1821, in Harold Moser, ed., *The Papers of Andrew Jackson, 1821-1824, vol. 5* (Knoxville: University of Tennessee Press, 1996), 27-28; 41-42. Hereafter referred to as *Jackson Papers, vol. 5*.

[167] Charles Francis Adams, ed., *Memoirs of John Quincy Adams, Comprising Portions of his Diary from 1795 to 1848, 12 volumes, vol. 5* (Philadelphia: J. B. Lippincott & Co., 1874-1877), 366.

[168] Remini, *Andrew Jackson: The Course of American Empire*, ch. 25; See also, editor's commentary in *Jackson Papers, vol. 5*, 93, 95-6.

being now in full operation, I have determined to take a little respite from the laborious duties with which I have been surrounded."[169] Jackson returned to Tennessee and by mid-November resigned the governorship.

PREPARING FOR 1824

Perhaps Jackson's first feelers for the presidency were revealed with the publication of *The Life of Andrew Jackson*, written by two of his military aides, John Reid and John Henry Eaton, in 1817. The book allowed the people to learn more about the great Hero of New Orleans. Moreover, the victorious battle was celebrated annually, always adding to Jackson's luster and presence. The General was also heralded at Independence Day events, like the one that occurred in 1822 when he accepted a commemorative sword from the Tennessee legislature for his services during the War of 1812. Jackson and nationalism simply went together. Later, in March of 1824, Congress presented the General with a gold medal (which had been voted on earlier) for his victory at New Orleans. The timing was perfect for Jackson and an additional example of how the battle constantly reminded of and renewed the Hero's popularity.

In late July and early August of 1822, the Tennessee House and Senate, respectively, nominated Jackson for the presidency. Having been informed shortly before the nomination, Jackson explained in a letter his views on the subject: "The people have a right to call for any mans services in a republican government—and when they do, it is the duty of the individual, to yield his services to that call. I will be silent—neither sayi[ng] aye, or nay, although I have been often solicite[d]."[170] Here, was Jackson's mantra: the staid, servant of the people. Under the surface, however, Jackson had always coveted the power and approval that elections, either political or military, represented, as well as the power and opportunity that victory promised.

The reality of this ambition and planning is revealed in Jackson's election to the United States Senate on October 1, 1823. His involvement in the contest became paramount because the incumbent senator, John Williams, was a member of the Sevier faction in Tennessee and had been critical of Jackson. This lent power to arguments that the General did not have the full support of

---

[169] Andrew Jackson to James Monroe, October 5, 1821, *Jackson Papers, vol. 5*, 110.
[170] See timeline in *Jackson Papers, vol. 5*, xxix, editor's comments on 196-7, and Andrew Jackson to Richard Keith Call, June 29, 1822, 199.

Tennessee in his bid for the presidency. It seemed that no other Jacksonian supporter in the state could compete with Williams, and it therefore fell to Jackson himself to crush the upstart senator. Jackson would have much preferred to stay out of the election and even expressed his concern that entering would look like political ambition on his part and thus tarnish his staid, republican, servant of the people image.[171] The move on Jackson's part also revealed the very active beginnings of a group, the Nashville Junto, soon to be a larger national party, built around support of the old Hero.

Jackson had no intention of really serving as a senator. His election was purely about politics and the presidency. His arrival in Washington on December 3rd and departure with a leave of absence on May 24, 1824 amply supports this fact, though he did return to his seat in December, but this was far more about being present for the presidential election than senatorial duties. Thus becoming a senator was a tactical move, and afforded Jackson both the opportunity for more attention and to mend old fences and forge future political alliances.

One of the first settling of past affairs occurred between Jackson and Winfield Scott, and is particularly worth noting because it embodies the duality of Jackson's personality that historian James Parton captured so well. Jackson and Scott, both serving in the military, had exchanged letters in 1817 in the midst of a disagreement that Jackson was having with the War Department. The exchange grew ugly and Jackson accused Scott of betrayal. Come 1823 and the arrival of Senator Jackson in Washington, Scott sent a letter noting, "One portion of the American community has long attributed to you the most distinguished magnanimity, & the another portion the greatest desperation in your resentments. Am I to conclude that both are equally in error?" Jackson responded immediately and, though without great warmth, put the matter to rest by insisting that he would be happy to meet on "friendly terms" and that "when you know me better, you will not be disposed to harbour the opinion, that anything like 'desperation in resentment' attaches to me."[172] Arriving in Washington was clearly about creating a positive public

---

[171] See editor's comments, *Jackson Papers, vol. 5*, 294-5, 297, and Andrew Jackson to Abram Maury, September 21, 1823, 298-9. See also, Remini, *Andrew Jackson: The Course of American Freedom,* 51-3. Interestingly, and revealing of his lack of political understanding, James Curtis asserted that Jackson's involvement in the Senate contest was put forth by supporters who were "willing to toy with Jackson's emotions to do so." See Curtis, *Andrew Jackson and the Search for Vindication*, 80.

[172] Winfield Scott to Andrew Jackson, December 11, 1823, and Andrew Jackson to Winfield Scott, December 11, 1823, *Jackson Papers, vol. 5*, 325-6.

perception and forging alliances. Jackson was tactical, clear-headed, and looked to the future.

John Henry Eaton certainly understood such a point and happily reported in a letter to Rachel the General's successes on this front. "He is constantly in motion to some Dinner party or other," wrote Eaton, and "all his old quarrels have been settled. The General is at peace & friendship with Genl. Scott, Gen Cocke—Mr. Clay & what you would never have expected Col. Benton."[173] Eaton's surprise at the reconciliation between Jackson and Benton is particularly understandable given the brawl that the two had engaged years earlier on the streets of Nashville, and the fact that Jackson still carried a bullet in his shoulder as a reminder. Nonetheless, Jackson actively pursued reconciliation, even visiting and leaving his card at Benton's residence, and Benton returned the courtesy.[174] The mending of this breach was a smart one on Jackson's part. Benton was quickly becoming a powerful force in Washington and would later be one of President Jackson's key allies in the Senate.

Nor were Jackson and his supporters merely focusing upon the nation's political elite. It was equally important to rally the citizenry to the General's candidacy. Thus in 1823 Eaton authored a series of thirteen anonymous letters published in the Philadelphia *Columbian Observer* in which he broached a variety of issues related to Old Hickory. The next year the various tracts were published in a single pamphlet, entitled *The Letters of Wyoming,* in which Eaton focused on two interlinked strategies: further development of Jackson's nationalism and explaining away within that nationalism the controversial, illegal acts he had engaged as a general.[175] At the very outset of the letters, Eaton trumpeted the General's nationalism: "He has saved, defended, and shielded his country....Storms and perils he has breasted, and borne her in safety through her angry trials." "Let the nation answer then," challenged Eaton, "where amongst them is there a republican like ANDREW JACKSON? Does he love his country?" And here, Eaton dropped the other shoe: "Let a head grown grey, a constitution impaired in the service of the country, declare!"[176]

---

[173] John Henry Eaton to Rachel Jackson, December 18, 1823, *Jackson Papers, vol. 5*, 327.
[174] Parton, *Andrew Jackson, vol. 3*, 47-8.
[175] Robert B. Hay, "The Case for Andrew Jackson in 1824: Eaton's Wyoming Letters," *Tennessee Historical Quarterly 29* (1970): 139-151.
[176] *The Letters of Wyoming, to the People of the United States, on the Presidential Election, and In Favour of Andrew Jackson* (Philadelphia: S. Simpson & J. Conrad, 1824), 14-15, 5, 103, 36, 14, 29-30.

Eaton also addressed the issue that Winfield Scott had raised, the darker, mean-spiritedness that manifested itself in Jackson's temper. For Eaton, however, temper was hardly a negative quality for a military leader, much less a president. "A wonderful manifestation of violence and temper, to be sure! God grant, should peril again assail us, that we may find some bold commander ready and willing to make precisely as strong a demonstration of his temper as did Jackson."[177] Eaton's arguments were risky in a nation that was traditionally obsessed with the protection of liberty, but it was the only way to explain the General's past acts, whether they were the execution of militia men, the imposition of martial law in New Orleans, or two invasions of Florida. And in reality, there was a legitimate argument to be made. In the view of many, all of these acts had ultimately benefited the United States even though they were violent and often patently illegal.

As with all things, however, especially in politics, there are always at least two sides to every story and the General's opponents viewed his candidacy in decidedly different terms than John Henry Eaton. Henry Clay had early on, long before Jackson was a real contender, questioned his conduct in the Seminole Affair and labeled Jackson a dangerous "military chieftain." Still, the reaction to such attacks, partly orchestrated by Jackson himself, caused Clay to be careful when it came to assaulting the nation's hero. In 1822, Clay wrote in a private letter that "it is uncertain whether it [Jackson's nomination] has been stimulated to produce division in the West, or was intended as a mere compliment to the Genl. from his own state." Clay's friends assured him, "Gen J will decline eventually—The public esteem him *only* for his military energy—He is too much of a Soldier to be a civilian." When Jackson's popularity as a candidate widened, even into Kentucky, Clay and his supporters continued to express doubt about Old Hickory's ability to ultimately win a nomination. Still, they considered the General's appeal when strategizing for Clay's candidacy: "Believing as we do that Gen Jackson will not finally be a candidate we have deemed it bad policy to give the Slightest offence to his friends in general as it will be very easy to turn the large majority of the people in your favour when he is out of view."[178]

Additional concerns about Jackson's military conduct arose when the presidential race heated up in 1823. Albert Gallatin, Thomas Jefferson's former secretary of the treasury, for example, wrote a friend in May of 1824,

---

[177] *The Letters of Wyoming*, 87, 42-43.
[178] Henry Clay to Peter B. Porter, 10 August 1822; Jonathon Meigs to Henry Clay, 3 September 1822; John McKinley to Henry Clay, 3 June 1823, Hargreaves and Hopkins, ed.s, *The Papers of Henry Clay, vol. 2*, 274, 427, 282.

remarking, "whatever gratitude we owe him [Jackson] for his eminent military services, he is not fitted for the office of first magistrate of a free people." "He entertains," continued Gallatin, "very sincere but very erroneous and most dangerous opinions on the subject of military and Executive power. Whenever he has been instrusted with the first, he has usurped more than belonged to him; and when he thought it useful to the public, he has not hesitated to transcend the law and the legal authority vested in him." But Gallatin also understood the Hero's immense popularity and feared that the people would be "dazzled by military glory."[179]

Jackson himself was quite aware of such concerns and the attempt by political opponents to expand upon such perceptions, writing to Samuel Swartwout in March of 1824, "my enemies prefer to call my acts by their strongest expressions, have in many parts of the country induced the belief, that I am in fact sort of a raw head & bloody bones, fit only to scar[e] children." In a letter to John Coffee only three months later, the General reiterated such sentiments: "Great pains had been taken to represent me as having a savage disposition; who always carried a Scalping Knife in one hand, & a tomahawk in the other; allways ready to knock down, & scalp, any & every person who differed with me in opinion."[180] It was these dichotomous Andrew Jacksons, the hero and the despot, that battled for votes in the November elections of 1824. And to be sure, there was some degree of truth to the criticisms, though they were also magnified by the burgeoning politics of the period.

THE ELECTION OF 1824 AND THE CORRUPT BARGAIN

The 1824 presidential election resulted in no clear winner. Five candidates originally entered the race: Jackson, Clay, John Quincy Adams, William Crawford of Georgia, and John Calhoun. Three of these men, Adams, Crawford, and Calhoun, all served in President Monroe's cabinet, as secretary of state, of treasury, and of the war department, respectively. Calhoun opted to drop out of the race fairly early on and run instead for the vice-presidency (at this time the two top administrative positions were not linked together.) In

---

[179] Albert Gallatin to Walter Lowrie, 22 May 1824, Henry Adams, ed., *The Writings of Albert Gallatin, vol. 2* (New York: Antiquarian Press, 1960), 289, 291.
[180] Andrew Jackson to Samuel Swartwout, March 25, 1824, and Andrew Jackson to John Coffee, June 18, 1824, *Jackson Papers, vol. 5,* 380-2; 416.

September of 1823, Crawford suffered a debilitating stroke that impacted his prospects, though he remained in the race.

When the returns came in, Jackson was the clear front runner with 43% of the popular vote and ninety-nine electoral votes. Adams achieved 30% of the popular vote and eighty-four electoral votes, Crawford 13% with forty-one electoral votes, and Henry Clay 13% with thirty-seven electoral votes. The problem was that victory required 131 electoral votes and with many candidates in the field the tally had been split so much that no clear winner existed. As per the Constitution, the election therefore devolved to the House of Representatives, where the top three electoral vote recipients – Jackson, Adams, and Crawford – were voted upon, with each state casting only a single ballot.

One might assume that Jackson, with the most votes from both the people and the electoral college, would have been a sure winner. Yet at this point the question came down to politicking and, importantly, the powerful speaker of the House, Henry Clay, who not only wanted to be the first president from the West, but also held genuine concerns over Jackson's past conduct. Almost immediately after the election Clay raised warning flags in letters that were widely reprinted in the nation's newspapers: "What I would ask, should be the distinguishing characteristic of an American statesman....

Should it not be a devotion to civil liberty?" "Is it then compatible with that principle," he continued, "to elect a man, whose sole recommendation rests on military pretensions?" In another letter he announced, "I cannot believe that killing 2500 Englishmen at N.Orleans qualifies for the various, difficult and complicated duties of the Chief Magistracy." It is wrong, he continued, "to establish the dangerous precedent of elevating, in this early stage of the Republic, a Military Chieftain, merely because he has won a great victory?"[181]

Clay's appeals were more a justification for openly moving against Jackson than they were any attempt to truly influence the electorate. For the people's role in the election was over. It was the representatives in the House who now held the presidency in their hands, and as speaker, Clay had tremendous sway over the vote. This is most evident in the fact that Clay's home state of Kentucky had not cast even one electoral vote for Adams and sent instructions for her representatives to support Jackson. On the day of the

---

[181] Henry Clay to George McClure, December 28, 1824; Henry Clay to Francis Preston Blair, January 29, 1825, Hargreaves and Hopkins, ed.s, *The Papers of Henry Clay, vol. 3*, 906; *vol. 4*, 47.

House vote, February 9, 1825, however, Clay made sure that Kentucky's choice was Adams. If only it was that simple.

A little over a week earlier, on January 28th, the Philadelphia *Columbia Observer* published an anonymous article accusing Clay of striking a deal with Adams in which he would receive the presidency and Clay would be appointed secretary of state, the traditional stepping stone to the executive office. It was a scandalous charge, but the two had indeed met on January 9th and, as Adams confided in his journal, engaged in "a long conversation explanatory of the past and prospective of the future."[182] There was nothing particularly incriminating in Adams' private entry, but the fact that the meeting occurred and shortly thereafter the *Observer* published a charge against the two, served to incite speculation and concerns over corruption.

On January 24th, Clay put an end to the speculation by coming out publicly for Adams. For many it seemed like a duplicitous alliance because in the past Clay had rarely been in agreement with Adams and clearly loathed him when the two worked together as peace commissioners negotiating the end of the War of 1812. This fact was not lost on outside observers. On January 27th the *Washington City Gazette* published an article entitled "Political Tergiversation" in which it announced that "Mr. Clay has deserted the cause of democracy; gone over to Mr. Adams; and, however incredible it may seem, is, with a bold hand, endeavoring to cast the die in his favor." The *Gazette* promised that if Clay "persists in his erratic course we shall not be wanting in our duty to lay bare every intrigue and bargain, that such doings may create." Other newspapers, such as the *Essex Register* of Salem, Massachusetts, in Adams' home state, picked up this news and reported that on "undoubted authority…the influences of Mr. Clay will be exerted in favor of Mr. Adams in the approaching election. If this should be the case, there is now no longer any doubt who will be chosen."[183]

Jackson also took note of the rumors, and once Clay came out publicly, wrote, "It shews the want of principle in all concerned—and how easy certain men can abandon principle, unite with political enemies for self agrandisement." Only a few days later he commented on the "intrigue, corruption, and sale of public office," adding, "How humiliating to the american charecter that its high functionaries should so conduct themselves, as

---

[182] Adams, *Memoirs of John Quincy Adams*, vol. 6, 464-5.
[183] "Political Tergiversation," *Washington City Gazette*, January 27, 1825; "The Presidency," *Essex Register*, February 3, 1825.

to become liable to the imputation of bargain & sale of the constitutional rights of the people."[184]

Clay strenuously denied such charges. Yet his influence seemed clear when the House vote occurred and Adams indeed won after Clay convinced Kentucky's representatives to cast their vote for Adams in opposition to the orders they had received from the Kentucky legislature. Thus the concerns over intrigue were more than mere suspicion. Two days later, on February 11th, Adams offered Clay the secretary of state position, and on the 20th, Clay accepted. It was the worst political decision of his long career.

Charges of "Corrupt Bargain" thundered throughout the nation. No smoking gun existed to absolutely prove such accusations, but perception was a mighty powerful force and well prior to the election Jackson's supporters had worried that some sort of political cabal would rob the General of victory. In January of 1823, John Henry Eaton lamented to the General that, "the Constitution has vested with the people the proud privilege of selecting a chief magistrate for themselves…and while the power is nominally theirs, they are but instruments in the hands of those who are commonly termed the *leading men* of the Country….We have seen enough of the ills resulting from this condition of things to desire a change."[185] Jackson was well aware of such realities, having witnessed for himself backroom political deals and brokering when he first arrived in the nation's capital as a representative and then a senator. Nor were his impressions at that time merely a product of his own inexperience as a legislator. Historian Joanne Freeman has shown with remarkable clarity the sordid power grabbing in the early years of the republic, explaining, "Political combat in the new national government was like a war without uniforms; it was almost impossible to distinguish friends from foes. National politics was personal, alliances were unpredictable, and victory went to those who trusted the right people at the right time in the right way. This was a politics of shifting coalitions and unknown loyalties, where an ally could become an opponent at the drop of a hat."[186]

With this reality in mind, it is no surprise that Jackson and his followers were concerned for the nation's future, even though he too had long been a part of Tennessee politics and the inevitable struggle for power and shifting

---

[184] Andrew Jackson to William Berkeley Lewis, January 24, 1824 and January 29, 1824, Harold D. Moser, ed., *The Papers of Andrew Jackson, 1825-1828, vol. 6* (Knoxville: University of Tennessee Press, 2002), 20, 22-3. Hereafter referred to as *Jackson Papers, vol. 6*.

[185] John Henry Eaton to Andrew Jackson, January 11, 1823, *Jackson Papers, vol. 5*, 235-9. See also, *John Henry Eaton to Andrew Jackson*, February 23, 1823, 254-6.

[186] Freeman, *Affairs of Honor*, xviii.

allegiances that existed there. In his mind, however, he was right and honorable. In the weeks leading up to the House vote he continually reiterated his now practiced avowal of republican simplicity and the will of the people: "If party or intrigue should prevail, and exclude me, I shall retire to my comfortable farm with great pleasure." He also insisted that he would not interfere or solicit deals with anyone.[187] Jackson's refusal to make deals was true, but no matter how much he spoke of retiring to the Hermitage, he really coveted the presidency and power. He always had. Such ambition was more than vanity, though that was certainly part of Jackson's personality. It was also about a vision for the Union, one that was long-standing and consistent in terms of his expansion and safeguarding of the frontier. He would soon add a firm commitment to majoritarian democracy as well.

When news of the final vote became known, Jackson blasted his disgust in a now famous letter to William Berkeley Lewis: "so you see the *Judas* of the West has closed the contract and will receive the thirty pieces of silver—his end will be the same. Was there ever witnessed such a bare faced corruption in any country before." Nor was Jackson alone in such reactions. John Pemberton wrote the General, remarking, "I have not the language to express to you, the deep sorrow and mortification I feel in the result of the Election....The Pride of Kentucky [Henry Clay] like Lucifer has fallen!"[188]

Once the news arrived that Clay had indeed accepted the role of secretary of state, Jackson knew that his conclusions about intrigue and corruption were true:

> "When we see the predictions verified on the result of the Presidential election —when we behold two men political enemies, and as different in political sentiments as any men can be, so suddenly unite, there must be some unseen cause to produce this political phenomena—This cause is developed by applying the rumors before the election, to the result of that election, and to the tendering of, and the acceptance of the office of Sec of State by Mr. Clay. These are facts that will confirm every unbiased mind, that there must have been, & were a secrete understanding between Mr Adams & Mr Clay of and concerning these scenes of corruption, that has occasioned Mr Clay to abandon the will, and wishes of the people of the west."[189]

---

[187] Andrew Jackson to John Overton, December 19, 1824, *Jackson Papers, vol. 4*, 455; Andrew Jackson to John Coffee, January 5, 1825, and January 6, 1825, *Jackson Papers, vol. 5*, 5-6, 7-8.

[188] Andrew Jackson to William Berkeley Lewis, February 14, 1825; John Pemberton to Andrew Jackson, February 15, 1825, *Jackson Papers, vol. 6*, 29-30, 30-1.

[189] Andrew Jackson to William Berkeley Lewis, February 20, 1825, *Jackson Papers, vol. 6*, 36-8.

Jackson's reactions to the "Corrupt Bargain" should hardly come as a surprise to readers. Who would not draw similar conclusions? Yet in considering how Jackson reacted, and how historians have perceived that reaction, one must keep in mind the competing historical interpretations of his personality. James Curtis, for example, insisted that Jackson's conduct following the election was marked by the standard psychological impotency that characterized him since his early days: "Rage, revenge, mission: the cycle began again....Jackson was hardly philosophical in defeat."[190] Though long on theory, such conclusions are practically devoid of historical context. Jackson's reaction regarding corruption in the election was hardly singular. Many believed it was an indication of much more widespread power grabbing and dishonesty in Washington. It is not that Jackson had never engaged in political maneuvering, but the level of dishonesty indicated by the "Corrupt Bargain" was astonishing.

What is equally problematic is Curtis' implication that Jackson's fledgling political organization, unstructured and unsophisticated, mirrored Jackson's lack of savvy and political understanding. For Curtis, everything for Jackson was personal, and thus his organization was not a "unified national party, not by modern definition at least."[191] Such statements reflect not only a misunderstanding regarding Jackson, but utter confusion over the nature of the party system. It was the election of 1824 that marked the beginnings of the second American party system, on which our current modern system was built. Moreover, the election cemented in Jackson a diehard commitment to democracy in the form of the popular votes of the people. From that point on he fervently believed in the will of the people and how the problem of corruption challenged that will. Such issues were hardly the products of Jackson's "inner demons." And to be sure, the coalescence of the new party and Jackson's focus on the people were determining factors in the rise of what has become known as Jacksonian Democracy.

THE ELECTION OF 1828

Considerations for the election of 1828 began within a week after the House seemingly robbed Jackson of the presidency. As Samuel Swartwout wrote, "The eyes of the whole union are upon you—The deepest solicitude

---

[190] Curtis, *Andrew Jackson and the Search for Vindication*, 84.
[191] Curtis, *Andrew Jackson and the Search for Vindication*, 85.

pervades all ranks of people. Jackson, greater in adversity than in prosperity, is the only man who can rally the Nation & restore the Govt to its primitive purity." Equally significant was Vice President John Calhoun's June 1826 letter in which he warned, "In my opinion liberty was never in greater danger." And though Calhoun had witnessed first-hand as secretary of war the degree to which Jackson could go when he thought it in the best interest of the nation – the Seminole Affair – Calhoun lauded the General as one who has always been "on the side of liberty."[192] Such comments were in part fueled by politicking on Calhoun's part. Years later he and Jackson had a major falling out that caused the South Carolinian to revise his perception of Jackson. Still, in the context of the politics surrounding the election of 1824, many, including Calhoun, viewed Jackson as a potential savior from the intrigue and corruption of Washington.

With such sentiments and Jackson's own understated desire to attain the White House, organization and preparations began right away. Moreover, one cannot read Jackson's correspondence for this period without recognizing the degree to which his supporters began serious organization and the degree that Jackson himself was involved. A major factor in the campaign was, understandably, animosity over the "Corrupt Bargain." That issue, combined with the fact that Adams and Jackson would certainly run against one another, promised to make the election one of the most competitive and dirty in American history.

Over the next four years Jackson prepared for the 1828 contest, constantly reminding the people of corruption. He spoke often of "the voice of the people," "the great body of the American people," and "the consent of the people." In a letter to Calhoun, the General announced, "I trust that my name will always be found on the side of the people."[193] Whereas Jackson had spent much of his life aspiring to rise beyond the common man and into the gentry class, he had now become the great defender of democracy. Nor were such professions mere "sound bites." The "Corrupt Bargain" revealed to Jackson a very real and dangerous threat to the future of the nation and as president he meant to reform the government. It is quite likely that Jackson's mission for democracy in government may have been very different had the "Corrupt Bargain" never occurred and he been elected in 1824.

Jackson's near victory in that election made him the clear contender in 1828 and this stimulated a stunning barrage of pamphlets and books attacking

---

[192] Samuel Swartwout to Andrew Jackson, February 18, 1825, and John Caldwell Calhoun, June 4, 1826, *Jackson Papers, vol. 6*, 32-4; 177-8.

[193] Andrew Jackson to John Caldwell Calhoun, July 18, 1826, *Jackson Papers, vol. 6*, 187-8.

him on everything from his temper, to dueling, to executing militia men, imposition of martial law, invading Florida, and even the earlier controversy over his marriage to Rachel. As James Parton noted, "General Jackson was accused of every crime, offense, and impropriety that man was ever known to be guilty of. His whole life was subject to the severest scrutiny."[194] Titles such as *Proceedings of the Anti-Jackson Convention, Held at the Capitol in the City of Richmond* and *Address from a meeting of Democratic Citizens of the City of Philadelphia, opposed to the election of General Jackson*, provided a clear indication of their sentiments about the General. There was also the infamous *Coffin Handbill: Some Account of Some of the Bloody Deeds of GENERAL JACKSON*, which depicted the caskets of militiamen executed for mutiny.[195]

In a book-length biography, one author, calling himself "A FREE MAN," devoted an entire chapter to the source of Jackson's national appeal, New Orleans, and castigated him for the despotism of martial law. The author lamented, "We wish it had not been so, and that every step of our hero's course had not conveyed pregnant proof of his unfitness to exercise civil-power. On the contrary, his conduct puts us in mind of the exasperated rhinoceros, wreaking his fury on every object that presents itself." Another writer denounced Jackson's "vindictiveness and cruelty," noting that he possessed "a total want of talent or acquirements, suitable for civil office."[196] One critic simply announced that "republicans cannot elevate such a man to office without laying the axe to the root of the Tree of Liberty!"[197]

If these were the only attacks, the campaign, though hotly contested, would not be recognized as so remarkably mean-spirited. Yet both sides stirred up issues that focused on questions of morality. When the editor of the Cincinnati *Gazette* published an article claiming that "Gen. Jackson prevailed

---

[194] Parton, *Life of Andrew Jackson, vol. 3*, 141.

[195] *Proceedings of the Anti-Jackson Convention, Held at the Capitol in the City of Richmond: With their Address to the People of Virginia* (Richmond: Franklin Press, 1828); *Address from a meeting of Democratic Citizens of the City of Philadelphia, opposed to the election of General Jackson* (Philadelphia: John Binns, 1827); *Coffin Handbill: Some Account of Some of the Bloody Deeds of GENERAL JACKSON*, (Philadelphia: John Binns,1828).

[196] J. Snelling, *A Brief and Impartial History of The Life and Actions of Andrew Jackson* (Boston: Stimpson and Clapp, 1831), 95; *A History of the Life and Public Services of Major General Andrew Jackson* (n.p., 1828), 37; another writer stated, "that from the irritability of his constitution, and an untoward disposition, he does not control the first impulse of his temper, but has indulged in repeated acts of violence." See *An Address to the People of the United States, on the Subject of the Presidential Election: with a special reference to the nomination of Andrew Jackson, containing public sketches of his public and private character. --By a citizen of the United States* (n.p., 1828), 7.

[197] *An Impartial & True History of the Life & Services of Major-General Andrew Jackson* (n.p., 1828), 14.

upon the wife of Lewis Roberts [Robards] of Mercer county, Kentucky, to desert her husband and live with himself, in the character of a wife," and then expanded upon the charge in a pamphlet entitled *Truth's Advocate and Monthly Anti-Jackson Expositor*, all hell broke loose. The competing Jacksonian paper, the Cincinnati *Advertiser,* called the "assertion a BASE, WANTON AND MILIGNANT FALSEHOOD."[198] Newspapers around the country picked up the story and lambasted Jackson as one who engaged in the "abduction of another man's wife."[199] If this was not enough, the Washington based *National Journal* announced that "General Jackson's mother was a COMMON PROSTITUTE, brought to this country by the British Soldiers! She afterward married a MULATTO MAN, with whom she had several children, of which number General JACKSON IS ONE!!!"[200]

For their part, Jacksonians charged Adams with a gambling addiction because he had purchased a billiard table for the White House, and with having an improper relationship with a female friend. Robert Remini explained, "other reports accused him of religious bigotry, alcoholism, Sabbath-breaking, and a string of other moral and ethical delinquencies." Certainly the most egregious charge was Jacksonian Isaac Hill's claim that while foreign minister to Russia, Adams supposedly provided an American virgin for Tsar Alexander's pleasure.[201] It was indeed a dirty campaign.

When the political dust settled, however, Jackson trounced Adams in the election with some 647,276 to 508,064 in popular votes and 178 to 83 electoral votes. Jacksonians viewed the victory as not only a personal vindication of the General's popularity, but a ringing denunciation of corruption in government. Both are revealed in the following letter from Jackson to Francis Preston:

> "It is true, as you remark, that with my enemies calumny was the order of the day. There is no parallel to their conduct for the last four years —no instance is heretofore recorded of as uniform a direction of the patronage of Government against the character of a private individual. The virtue of the people became aroused by such unwarrantable procedure, and regarding it as a stain upon our national fame, have, in the majesty of their strength pro[n]ounced a verdict that, I trust, in all future time will be a solemn warning to politicians never to depart from principle, or disobay the will of

---

[198] Quoted in Remini, *Andrew Jackson: The Course of American Freedom*, 118-9.
[199] See, for example, the *Essex Register* (Salem, MA), April 16, 1827.
[200] *National Journal*, September 4, 1828.
[201] Remini, *Andrew Jackson: The Course of American Freedom*, 133-4; Robert Remini, *The Election of Andrew Jackson* (Philadelphia: J.B. Lippincott, 1963), 117-8.

their constituents, in order to gain office and power. To the people, for the confidence reposed in me, my gratitude & best services are due; and are pledged to their service."

Jackson's letter most certainly mixed his own biased, almost sanctimonious views, about his reputation and the will of the people. One must also recognize the degree to which Jackson's partisans engaged in "calumny," and challenged the notion that the General was merely a "private individual." He was distinctly a political actor and immersed in the quest for the presidency. Nonetheless, he rightly viewed the election as a statement about corruption and the will of the people. Interestingly, he concluded the letter by noting, "I cannot calculate that my administration will be undisturbed by the agitations of party—but based on the constitution and devoted to the prosperity of our common country, I cherish the hope that I shall forget no cardinal principle, and that any error which I may commit, will be ascribed to the head, and not to the heart."[202]

Jackson's calculations regarding the "agitations of party" were a whopping understatement. The next eight years were marked by the most aggressive party organization and combat the nation has perhaps ever witnessed. And the battles stemmed directly from a rather vain Jacksonian principle: the new president would do whatever he believed best for the country's prosperity, even if that meant challenging the Constitution itself. This, after all, was the precedent on which he had succeeded as a general. First, however, an inauguration that ushered in the Age of Jacksonian Democracy needed to take place.

The story of Jackson's inauguration is well known. Whereas in previous such ceremonies the people had been all but a distant thought, at Jackson's inauguration they were central to the event. On March 4, 1829, Americans from all walks of life crowded the streets to watch Jackson ride to the Capitol building and take the oath of office. What had previously been a private reception at the executive mansion for the social elite was now opened to the people, who flocked to the president's residence in unprecedented numbers. Supreme Court Justice Joseph Story bemoaned that the crowd represented the "highest and most polished…down to the most vulgar and gross in the nation." "I never saw such a mixture," concluded Story, "The reign of KING MOB seemed triumphant."[203]

---

[202] Andrew Jackson to Francis Preston, December 18, 1828, *Jackson Papers, vol. 6*, 545.
[203] Joseph Story to Mrs. Joseph Story, March 7, 1829, in William W. Story, ed., *Life and Letters of Joseph Story, vol. 1* (Boston: Charles C. Little and James Brown, 1851), 563.

When the people flocked to the White House they literally pressed themselves into the mansion, breaking china and glassware, almost crushing Jackson in their desire to wish him well. Diarist Margaret Bayard Smith recorded the day's events: "The mob broke in, in thousands—Spirits black yellow and grey, poured in in one uninterrupted stream of mud and filth, among the throngs many fit subjects for the penitentiary." "What a scene did we witness!" she continued. "The Majesty of the People had disappeared, and a rabble, a mob, of boys, negros, women, children, scrambling, fighting, romping. What a pity what a pity."[204]

Jackson had arisen from this rabble. Granted, he had early on committed himself to overcoming his common origins and pulling himself up to join the higher classes. Yet he never fully shed his back country upbringing. Indeed, some of his campaign biographers capitalized on this fact. This, and the General's constant comments about the voice of the people, made him a symbol of what restless, common Americans might achieve.

CONCLUSION

Jackson could not have risen to the White House in 1828 without a savvy understanding of politics, an ability to inspire the people, and a track record of real accomplishment. Still, those accomplishments often included dark moments for the Constitution, Indians, and Spain, among others. Jackson was hardly the philosopher diplomat. He was a man of action, dangerous at times, even unwieldy to his own government. There was good reason for Henry Clay's charge of "military chieftain." Yet with each seemingly despotic episode Jackson also carried the United States forward, securing the Union's future with each troubling step. He trampled upon civil liberties, but saved New Orleans. He crushed the Creeks and forced them to sign away millions of acres, but expanded the geographic borders of the southern United States and opened it for settlement. He violated his military orders, the Constitution, and an international treaty by invading Florida in 1818, but achieved American dominance over Spain and forced them to sell Florida and once again increase the nation's expansion. Is there any wonder why the duality of Jackson's image continues to confound historians? Was Jackson the greatest of heroes or the most dangerous of despots?

---

[204] Margaret Bayard Smith, as quoted in Remini, *Andrew Jackson: The Course of American Freedom*, 178.

Jackson and his followers obviously focused on heroism and the extent to which he had safeguarded the nation. They even confronted directly the problematic constitutional and legal violations related to the General's record. In the midst of the 1824 election Jackson wrote that many considered him "a most dangerous and terrible man....and that I can break, & trample under foot the constitution of the country, with as much unconcern & careless indifference, as would one of our backwoods hunters, if suddenly placed in Great Britain, break game laws." He continued, "it has been my lot often to be placed in situations of a critical kind" that "imposed on me the necessity of Violating, or rather departing from, the constitution of the country; yet at no subsequent period has it produced to me a single pang, believing as I do now, & then did, that without it, security neither to myself or the great cause confided to me, could have been obtained."[205]

Here was a bold Jacksonian assertion. For those who prized the sanctity of the Constitution and the strictures of law against all else, Jackson was an unrestrained monster for whom the end could not justify the means. Others held a decidedly different opinion, believing that the form of law should not hamper the nation's ability to defend itself. This ideological quandary continues into twenty-first century America. The question remains: what is more important, winning the war or the means by which one wins it?

Such imposing issues were at the heart of Jackson's run for the presidency in 1824. Yet that election also brought new and important concerns to light. The "Corrupt Bargain" warned Americans that conspiracy was rife in Washington, and both Jackson and his followers capitalized on this point while feverishly preparing for 1828. In the process, Jackson could claim not only the mantle of national hero, but that of victim and man of the people. He consistently spoke of the people's will and their right to choose a leader. Jackson thus became the harbinger of democracy and today the Age of Jacksonian Democracy bears his name.

In considering such points it is important to understand that Jackson did not create the beginnings of this burgeoning democracy. It had been underway since the Revolution when the great men of the nation pronounced again and again that "all men are created equal" and that freedom and liberty were natural rights. These were the ideas that broke the flood gates of democracy. From then until today, each generation of Americans has struggled to define and defend the nature of that right. Jackson appeared at a time when this movement was just underway and as a recipient of what America had to offer,

---

[205] Andrew Jackson to Samuel Swartwout, March 25, 1824, *Jackson Papers, vol. 5*, 381.

and as its defender, he was viewed by many as a symbol of the nation's grit, determination, and energy. Such traits were not always pretty, as observers of Jackson's inauguration duly noted. Democracy was a mixture of the grand and the horrible. Jackson represented it well.

Chapter 6

PRESIDENCY: THE FIRST TERM

For Andrew Jackson, becoming president was far easier than being president. His march to the White House had been largely about image, symbolism, and a rather broad nationalism that stemmed from New Orleans, first, and the "Corrupt Bargain," second. None of this had required much in the way of defining policy, except in regard to national self-defense. And even here, Jackson had relied far more, perhaps solely, on action than on building political support. As a general, he had been able to make his own decisions and exert control through sheer determination, often at the point of a musket. Jackson's vanity, enlarged by his military successes, encouraged his belief that he *knew* the correct course for the nation, regardless of whether that course was politically wise or strictly legal. Still, he knew enough about politics to correctly surmise that military success and the resulting nationalism would shield him from the slings and arrows of political enemies. Thus he marched away freely from New Orleans after imposing martial law and weathered the Florida storm in Congress. Even after he suffered defeat in the 1824 election, his supporters, and Jackson himself, turned the loss into another important symbolic statement, this time about the "will of the people" and the need to clean up corruption in Washington. This is not to say that Jackson failed to believe in these things, but he and the political machine coalescing around him needed to market such ideas directly to the electorate.

Thus Jackson's rise to the presidency had required virtually no success as an actual politician, at least as it related to devising and enacting legislation, and, very importantly, engaging in the art of compromise so integral to American politics. To be sure, Jackson had revealed political skill in his life. His rise through the power structure of Tennessee and his ability to win the presidency had indeed shown a degree of sagacity. Yet his time as a representative and senator had indicated no great promise as, or real interest in, being a politician. This was far different from virtually every other president who had served previously, many of whom had held important governmental positions, in particular secretary of state.

The simple fact is that the intricacies and politicking of Washington required, at least on the surface, a far more delicate and nuanced approach to problem solving than Jackson had thus far displayed. He would not be able to mount a horse and ride headlong into battle, imposing his will and hanging those who failed to fall in line. Opponents had specifically argued that Jackson was unsuited for civil office, and worried that he would attempt to create a military dictatorship.

The eight years that Jackson spent in the White House have caused historians to arrive at markedly different conclusions about his success or failure as a president. Arthur Schlesinger, in his seminal work *The Age of Jackson*, presented the General as a prototypical Franklin Delano Roosevelt, and the first of our modern presidents. Robert V. Remini has concurred, arguing in many books that Jackson was the first chief executive to truly recognize the power of the presidency, and that he brought a vigor and strength cemented with a real concern for the common man and democracy.[206]

Others have disagreed. James C. Curtis and Andrew Burstein insisted that Jackson was more bluster than success, and that he did little to modernize the presidency or move the nation forward. Curtis' conclusions have certainly influenced others. In an excellent and detailed study of Jackson's presidency, Donald B. Cole noted in particular his debt, remarking, "Although I do not carry my analysis of Jackson's uncertainties as far as James C. Curtis, I have been guided by the insights in his *Andrew Jackson and the Search for Vindication*." Thus Cole presents "a different Jackson, a man less sure of himself than imagined, a man more controlled by the political and economic forces of his age than the reverse." Cole's is an "ambivalent" Jackson, whose presidency was marked by "his inconsistent and unsuccessful battle to resist the market revolution."[207]

It should be no mystery to readers at this point in the book that I am not enamored of Curtis' psychologically driven theories regarding Jackson's inner

---

[206] Schlesinger, *The Age of Jackson*; Remini, *Andrew Jackson*; Remini, *Andrew Jackson: The Course of American Democracy*.

[207] Curtis, *Andrew Jackson and the Search for Vindication*; Burstein, *The Passions of Andrew Jackson*; Donald B. Cole, *The Presidency of Andrew Jackson* (Lawrence: University of Kansas Press, 1993), x.

demons and that the great tragedy of his life, the death of his mother and brothers, caused him to react to everything that followed in some sort of simplistic lashing out at all challenges that followed. Jackson was a more thinking and calculating man than Curtis' interpretation allows. For Cole's part, though he provides a richly nuanced study of Jackson's presidency, he misses to some extent the integral meaning of what he himself presented: "brought to the presidency by a broad coalition of conflicting interest groups, Jackson was involved in constant battles not only against his opponents but also among his supporters."[208] This is a key contextual point that must be understood.

Not only had the meanness of the 1828 election, with the nation broken into broadly defined pro- and anti-Jackson camps, ensured that there would be serious political battles for Jackson to face, but the very makeup of his fledgling party consisted of an almost paralyzing jumble of competing interests: North versus South; East versus West; states' rights versus nationalists; supporters and opponents of the Bank of the United States, of federally sponsored internal improvements, tariffs, Indian removal, and slavery.

That Jackson was unable to exert "control" over the political and economic forces of his age should be of no great surprise. No one could. John Quincy Adams, surely an astute and seasoned politician, had failed rather miserably as president, yet historians have not attempted to explain away his time as chief executive in terms of a psychologically driven lack of control. Surely some of these arguments regarding Jackson's control stem from a reaction to historians who have fallen too far to the side of Jackson dominating every situation and, as Remini has too often argued, that he was politically "masterful" in virtually all that he did. This was most certainly not the case. Jackson made mistakes. He also came to a Washington that was fearful of and hostile to his arrival with a well deserved reputation for acting despotically and running rough shod over the Constitution. Combine these factors with the virtual impossibility of balancing the competing interests in the quickly formed Jackson party, and it is a wonder that he accomplished anything as president. And here is the key point. Though nothing went smoothly, it is remarkable what Jackson *did* accomplish, whether or not it was popular or controversial. Jackson exploded at times, but on the whole, especially considering his lack of a track record in legislating and compromising, he did

---

[208] Cole, *The Presidency of Andrew Jackson*, x.

Building a Cabinet

The story of Jackson's troubled cabinet is infamous. Though Thomas Jefferson had resigned his position as secretary of state in George Washington's administration, and other presidents had made changes in appointments, no previous president had suffered the problems that Jackson faced. For the most part, historians agree that Jackson's was a rather weak cabinet. Remini insisted that Jackson meant to dominate it, whereas Donald Cole imparted that the new president "appeared defensive and unsure" in determining who would serve.[209]

A problematic cabinet was hardly how Jackson planned on starting his presidency. Like all chief executives, he considered both ideological and sectional issues when selecting advisors. More than any other previous president, however, Jackson was forced to balance the needs of his newly forged and still unstable party, ensuring that those who made the victory possible were rewarded. As historian Richard Longaker pointed out, Jackson's original cabinet was a smattering of disparate John Quincy Adams and Henry Clay foes, most of whom were appointed to the cabinet because of sectional demands and political debts owed as a result of the campaign of 1828.[210] At the same time, Jackson was particularly wary of the Washington political environment and looked to trusted advisors, primarily from Tennessee, for advice on the cabinet. No matter what Jackson decided, there were sure to be some who resented certain appointments.

When the dust settled, Martin Van Buren of New York, a key organizer in the North/South Jackson alliance, was appointed secretary of state. John Henry Eaton of Tennessee, Jackson's former military aide and confidant, served as secretary of war. Samuel D. Ingham of Pennsylvania, a key player in delivering his state's votes and heavily supported by his home state coalition, served as secretary of the treasury. John Berrien of Georgia, a former William

---

[209] Remini, *Andrew Jackson*, 122; Cole, *The Presidency of Andrew Jackson*, 31.

[210] Richard P. Longaker, "Was Jackson's Kitchen Cabinet a Cabinet?" *The Mississippi Valley Historical Review* 44, no. 1 (June 1957): 94-108. Lonaker notes that "political demands rather than his free choice dictated the cabinet membership in the early years of the administration." See also, Richard B. Latner, "The Kitchen Cabinet and Andrew Jackson's Advisory System," *The Journal of American History* 65, no. 2 (September 1978): 367-388.

Crawford supporter, served as attorney general. John Branch of North Carolina took the role of secretary of the navy, and William T. Barry served as postmaster general. In all, these men represented, broadly, the Jackson coalition. As Cole noted, "Jackson had done a remarkable job of balancing the varied interests of his coalition in his cabinet. With members from six different states representing almost all sections of the country, he had secured good geographic balance....The outpouring of criticism that greeted the cabinet showed the impossibility of satisfying all elements of the coalition."[211]

What was also particularly troubling, and surfaced almost immediately, was the political rivalry between Van Buren and John C. Calhoun, who served as vice-president. Both men were remarkably bright, equally ambitious, and politically shrewd. With many believing that Jackson, at sixty-one, was too old and frail to serve more than one term in office, the man closest to the president might very well rise to the executive chair. This rivalry framed every subsequent issue that surfaced during Jackson's first term.

SEXUAL SCANDAL AND THE CABINET'S DOWNFALL

The difficulty of moving from campaigning and a loosely defined Jackson party to creating a working administration was compounded by personal tragedy. Shortly after his election and just days prior to his departure for Washington, Jackson's wife of more than thirty years died abruptly from a heart attack. The loss of Rachel was bad enough, but it was markedly worsened by Jackson's belief that his political opponents had essentially killed her. The nastiness of the campaign engendered attacks on the difficulties of the Jacksons' marriage, and though the General had attempted to shield Rachel from such barbs, it proved impossible. Jackson never forgave his enemies, from then onward wore a black mourning band on his hat, and allowed the matter to influence his judgment when problems arose in his presidential cabinet.

The cabinet troubles stemmed from his long relationship with and appointment of John Henry Eaton as secretary of war. The difficulty came in Eaton's choice of a bride. Margaret O'Neale Timberlake was a spirited, vivacious young woman who grew up amidst the bustle of politics in her father's Washington boarding house. In the mid-1820s, Eaton and Jackson had roomed at O'Neale's establishment, Franklin House, and came to know both

---

[211] Cole, *The Presidency of Andrew Jackson*, 29.

Margaret and her husband John Timberlake. Margaret had a rather spotty reputation when it came to men: liaisons, contemplated elopements, narrowly avoided conflicts among suitors, and marriage to Timberlake at the age of sixteen. Timberlake and Eaton became friends in 1818, which later resulted in then Senator Eaton's influence in Timberlake regaining appointment as a Navy purser. To make a long, intriguing, and decidedly Hollywoodesque story brief, Timberlake went to sea, Eaton lavished the young Margaret with attention, and in April of 1828 Timberlake committed suicide by slashing his own throat. Custom necessitated that Margaret mourn her husband for at least a year, perhaps two, wearing black and avoiding social engagements. This was not to be. She was frequently in the company of Eaton, who proposed marriage in December, a short nine months after Timberlake's death. There is little reason to question why tongues in Washington wagged with gossip of the soap opera.[212]

As furor over the matter continued to build immediately after Jackson's election victory, Eaton turned to the president for advice. No stranger to controversies over love and liaisons, Jackson counseled immediate marriage, believing that it would hush the matter. The General should have known better considering that the circumstances of his own marriage had darkened the recent election. He surely knew that politics was a nasty business and the matter would be used against Eaton and perhaps the new administration. A quote from the period aptly described the connections that Jackson should have made. Unaware of Rachel Jackson's recent death, Margaret Bayard Smith, commented on Eaton's appointment as secretary, announcing, "The General's personal and political friends are very much disturbed by it; his enemies laugh and divert themselves with the idea of what a suitable lady in waiting Mrs. Eaton will make to Mrs. Jackson and repeat the old adage, 'birds of a feather will flock together'."[213]

When the other cabinet wives, including Jackson's own niece, Emily Donelson, who served as White House hostess, refused to associate with Margaret, matters worsened and what had started out as merely a social scandal progressed into a political firestorm that threatened to paralyze Jackson's cabinet and most certainly made the president look unbalanced and petty. In a cabinet meeting Jackson blasted his secretaries, telling them to make their women behave. In opposition to rumors that Margaret had undergone an abortion prior to her marriage with Eaton, Jackson exploded that

---

[212] Marszalek, *The Petticoat Affair*.
[213] Quoted in Marszalek, *The Petticoat Affair*, 49.

she was as "chaste as a virgin!" Donald Cole insisted that Jackson "personalized the entire affair" (Curtis also asserted this) and that the episode dominated the first part of Jackson's presidency, explaining that "about half of Jackson's published letters between the inauguration and September 1831 concern either the Eaton affair or the related subject of Jackson's deteriorating relationship with Calhoun."[214] Most recently, Jon Meacham's book *American Lion* does an outstanding job of presenting the personal and political intricacies of Jackson's struggle over the Eaton Affair and how it affected his relationship with Emily Donelson.[215]

If ever there was an episode that invites psychological speculation regarding Jackson, the Eaton Affair is it. To put it plainly, the president became obsessed with the issue. Rachel's death certainly compounded his emotions and was surely a more significant psychological factor than Curtis' great adolescent tragedy theory. Nonetheless, even his most supportive biographer, Robert Remini, admitted that the entire matter "was a farce….Sheer madness. The President was engaged in a lunatic campaign in which he had absolutely no business." Andrew Burstein concluded, "The devastating loss of Rachel, fresh memories of the slanders leveled at her during the presidential contest, plus Jackson's constant perception that enemies swarmed about him, stimulated his martial inclination to seek justice and personal vindication at any cost."[216] Add to this, two additional factors: one, Jackson possessed an undying loyalty to friends and Eaton was among his closest friends in Washington; and two, the president believed political enemies were attempting to force Eaton from the cabinet. As a result, Jackson dug in his heels and attempted to force cabinet members to follow his dictates, much as he had ordered junior officers to follow his military orders. Jackson appeared to do what many feared, figuratively mount his horse and carry his decrees by storm. It was a poor way to begin the presidency.

A number of historians have concluded that the Eaton Affair essentially destroyed Jackson's cabinet. He stopped meeting with cabinet members for advice and instead instituted the "Kitchen Cabinet," a group of advisors made up of friends and political allies. Jackson then ultimately requested the resignation of his official cabinet. Moreover, some historians have asserted

---

[214] Cole, *The Presidency of Andrew Jackson*, 35-9; Curtis, *Andrew Jackson and the Search for Vindication*, 98.
[215] Jon Meacham, *American Lion: Andrew Jackson's White House Years* (New York: Random House, 2008).
[216] Remini, *Andrew Jackson and the Course of American Freedom*, 209; Burstein, *The Passions of Andrew Jackson*, 174.

that Jackson was heavily influenced by members of the Kitchen Cabinet, revealing that the president possessed little real control over his administration.[217] If this was indeed the case, Jackson's first term may very well have been paralyzed and one can judge the Eaton Affair as the dominating influence, consuming the President, stopping him from achieving anything, and leaving him to the domination of more experienced, shrewd political actors.

Such conclusions, however, are incorrect. In the most detailed studies of the cabinet situation, historians Richard Longaker and Richard Latner have proven that Jackson continued to bring substantive issues to his official cabinet. Nor did he utilize the Kitchen Cabinet as an alternative to his regular advisors. Rather, Jackson actually revealed a degree of political sagacity in dealing with the cabinet situation, both in terms of the problems caused by the Eaton Affair and the overall weakness of the cabinet due to political appointments. He brought in others whom he trusted, and thereby increased his options in terms of advice. Moreover, as Latner explained, Jackson's use of additional advisors was actually a mark of his modernizing the presidency: "conceptualize it as an early prototype of the President's White House staff, a group of personal aides providing the president with a variety of services. The staff includes policy advisors, lobbyists, liaison people, publicity experts, speech writers, and friends." Finally, in analyzing the president's interactions with his many advisors and their comments regarding his role, Latner concluded, "The picture that emerges is not that of an inexperienced and vacillating executive, prone to manipulation by those who gained his confidence. Rather, it is that of an astute and skillful President, who consulted widely on matters of policy and politics and who reached beyond the formal institutions for assistance."[218]

Jackson was well aware that some believed him to be the dupe of others, and in a letter to John Randolph, announced, "to these complaints and others of a similar character founded on a pretended distrust of influences near or around me, I can only say that they spring from the same false view of my character. I should loath myself did any act of mine afford the slightest colour for the insinuation that I follow blindly the judgement of any friend in the

---

[217] Leonard D. White, *The Jacksonians: A Study in Administrative History*, 1829-1861 (New York: Macmillan, 1954); Mary L. Hinsdale, *A History of the President's Cabinet* (Ann Arbor: University of Michigan Press, 1911); Marquis James, *Andrew Jackson: Portrait of a President* (Indianapolis: Bobbs Merrill, 1937).

[218] Longaker, "*Was Jackson's Kitchen Cabinet a Cabinet?*"; Latner, "*The Kitchen Cabinet and Andrew Jackson's Advisory System,*" 378; 384.

discharge of my proper duties as a public or private individual." Two of Jackson's closest informal advisors, Francis Preston Blair and Amos Kendall, confirmed this point. Blair insisted, "Whenever anything involves what he conceives the *permanent interest* of the country, his patriotism becomes an all-absorbing feeling, and neither *kitchen* nor *parlor* cabinets can move him." Amos Kendall made the same assertion: "They talk of a Kitchen Cabinet, etc....There are a few of us who have always agreed with the President in relation to the Bank and other essential points of policy, and therefore they charge use with having an influence over him! Fools! They can not beat the President out of his long-cherished opinions, and his firmness they charge to our influence!"[219]

THE SEMINOLE AFFAIR AND FALL OF JOHN C. CALHOUN

One of the important items to consider regarding Jackson's cabinet woes is that the Eaton Affair was not the only source of problems. Though the dispute over Margaret Eaton was certainly not some sort of machination designed solely to disrupt the administration and pit the political ambitions of Martin Van Buren against those of John Calhoun, there is little question that the issue was quickly enveloped in exactly this sort of political intrigue. Both men had massive ambitions and there were concerns on Calhoun's part that Eaton, who was close to the president, favored Van Buren and supported tariffs. The fear was that this might sway Jackson and hurt both Calhoun's presidential hopes and South Carolina's opposition to the tariff.[220]

In 1828, Calhoun had anonymously authored the "South Carolina Exposition and Protest," in which he argued that the tariff was unconstitutional because it protected northern manufacturing at the expense of the South. He insisted further that states had the right to judge the constitutionality of federal laws, nullify them if they were found unconstitutional, and secede from the Union if the federal government attempted to coerce compliance. Calhoun and other nullifiers hoped that the "Exposition" would sway legislators to rethink protective tariffs and that the vice-president would be able to influence

---

[219] Andrew Jackson to John Randolph, November 11, 1831, *Correspondence, vol. 4*, 372; Thomas H. Clay, "Two Years with Old Hickory," *Atlantic Monthly 55* (August 1887): 198; William E. Smith, "Francis P. Blair, Pen-Executive of Old Hickory," *The Mississippi Valley Historical Review 17, no. 4* (March 1931): 543-556.

[220] Richard B. Latner, "The Eaton Affair Reconsidered," *Tennessee Historical Quarterly 35* (Fall 1977): 330-51.

Jackson on the matter. Short of that, they strategized that Jackson would serve only one term and Calhoun would be next in line for the presidency.

The Eaton Affair, along with disagreements over Nullification and Calhoun's potential connections to nullifiers, made the political jockeying for power within the administration serious business, especially after Jackson very publicly denounced Nullification at the Jefferson Birthday Dinner. (Nullification will be discussed in greater detail in the next chapter.) Equally detrimental to Calhoun was the resurgence of the Seminole Affair and whether, as secretary of war in 1818-19, he had or had not supported Jackson's invasion of Florida. This came to light in the midst of the Eaton Affair, when Jackson received a copy of a letter written by William Crawford, who had served as President Monroe's secretary of the treasury and was privy to the cabinet discussions over Jackson's conduct. Jackson wrote Calhoun, noting, "the statements and facts it [the letter] present being so different from what I had heretofore understood to be correct requires that it should be brought to your consideration." Jackson continued, expressing his "great surprise" and desired "to learn of you whether it be possible that the information given is correct...that any attempt seriously to affect me was moved and sustained by you in the cabinet council."[221]

After Calhoun sent a reply essentially confirming that he had discussed censuring the General, Jackson responded with a damning letter that surely ended any alliance that may have existed: "I had a right to believe that you were my sincere friend, and, until now, never expected to have occasion to say to you, in the language of Caesar, *Et tu Brute*....Your letter to me of the 29th, handed today, and now before me, is the first intimation to me that *you*, ever entertained any other opinion....Understanding you now, no further communication with you on this subject is necessary."[222]

The fact that the letter sparking the dispute came from Crawford, who Van Buren had supported for the presidency in 1824, has caused many, in both Jackson's day and historians who followed, to surmise that Van Buren was at the bottom of the leak and his desire was to politically damage Calhoun. This was certainly what Calhoun believed, and in order to defend himself, the vice-president decided to publish in the newspapers and in pamphlet form all of the correspondence related to the Seminole Affair, much of it private letters between himself and Jackson. One of Calhoun's goals was to implicate Van Buren as the instigator of the entire dispute. The result, however, was a final

---

[221] Andrew Jackson to John C. Calhoun, May 13, 1830, *Correspondence, vol. 4*, 136.
[222] Andrew Jackson to John C. Calhoun, May 30, 1830, *Correspondence, vol. 4*, 140-1.

break with the president and Calhoun's virtual banishment from the Democratic Party until well into the 1840s.

It is impossible to cleanly separate the animosities and political maneuvering engendered by the Eaton and Seminole affairs. The matter over Margaret Eaton may have started out as personal in nature, but it quickly accelerated into a serious political struggle, the undercurrents of which had to do with power and its ability to influence very real political issues. Jackson certainly exacerbated the Eaton Affair by personalizing it, but one is tempted to question how it would have played out had Jackson done nothing. Surely, with the personalities involved, the lack of decorum among cabinet members and their wives would have become increasingly worse and actually required the president to address the matter. This, to be sure, is speculative.

Nonetheless, the really key factor in all of this was the degree to which politics was at play, Jackson's understanding of this fact, and his often repeated belief that a conspiracy was afoot. Some historians have been quick to criticize his concerns, arguing that they revealed the defensiveness and paranoia that betrayed Jackson's deeper insecurities, but it is hard to escape the fact that real conspiracies, or at the very least, political power plays, did exist.

The dissolution of Andrew Jackson's presidential cabinet in 1831 followed just a couple of months after the publication of the Seminole correspondence. The initial impetus for the resignations came from Van Buren, who felt it best for his own political fortunes to get out of the cabinet. After he finally convinced Jackson, the president spoke with Eaton who also decided to resign. It was then easy for Jackson to request the resignations of his other cabinet officers: Ingham, Branch, and Berrien.

Yet the intrigue did not end there. Van Buren had suggested that Jackson appoint him foreign minister to England following the resignation, a post that Jackson dutifully approved. Van Buren even packed his bags and departed for Great Britain prior to the Senate confirmation of his new position. This is where John Calhoun exacted his revenge. As vice-president, Calhoun cast the deciding vote in the Senate should a tie exist. This is precisely what occurred, and when Calhoun killed Van Buren's confirmation, he gleefully boasted of the vote's effect on Van Buren: "It will kill him, sir, kill him dead. He will never kick sir, never kick." Yet the reality was more accurately described by Thomas Hart Benton, the imposing senator from Missouri, who, after the vote, turned to a colleague and announced, "You have broken a minister, and elected a Vice-President."[223] The senator was of course correct. Van Buren became Jackson's vice-president and followed him into the presidency after Jackson's retirement in 1837. For Calhoun's part, he resigned as vice-president late in 1832, both because of the break with Jackson and because Calhoun and his supporters in South Carolina believed he could do more to aid the cause of Nullification as a U.S. senator, for which he was duly elected.

FORGING A PROGRAM AMIDST THE POLITICKING

In considering the degree of turmoil that engulfed the first years of Jackson's presidency, it is a wonder that he managed to get anything done in terms of policy. He had come into the presidency with only one clearly defined plan: to reform Washington by rooting out corruption. No one knew exactly how he would do that. Nor did they know his views on the many and complicated issues facing the nation. If he was merely a symbolic figurehead, or a military man playing civilian chief, would Jackson have the ability to identify problems and formulate a plan of action? It is, arguably, the president's "Inaugural" and "Annual Addresses" that best answer such questions. For in these speeches, he outlined specific items that needed attention. Moreover, one can judge Jackson's effectiveness or ineffectiveness as a chief executive by determining whether or not he pushed through policies that dealt with those items mentioned.

In making such considerations, one must ultimately accept that Jackson was amazingly successful in implementing policies that reflected his views of what would move the nation forward. This, of course, does not mean that one condones his policies, just that an objective consideration of what Jackson wanted to do and succeeded in doing reveals his effectiveness as a president.

In his "First Inaugural Address," Jackson defined broadly his areas of interest in terms of managing the public revenue so that the national debt could be extinguished, supporting the tariff for items that were integral to national independence, engaging internal improvements that were consistent with the Constitution, following dictates regarding the will of the people, liberality and humanity toward the Indians, and the reform of government to remove power from those who were unfaithful or incompetent.[224]

---

[223] Thomas Hart Benton, *Thirty Years View, vol. 1* (New York: D. Appleton and Co., 1856), 215; 219.

[224] Andrew Jackson, "Inaugural Address," March 4, 1829, *Avalon Project*, Yale Law School, http://www.yale.edu/lawweb/avalon/avalon.htm.

He expanded and added to these items in his "First Annual Address," focusing considerable attention on negotiating with foreign powers (especially in regard to addressing monetary claims against England, Spain, and France), amending the Constitution to address problems in the election of the president and vice-president, as well as doing away with the electoral college so that the people's will in choosing their chief executive would not be thwarted by a powerful minority. The president also discussed the simplicity of government and the idea of limiting service in public positions, and once again addressed the tariff, suggesting modification for those items not essential in time of war, as well as the need to extinguish the national debt and engage internal improvements that were authorized by the Constitution. He also addressed the problem of fiscal corruption within the government, as well as a policy that encouraged Indians to move west of the Mississippi, and, finally, the constitutionality of the Bank of the United States.[225] Jackson did not offer much if anything in the way of specificity on these items. Rather, he presented them as issues to be dealt with. And he dealt with many of them.

REFORM IN GOVERNMENT

Reform under Jackson consisted of two primary themes. The first was investigating theft by government office holders and prosecuting those found guilty. Only weeks after his inauguration, the president wrote to his friend John McLemore: "A rat that has been marauding on the Treasury, finding that he was detected, left this place, and I am ingaged in preparing legal process to pursue and arrest him."[226] The rat was one Tobias Watkins, whose accounts as fourth auditor of the Treasury Department were off by $7,000. Ten other fraudulent treasury agents were also discovered, and within twelve months investigators learned that some $280,000 had been stolen. Jackson ultimately learned that the amount totaled $500,000. There were also problems with some customs collectors, as well as major issues in the Navy Department, for which Amos Kendall determined that within a year $1 million had been saved and would continue to be saved annually.[227] Although on the whole Jackson proved

---

[225] Andrew Jackson, "First Annual Message," December 8, 1829, *The American Presidency Project*, http://www.presidency.ucsb.edu.
[226] Andrew Jackson to John McLemore, April, 1829, *Correspondence*, 20.
[227] Albert Somit, "Andrew Jackson as Administrative Reformer," *Tennessee Historical Quarterly 13* (September 1954): 205-223; see also, Remini, *Andrew Jackson and the Course of American Freedom*, 187.

his contention that serious problems of corruption existed, there were also unanticipated black spots for his own administration. Whereas the president remained committed to reform and rooting out corruption, not all of his appointees followed a similar view. It was discovered in 1838 that Samuel Swartwout, appointed by Jackson to the important post of New York customs collector, had absconded to Europe with some $1.2 million.

Jackson's second reform program focused on dismissing inefficient or incompetent office holders. He insisted that any person of intelligence should be able to serve the public's interest, noting in the "Annual Address" his concern that "Office is considered as a species of property, and government rather as a means of promoting individual interests than as an instrument created solely for the service of the people." Jackson thus instituted the principle of rotation in office, which he believed would secure liberty and further democracy by "promoting that rotation which constitutes a leading principle in the republican creed, [and] give healthful action to the system." He continued, "In a country where offices are created solely for the benefit of the people no one man has any more intrinsic right to official station than another. Offices were not established to give support to particular men at the public expense. No individual wrong is, therefore, done by removal, since neither appointment to nor continuance in office is a matter of right."[228] His pronouncements in this regard were further indications of and an advertisement for a democratic principle in government, especially the idea that public office was not meant to be the sole arena of the privileged few. This was a decidedly different idea from the deferential and elitist politics at the time of the nation's founding and is one of the reasons that Jackson is credited by some historians with expanding democracy.

In all, Jackson turned out some 919 of 10,093 government workers in the first eighteen months of his presidency. During his eight year administration he removed a total of about ten percent. Critics at the time and historians ever after have debated the meaning of Jackson's rotation policy. Some argued it more properly represented a spoils system, the primary point of which was to allow the incoming president and his party to take control of federal patronage by sweeping out their political enemies and reward the party faithful. Yet some scholars insist that it was actually Thomas Jefferson who initiated such an idea in the aftermath of the 1800 election. There is little doubt that this feature of the system was abused by parties, to the extent that in 1883 Congress enacted civil service reform. Yet Jackson's intent was to actually

---

[228] Jackson, *"First Annual Message."*

reform the system and democratize its features, not engage in a wholesale house cleaning, and his letters indicate concern over selecting "honest men."[229]

In all, one can conclude that Jackson's reform policies were a mixed bag. He without a doubt took seriously the missions of rooting out corruption and democratizing government, but he also utilized, to an extent, the opening of positions to reward the party faithful. That, after all, was part of building a newly forged party in the nineteenth century. Patronage had always been used. That was politics. Yet Jackson, without question, increased the nature of patronage in relation to party power. Hence the reason that historians have debated the degree to which the system should be called rotation versus spoils. Whatever the conclusion, one can hardly escape the fact that Jackson had a clear plan of attack and succeeded in implementing it.

THE NATIONAL DEBT, INTERNAL IMPROVEMENTS, AND THE VETO POWER

When Andrew Jackson arrived in office, the United States national debt stood at $58,421,413.67, which translates to approximately $1.13 billion in 2007 dollars.[230] The debt was the total amount that the government was in arrears, as opposed to the deficit, which is the amount that the government is in arrears in a single year. During his life, Jackson had been no stranger to debt and the realizations caused by America's most serious financial collapse, the Panic of 1819, had further instilled in him a belief that debt was a great evil, and that banks, with their excessive use of paper money, were a potential problem. In the midst of the 1824 presidential election, Jackson stated forcefully that the debt was "a national curse" and that should he be elected, "my vow shall be to pay the national debt, to prevent a monied aristocracy

---

[229] For more on the origins of civil service, Jackson's removals, and the arguments among historians, see, Carl E. Prince, *The Federalists and the Origins of the U.S. Civil Service* (New York: New York University Press, 1977); Carl Russell Fish, *The Civil Service and the Patronage* (New York: Longman, Green, and Co., 1904); Eric M. Erikson, "The Federal Civil Service under President Jackson," *Mississippi Valley Historical Review 13* (March 1927): 517-40; Sidney H. Aronson, *Status and Kinship in the Higher Civil Service: Standards in Selection in the Administrations of John Adams, Thomas Jefferson, and Andrew Jackson* (Cambridge: Harvard University Press, 1964); William F. Mugleston, "Andrew Jackson and the Spoils System: An Historiographical Survey," *Mid-America 59* (1977): 113-125; Andrew Jackson to John Coffee, May 30, 1829, *Correspondence, vol. 4*, 39.

[230] The exact amount is $1,342,928,243.14. See *"Measuring Worth,"* http://www.measuringworth.com/uscompare/ (accessed September, 2008).

from growing up around our administration that must bend it to its views, and ultimately destroy the liberty of our country."[231] The problem of a moneyed aristocracy was directly tied to the power of banks, especially the Bank of the United States.

With this pledge to eradicate the national debt, Jackson focused carefully on any potentially wasteful spending, especially internal improvements that not only spent precious resources, but violated the Constitution by being too local in scope. Jackson, like many previous presidents, supported an improved infrastructure, but noted that it must be done in accordance with the Constitution. Madison and Monroe had actually called for amendments in this regard. Jackson concluded that the federal government could fund projects that he deemed national in scope, especially on federally owned lands. Along these lines, he actually spent more on internal improvement projects than any of the previous presidents combined, keeping in mind the need to reduce the debt. Thus Jackson was not opposed to internal improvement projects in the abstract. Rather, there was a fairly clear policy issue.

Certainly his most controversial internal improvement veto was on the Maysville Road, a project largely in Kentucky. It was a delicate situation both because it was in the West, one of Jackson's strongholds, and because it was Henry Clay country. Many of the president's supporters feared that Clay would use the veto as a political tool to harm Jackson's support. Nonetheless, Jackson vetoed the measure, specifically with an eye to paying down the debt and abiding by the Constitution. With the twin vision of debt eradication and national internal improvements, Jackson consistently flexed his veto muscle, utilizing it more than any of the previous presidents combined, a total of twelve times, and engaging the pocket veto by denying his signature on a bill prior to Congress adjourning. His vetoes killed a Washington Turnpike Bill, canceled appropriations for light houses and coastal improvements, and for buying stock in canal companies.[232]

The issue of Jackson's vetoes have sparked disagreement among historians regarding the nature of the veto itself. Robert Remini argued that it revealed "Jackson's profound understanding of his presidential powers" and that the veto was "a positive weapon to implement his executive purpose."

---

[231] This figure was actually for January, 1829. *Bureau of the Public Debt, U.S. Treasury Department*, "Historical Debt Outstanding," http://www.treasurydirect.gov/govt/reports/pd/pd.htm (accessed March 20, 2008); Andrew Jackson to William S. Fulton, July 4, 1824, *Correspondence, vol. 3*, 139.

[232] See Daniel Feller, *The Public Lands in Jacksonian Politics* (Madison: University of Wisconsin Press, 1984); Remini, *Andrew Jackson and the Course of American Freedom*.

James Curtis offered a decidedly different and equally forceful argument that the veto was a purely "defensive weapon," and that "each application of the veto power was a tacit admission of weakness, of failure to manipulate committees and marshal votes. This was a weakness that Jackson would be forced to admit more often than all his predecessors combined."[233] Political scientists have wrestled with this contradiction and arrived at no clearly accepted conclusion, imparting that the veto is often a negative weapon, but one that frequently reveals presidential strength and policy.[234]

In reality, the truth of Jackson's veto power lay in a sort of dichotomy, a middle ground between Remini and Curtis. It is true that Jackson did not have enough control of Congress to force its adherence to his views. At the same time, however, one must accept that to a large extent Jackson was forging new presidential territory at a time when party solidarity was tenuous at best, with multiple and often competing interests at play within his own party. In this atmosphere there was little possibility of a clearly articulated Democratic legislative program. With this in mind, Jackson followed through on his own beliefs. This signaled the force of his convictions, and the veto was the weapon through which he often compelled Congress to abide by those convictions.

Jackson's plans also ensured payment of the national debt. He announced this fact in his "Sixth Annual Message," noting that by January 1, 1835, not only would the debt be paid, the treasury would soon enjoy a $440,000 surplus. In all, Jackson had focused steadfastly on fiscal responsibility and proved to be the only president in American history to pay off the nation's debt. He announced in his message, "Free from public debt, at peace with all the world, and with no complicated interests to consult in our intercourse with foreign powers, the present may be hailed as the epoch in our history the most favorable for the settlement of those principles in our domestic policy which shall be best calculated to give stability to our Republic and secure the blessings of freedom to our citizens."[235]

---

[233] Remini, *Andrew Jackson*, 160; Curtis, *Andrew Jackson and the Search for Vindication*, 131.

[234] Jong R. Lee, "Presidential Vetoes from Washington to Nixon," *The Journal of Politics 37, no. 2* (May 1975): 522-46; Gary W. Copeland, "When Congress and the President Collide: Why Presidents Veto Legislation," *The Journal of Politics 45, no. 3* (August 1983): 696-710; David McKay, "Presidential Strategy and the Veto Power: A Reappraisal," *Political Science Quarterly 104, no. 3* (Autumn 1989): 447-61. Most recently, constitutional scholar Gerard N. Magliocca argued that Jackson shaped the veto into a powerful weapon. See *Andrew Jackson and the Constitution: The Rise and Fall of Generational Regimes* (Lawrence: University of Kansas Press, 2007.)

[235] Andrew Jackson, "First Annual Message," December 1, 1829, *The American Presidency Project*, http://www.presidency.ucsb.edu.

JACKSONIAN FOREIGN POLICY

One might reasonably surmise that Jackson's often combative, frontier personality would be a detriment to a successful foreign policy. His often aggressive nationalism was revealed in two wars against the British, his continual aspersions towards the Spanish Dons, two invasions of their territory in Florida, as well as a consistent criticism of foreign influence upon the Indians. It might then be a surprise to know that a third, sometimes half, of Jackson's annual messages focused wholly and intricately on foreign policy. In the sole book length study of the subject, John M. Belohlaveck argued, "Andrew Jackson formulated and exercised the most expansive and aggressive foreign policy between the presidencies of Thomas Jefferson and James K. Polk. In so doing, he developed the power of the chief executive beyond the horizon of domestic affairs for which he is usually credited, and helped to lay the foundations for the more dynamic diplomatic actions of the modern presidency."[236]

Jackson focused on two areas of foreign policy. First, he set about settling assertions, known as spoliation claims, against European powers that had seized American ships and cargoes during the Napoleonic Wars. This was an issue that previous administrations had unsuccessfully attempted to settle for a quarter of a century. Second, he established trade agreements that increased foreign commerce and expanded the rapidly developing market economy. In both, the president looked to defend and bolster America's standing in the world community. Jackson was always a nationalist. And he was remarkably successful in achieving his goals. By midway through his first term, the president's ministers had succeeded in achieving spoliation agreements of $4.5 million from France, $2 million from Naples, and about $600,000 each from Denmark and Spain. France later attempted to renege on its pledge and Jackson, not uncharacteristically, blustered, making the situation tense, but ultimately forcing them to pay.

In terms of commerce, revisions of, or new trade agreements were made with England, France, Russia, and Spain. As Belohlaveck explained, "By 1836, United States exports had increased by more than 75 percent and imports 250 percent over those of Jackson's first year in the White House. Critically, two-thirds of the exports and imports involved the Continental

---

[236] John M. Belohlaveck, "Let the Eagle Soar!" *The Foreign Policy of Andrew Jackson* (Lincoln: The University of Nebraska Press, 1985), 275.

trade."[237] Perhaps most importantly, Jackson's representatives negotiated the British West Indies trade, something that had eluded America and been a source of aggravation since the 1790s. America also gained considerable trading rights in the Mediterranean, and Jackson added new diplomatic positions in Naples, Turkey, Brussels, Prussia, Venezuela, and Texas.

One might argue that credit in foreign relations more properly belonged to the secretary of state or the individual ministers who negotiated claims and trade treaties, but Belohlaveck explained specifically, "The President so wove his thread into the fabric of everyday affairs of the State Department that literally no appointment, regardless of level, could be made without his approval." Moreover, Belohlaveck insisted,

> "Jacksonian diplomacy was personal—it had the markings of the President, not of his Cabinet or even his secretaries of state. Old Hickory believed that the chief executive held the constitutional reins in determining policy....Historians have been reluctant to see that his 'iron will' was also applied to foreign affairs in a calculated and often successful fashion....Old Hickory proceeded with a vigor that bordered on the precipitous. His foreign programs often presented a mirror image of his domestic policies. In each he appears headstrong, impetuous, brash, and uncompromising. Yet this same man possessed tact, patience, and finesse. His moods were mercurial. Jackson was an emotional but intelligent man."[238]

Finally, and of particular note regarding one of the underlying themes of this book – that of Jackson's psychology and the alleged effects of his childhood trauma – Belohlaveck comments in particular on the psychological theory espoused by Michael Paul Rogin: "Rogin has gone so far as to suggest that Old Hickory's knee-jerk emotional responses to Mother England were reflections of deeply rooted psychological problems. It would perhaps then be logical to assume that the hot-tempered General would be eminently unsuccessful in his conduct of diplomacy toward Great Britain." Yet, Belohlaveck concludes, this was not the case. Rather, "Jackson made Anglo-American relations a high diplomatic priority. In doing so, and with the successes that would follow from this decision, Jackson fostered one of the greater ironies in early American diplomatic history."[239] There can be little doubt that Jackson proposed and achieved a successful foreign policy.

---

[237] Belohlaveck, "Let the Eagle Soar!," *43*; 53.
[238] Belohlaveck, "Let the Eagle Soar!," *39*; 251; 253.
[239] Belohlaveck, "Let the Eagle Soar!," *54*.

INDIAN POLICY

Andrew Jackson's Indian policy was atrocious. In his "Inaugural Address" the president insisted on the need for a "liberal policy, and to give that humane and considerate attention to their rights and their wants."[240] Yet the racism that defined much of nineteenth century America and which influenced Jackson's outlook, along with his experiences on the frontier, made his definition of liberality and humanity a farce by today's standards. The fact is that Jackson and his supporters in Congress pushed through the Removal Act of 1830 and ultimately forced tens of thousands of Native Americans from their lands in the East to areas west of the Mississippi River. Most infamously, some 18,000 Cherokee were forced to flee their homes at the point of a bayonet. Thousands died along the way. The Trail of Tears, as it has come to be known, occurred after Jackson left the presidency. Yet he was as responsible for the atrocities that occurred as he would have been had he still occupied the executive chair. His desire for a speedy, cost-saving removal – his desire for removal in the first place – resulted in the atrocity.[241]

Moreover, there is no question that Jackson engaged in all the political wrangling that he could muster in order to achieve passage of the Removal Act. Once successful, he continued the same tactics that Americans and Europeans had utilized for centuries. Corruption and bribery, bullying and bluster were employed to force Indians to leave the East. Whites, including Jackson and his friends, profited financially from the speculation related to this newly opened land. There is simply no denying Andrew Jackson's complicity in the horrors of Indian removal, and Native Americans today are justified in their hatred of and outrage towards him. Yet this is not the end of the story, nor is it the only lens through which it can be viewed.

In the preface to his book, *The Long, Bitter Trail: Andrew Jackson and the Indians*, Anthony F.C. Wallace writes that as an anthropologist he

---

[240] Jackson, *"Inaugural Address."*
[241] A great deal has been written on Jackson's removal policy. It is impossible for the purposes of this book to delve into every detail of that policy. The following works are a good place to begin, presenting views that both criticize Jackson and attempt to explain the context of what occurred: Ronald N. Satz, *American Indian Policy in the Jacksonian Era* (Lincoln: University of Nebraska, 1975); Francis Paul Prucha, *Indian Policy in the United States: Historical Essays* (Lincoln: University of Nebraska Press, 1981); Burstein, *The Passions of Andrew Jackson*; Anthony F.C. Wallace, *The Long Bitter Trail: Andrew Jackson and the Indians* (New York: Hill & Wang, 1993); Robert Remini, *Andrew Jackson and His Indian*

"cannot resist seeing events, as well as cultures, in some sort of comparative perspective. One comparative observation is unavoidable. The removal of inconveniently located ethnic groups and their resettlement in out-of-the-way places is, and has been for thousands of years, a common phenomenon in the history of states and empires. The removal of the Eastern Indians is a typical case. Nations all over the world today face the need to find ways of organizing diversity instead of trying to remove it."[242]

Another author, John Buchanan, noted, "Like Arabs and Vikings and Mongols and Aztecs before them, frontier Americans were conquerors, and they had the conqueror's self-confidence, convinced that their cause was just….Restless, aggressive, land hungry, they saw before them millions upon millions of acres that by their lights were unused."[243]

The issues of context and history emphasized by such statements are often difficult to embrace or rationalize when considering the troubling paradoxes of America, a nation born of liberty but one whose very foundations were built upon slavery and Native American dispossession. This realization is particularly problematic in the wake of the Civil Rights movement. If Jackson supported slavery and forced Indians to move West, then surely he was a monster, an evil man, a racist who did not appreciate diversity. He could not possibly have represented the highest ideals of liberty and Union.

As bizarre as it might seem, Jackson actually believed that he was treating the Indians with liberality and humanity. In his mind, removal offered at least a chance for Native Americans to continue their culture west of the Mississippi River, relatively undisturbed by white encroachment. The alternative was for Indians to stay where they were and succumb to state laws and land greedy whites. European and Euro-American greed had, after all, been the driving force of relations with the indigenous peoples of the new world for some 300 years before Jackson was born. The reality in the early republic is that short of constant military protection, which in itself would have been impossible, Indians would have been preyed upon by settlers, resulting in retaliation, and thus an excuse for wholesale slaughter of the tribes. Even had he wanted to, Jackson could not have protected the Indians from this any more than George Washington, who came to despise slavery, could have convinced his fellow southerners to abolish the peculiar institution at the birth of the new republic.

Wars (New York: Viking, 2001); John Buchanan, *Jackson's Way: Andrew Jackson and the People of the Western Waters* (New York: John Wiley and Sons, 2001).
[242] Wallace, *The Long Bitter Trail*, viii.
[243] Buchanan, *Jackson's Way*, 36.

As explained in previous chapters, Jackson's overriding conviction since his early arrival in Tennessee and involvement in the Creek Wars was that frontier security necessitated control of Indian lands in the East and ultimately separation of the two races. Similar security concerns influenced later American policies. Consider the Supreme Court sanctioned internment of Japanese-Americans in the midst of World War II, or the current treatment of Palestinians in Israel. Security rationales often justify oppression.

In terms of Indian removal, Jackson was hardly the originator of the idea. As described in the introduction to this work, Thomas Jefferson and James Monroe had early on determined that removal was the policy of choice for those tribes that could not be cowed into submission. For Jackson, the real change was expanding the use of removal and, importantly, making it a congressionally sanctioned act. As Robert Remini accurately explained, early presidents had forced removal through executive order. "What Jackson did was force the Congress to face up to the Indian issue and address it in the only way possible. And what it did at his direction was harsh, arrogant, racist—and inevitable. There was no way the American people would continue to allow the presence of the tribes in the fertile hills and valleys that they coveted. Sooner or later, white culture and life would engulf them."[244] John Buchanan came to much the same conclusion, noting that movement west among white settlers was "an irresistible flood": "To deny that this was a people's movement and argue that big land speculators or colonization companies or especially the government were the driving forces behind the conquest is to miss the point. For it was not, as some claim, primarily a political movement. It was then as it is today—an unstoppable folk movement."[245]

The fact that Indian removal and land dispossession was spurred by the American people does not change Jackson's role or culpability. It merely contextualizes the movement. Jackson, as Indian fighter and president, represented the views of the South and West in his removal policy. He did not devise the policy, but he did push it through with a devotion and political skill that others had lacked. Even when the Supreme Court attempted to provide some degree of protection through its *Worcester v. Georgia* decision, which argued that tribes retained a degree of sovereignty and could be protected from state laws, Jackson did nothing to support such a view and managed to have the problems related to the case settled internally within Georgia.

---

[244] Remini, *Andrew Jackson and His Indian Wars*, 237.
[245] Buchanan, *Jackson's Way*, 37.

For those who want to see the worst in Andrew Jackson and portray him as a nineteenth century Hitler, there is no need to go beyond his Indian policy, especially removal. To take this view, however, distorts the cultural, racial, and historical realities that existed in Jacksonian America. As Paul Finkelman wrote, "Had he [Jackson] been the genocidal Indian hater his fiercest critics claim he was, it is doubtful there would be large number of Indians in Oklahoma today living on tribal lands....While modern critics might accuse him of ethnic cleansing, his was not the cleansing of the Bosnian killing fields. He removed Indians to Oklahoma, not Auschwitz."[246]

Considering such arguments does not mean that one condones the ideas of Jackson or his contemporaries. It merely means that we understand those ideas and work harder to eradicate them from our society. In this sense, much works remains undone. Finally, and interestingly, it was, perhaps, Martin Van Buren who in his autobiography best stated how removal might continue as a moral dilemma for the nation's future: "Unlike histories of many great questions which agitate the public mind in their day [removal] will in all probability endure as long as the government itself, and will in time occupy the minds and feelings of our people."[247]

THE BANK WAR: ROUND ONE

The Bank of the United States was the brainchild of George Washington's secretary of the treasury, Alexander Hamilton, who viewed its establishment as integral to the creation of a mercantile society focused on manufacturing and trade. Thomas Jefferson, then secretary of state, strenuously opposed such a bank, insisting that it was unconstitutional and unnecessary for a largely agricultural society. Hamilton countered with a broad conception of constitutional authority, insisting that the "necessary and proper clause" authorized the government's charter of a bank. Hamilton won the argument and the First Bank of the United States was established in 1791with a twenty year charter, expiring in 1811. When the War of 1812 began shortly thereafter and the nation was left with no central financial institution to either stabilize currency or provide loans to pay for the war, Jeffersonian Republicans

---

[246] Paul Finkleman, ed., *Congress and the Emergence of Sectionalism: From the Missouri Compromise to the Age of Jackson* (Columbus: Ohio University Press, 2008), 15.
[247] Van Buren, *Autobiography*, 275-6.

reversed their ideas on the value of a bank. In his "Seventh Annual Message," James Madison advocated the creation of a new bank.

The Second Bank of the United States, often referred to as the BUS, was established in 1816 with a twenty year charter. It carried a stock of some $35 million dollars and operated as a semi-public/private enterprise, with five of its twenty-five directors appointed by the government, which used the BUS as a depository, receiving interest on all monies, and also as a fiscal agent that made payments for the government in exchange for an annual payment of $1.5 million. The BUS benefitted by loaning out a portion of the federal deposits and receiving interest from the loans. It also produced paper notes and was free from state taxation, a fact that was determined conclusively in the Supreme Court's 1819 *McCulloch v. Maryland* decision in which Chief Justice John Marshall not only denied Maryland's right to tax the bank, but deemed it wholly constitutional. In all, the BUS wielded tremendous economic power, more than any other entity, including the government.[248]

Criticisms of the bank's power and constitutionality did not, however, disappear, and were expanded when the nation was struck by the financial Panic of 1819. Land speculation, inflation, unsound loans, and over-extension of credit led to a precipitous contraction by the bank and worsened the economic downfall. In the end, the BUS was left holding titles on massive amounts of property, and was seen by many as the culprit in the financial collapse. Many Americans, Jackson among them, were in debt and viewed the lending practices and extensive use of paper money by the bank as sources of the problem. Though the bank's new director, Nicholas Biddle, restored the bank's fiscal responsibility, his arrogance and aristocratic demeanor did little to allay concerns over the institution's power. Biddle once remarked in 1824, "No officer of the Government, from the President downwards, has the least right, the least authority, the least pretense, for interference in the concerns of the bank."[249] Jackson's ideas about democracy and the government's responsibility to the people contrasted such a sentiment. His suspicion of the bank's power led him to challenge its very existence.

In his "First Annual Message," the president commented on the approaching 1836 re-charter of the bank, noting, "Both the constitutionality

---

[248] For more on banking in the early republic, see, Bray Hammond, *Banks and Politics in America from the Revolution to the Civil War* (Princeton: Princeton University Press,1957); Robert V. Remini, *Andrew Jackson and the Bank War: A Study in the Growth of Presidential Power* (New York: W.W. Norton & Company, 1967); Howard Bodenhorn, *A History of Banking in Antebellum America: Financial Markets and Economic Development in an Era of Nation-Building* (Cambridge: Cambridge University Press, 2000).

[249] Nicholas Biddle to Thomas Swann, March 17, 1824, quoted in Wilentz, *Andrew Jackson*, 77.

and the expediency of the law creating this bank are well questioned by a large portion of our fellow citizens, and it must be admitted by all that it has failed in the great end of establishing a uniform and sound currency."[250] Jackson had fired the first salvo, and though he quickly became preoccupied with the Eaton Affair and Indian removal, the president never lost sight of the bank. Louis McLane, who ultimately became secretary of the treasury after the cabinet reshuffle, attempted to arrive at a compromise between Biddle and Jackson, but it fell apart when anti-bank forces within the Democratic Party exerted pressure. (Once again an indication of the loose coalition that made up Jackson's still developing party.) The bank war then became fully engaged when Biddle followed the advice of Henry Clay and Daniel Webster by pushing for early re-charter and thereby making the issue a central component of the 1832 presidential election. Clay surmised that Jackson would lose support within his own tenuous coalition whether he supported or vetoed the re-charter. Either way, he would lose the election and if vetoed, the bank would simply be re-chartered once Clay became president. The strategy seemed flawless.

Clay underestimated Andrew Jackson. Tenacious as ever, Old Hickory refused to be beaten. On a late evening in July 1832, Martin Van Buren arrived at the White House and found Jackson laying on a couch, once again struggling with his health. The president reportedly croaked, "The bank, Mr. Van Buren, is trying to kill me, *but I will kill it.*"[251] Three days later, he delivered his veto message.

Some historians have interpreted Jackson's statement to Van Buren as the ultimate indicator of a personal rather than a principled or policy based view on the bank. Jackson was merely lashing out, flailing at his enemy. Nicholas Biddle remarked that the veto "has all of the fury of a chained panther, biting the bars of his cage," and attempted to crush Jackson with his own words by having 30,000 copies of the Veto Message printed and distributed throughout the country.[252] He also used the bank's tremendous financial resources, to the amount of $100,000, to influence the presidential election.

Though there is no doubt that Jackson ultimately personalized the battle, as he always did, that did not mean he failed to have serious constitutional and policy driven criticisms of the BUS. His veto was replete with a Jeffersonian

---

[250] Andrew Jackson, "First Annual Message," December 1, 1829, *The American Presidency Project*, http://www.presidency.ucsb.edu.
[251] Van Buren, *Autobiography*, 625.
[252] Nicholas Biddle to Henry Clay, August 1, 1832, in John F. Hopkins, ed., *The Papers of Henry Clay, vol. 8* (Lexington: University of Kentucky Press, 1984), 556.

strict construction of the Constitution, warnings about the moneyed aristocracy, and the dangers to democracy and the common people from an institution that wielded unprecedented power with no balancing check or oversight:

> "It is to be regretted that the rich and powerful too often bend the acts of government to their selfish purposes. Distinctions in society will always exist under every just government. Equality of talents, of education, or of wealth can not be produced by human institutions. In the full enjoyment of the gifts of Heaven and the fruits of superior industry, economy, and virtue, every man is equally entitled to protection by law; but when the laws undertake to add to these natural and just advantages artificial distinctions, to grant titles, gratuities, and exclusive privileges, to make the rich richer and the potent more powerful, the humble members of society-the farmers, mechanics, and laborers-who have neither the time nor the means of securing like favors to themselves, have a right to complain of the injustice of their Government. There are no necessary evils in government. Its evils exist only in its abuses. If it would confine itself to equal protection, and, as Heaven does its rains, shower its favors alike on the high and the low, the rich and the poor, it would be an unqualified blessing. In the act before me there seems to be a wide and unnecessary departure from these just principles."[253]

Such a message resonated with many Americans. Biddle's politicking in printing the Veto Message turned it into a club with which he was beaten into submission. Jackson won re-election and the first round of the Bank War. The president now believed that he had a mandate to finish the bank once and for all.

CONCLUSION

When Andrew Jackson arrived at the White House few in the nation, much less in Washington, knew what he stood for other than a broadly defined and somewhat amorphous call to root out corruption in government. Reform was the word, but how it would take place was a mystery, as was the question of how Jackson would control his new and quickly organized coalition. One of the key problems was the very broadness of that coalition. The Jacksonian Democratic Party was made up of a disparate number of groups, often

---

[253] Andrew Jackson, Bank Veto Message, July 10,1832, *Avalon Project*, Yale Law School, http://www.yale.edu/lawweb/avalon/presiden/veto/ajveto01.htm

conflicting over banking, tariffs, internal improvements, and Indian policy, to name but a few issues. Jackson faced immediate problems within his cabinet when the Eaton Affair went from social ostracization to a full-fledged political conflagration, in part fueled by the president's own obstinate reaction, but also because John Calhoun and Martin Van Buren were jockeying for power. The problem engulfed his administration, but not so much that Jackson was unable to work on a wider agenda, which was fairly clearly broken down in his "Inaugural" and "Annual Messages."

The president focused on finding corruption in the form of theft, removing from office those who were incompetent or dishonest, paying down the national debt, engaging in internal improvements where constitutionally feasible, focusing on foreign trade and negotiating spoliation agreements with European powers, removing the Indians west of the Mississippi River, and challenging the constitutionality of the Bank of the United States. In all of these things he was amazingly successful. This does not mean that Jackson was correct in all his views or that everything was done perfectly. Jackson's reform efforts were hurt by Samuel Swartwout's theft from the New York Customs Office, and rotation in office took on an entirely different aspect as the spoils system. Removal of the Indians was hardly "liberal" or "humane," words that Jackson utilized in the "Inaugural" to define the nation's duty to Native Americans. Nonetheless, Jackson achieved all of these things within a nineteenth century rationale of what was good for the nation in terms of fiscal policy and national security. Some at the time did not agree with the president's views, just as there are vastly differing ideas about what is good policy in America today. Yet one can hardly deny that Jackson was successful during his first term, or that he mapped out a fairly ambitious plan and achieved the majority of it.

Such ideas stand in stark contrast to James C. Curtis' conclusions regarding Jackson's first term: "Doubts far more than any concern for ideology or party policy determined Andrew Jackson's behavior during his first term of office. Whether as spoilsman, government reformer, defender of strict construction, architect of Indian removal, or enemy of the Bank, the president acted more in self-defense than out of loyalty to the Democratic coalition."[254] Curtis' assertions fail to give Jackson any due for the policies that he did push through – whether or not one agrees with those policies – and fails to fully understand the unsettled nature of the Jackson party at the start of his presidency. In all, Jackson expanded his notions of Jacksonian democracy and

---

[254] Curtis, *Andrew Jackson and the Search for Vindication*, 101.

during his second term in office he furthered those ideas, both in terms of burying the bank and safeguarding the Union that he had fought so hard to build.

Chapter 7

PRESIDENCY: THE SECOND TERM

Andrew Jackson viewed his victory in the 1832 presidential election as both a mandate for his policy of reform, which included vetoing the re-charter of the Bank of the United States, and a message from the people about the nature of democratic government and his commitment to it. Jackson trusted in the people to make the right decision, even with Henry Clay and Nicholas Biddle doing all they could to make the election a referendum on the Bank Veto. Writing of the election to his old friend and military protégé General John Coffee, Jackson stated calmly, "the virtue of the people will meet the crisis and resist all the power and corruption of the bank."[255] Jackson's repeated declarations about the people's will had, in large part, been generated by the difficulties of the 1824 election and the ensuing Corrupt Bargain. His faith continued into the 1828 contest and he remained supremely confident that the people would once again do their duty so that Jackson could reclaim the executive chair and do his duty to crush the bank and defend the Union.

The election of 1832 was not nearly as nasty as 1828. Still, the campaign literature and activities from both sides revealed the incredible duality of Jackson's image. Democrats lionized him as the defender of democracy and servant of the people. Hickory Clubs were created throughout the nation and barbecues, hickory pole raisings, and the wearing of hickory leaves became the activities of choice for those who supported the president. Such symbolism was fitting for a man who had come to represent much of the nation through his common origins and devotion to the Union. Jackson's statements about the ability of common men to serve in office and his willingness to fight the

---

[255] Andrew Jackson to John Coffee, October 1832, in Remini, *Andrew Jackson: The Course of American Freedom*, 374.

seemingly corrupt BUS heightened his allure. The president's opponents, however, were equally resolute in their opposition to the old "hero." To anti-Jacksonians, soon to coalesce under the banner of Whig, Jackson was a monster who had brought his lawless, Constitution-defying ways to the nation's capitol. As one campaign document put it bluntly, Jackson "is an Usurper and a Tyrant; and our constitution and laws, under his Chief Magistracy, are but a dead letter."[256]

It appears from Jackson's correspondence that he did not have much apprehension about the election. His letters from the fall and winter of 1832 reveal far more focus on problems connected to the bank and the dangers of Nullification in South Carolina, than on the election. He wrote as a president planning his next move. Jackson was certain of his reelection. When the returns came in he was proven correct, winning 688,242 popular votes, 55% of those cast, to Henry Clay's 473,462, 37%, and William Wirt's 101,051, 8%. Clay had run as a National Republican and Wirt as the candidate for America's first third party movement, the Anti-Masons, which evolved from a movement in New York State in opposition to the power and secrecy of the Order of Free Masonry.

In many ways, Jackson's second term began with as much difficulty as his first. There were no more Eaton Affairs, but the Bank War had been a difficult battle that placed the president in a tricky position and revealed cracks within the still forming Democratic coalition. Not all members of Jackson's party agreed with his veto, and this fact became evermore clear when he unleashed another attack by removing the federal deposits in an attempt to deliver a finishing blow. Jackson was never one to do things halfway. He had refused to retreat from the field during the Creek Wars, believing that the Indians would regroup and launch another attack in the future. Better to finish the job when the opportunity was at hand. He had refused to relinquish martial law in New Orleans lest the British attack again and take the city. The same mentality motivated Jackson to fulfill his ode to Martin Van Buren. Jackson would kill the bank once and for all. Removing the deposits, he believed, would carry out that task. The difficulty was in how he went about doing it, ultimately removing two secretaries of the treasury until he settled on a third who was willing to do his bidding. The actions revealed the single-mindedness, the uncompromising nature, and aggressive power that Jackson had used in the past and which critics had worried about when he became president. Equally

---

[256] *A Retrospect of Andrew Jackson's Administration*, (n.p., 1832), 9-10.

problematic was that Jackson focused far more on destroying the bank than he did on coming up with a viable, economically sound alternative.

The other major problem that confronted Jackson was the specter of Nullification. The fallout between the president and John Calhoun had placed South Carolina in a dire position, made worse by Congress' failure to reduce tariff rates in a significant way. The 1828 "South Carolina Exposition and Protest" had offered both a warning and a means through which that warning could be carried into action, arguing that states possessed the right to hold a convention and literally vote to declare a law null and void. Once they did so, if the federal government attempted to coerce the state into compliance, that state had the right to secede, argued nullifiers. Thus Nullification was far more than a challenge to federal authority in terms of its law-making powers. South Carolina's actions were a challenge to the Union's very existence. Jackson faced the biggest threat to the nation up until the Civil War. In this sense, his response to the nullifiers, especially his "Nullification Proclamation," became a manifesto on the Union's perpetuity.

Many historians have concluded that the Bank War was the defining moment of Jackson's presidency because it had to do with the bank's constitutionality and the nation's economic future. Yet Nullification was at least equally important because it revealed the seriousness of challenges to the Union's existence and how a strong president might go about meeting those challenges. In many ways, Jackson became something of a model to Abraham Lincoln's defense of the Union during the Civil War. Though the two would have certainly disagreed on the institution of slavery and which section had pushed the nation to war, they would have agreed that the Union could not be broken.

It is also important to note that historians, as with his first administration and earlier career, debate the extent to which Jackson lucidly and effectively mapped out and carried through a policy to deal with the Bank and Nullification. Robert Remini believed that Jackson acted masterfully in both instances, whereas James C. Curtis and Andrew Burstein questioned the president's motivations and demeanor.

Additionally, the second round of the Bank War and the Nullification crisis revealed, once again, the incredible duality of Andrew Jackson. Depending on one's political affiliation at the time, Jackson could be seen as the greatest of heroes or the worst of despots. His handling of the bank was either a principled, democratic, constitutionally-based defense against a moneyed aristocracy that threatened the republic through its vast economic power, or it was a vengeful, narrowly conceived, personal vendetta to destroy an important economic institution. Jackson's handling of Nullification was equally controversial. He was either the savior of the Union, the great national defender who stood up to nullifiers and secessionists bent on looking to their own selfish interests over those of the nation at large, or Jackson was a tyrant who coerced South Carolina through the threat of force and in the process robbed a sovereign state of her rights.[257]

As always with Jackson, there was some degree of truth in each of these charges. For it was not just about what Jackson believed, but how he went about putting those beliefs into action. Never one to tread lightly, he moved with swiftness to crush any opposition. Though Jackson was often correct in principle, his methods were far from conventional.

THE BANK WAR AND REMOVAL OF THE FEDERAL DEPOSITS

In his 1832 "Annual Message" to Congress, Jackson explained in brief a troubling occurrence related to the Bank of the United States. The government planned to make significant payments, some $13 million, toward reducing the national debt by redeeming bonds held by the BUS. The problem was that Biddle did not actually have the money. It was loaned out in various forms and he did not want to contract currency or call in loans in the midst of the presidential election. The payment would have to wait while Biddle worked out a plan to borrow money from the foreign stockholders who held the bonds. One of Jackson's veto criticisms was that foreign stockholders possessed too much power over the American economy. Not only did the situation confirm, in Jackson's mind, this criticism, but it delayed the payment of the debt, something he had focused on since the beginning of his presidency.[258]

Jackson thus informed Congress of his "duty to acquaint you with an arrangement made by the Bank of the United States with a portion of the holders of the 3% stock [the bonds in question], by which the Government will be deprived of the use of the public funds longer than was anticipated." He

---

[257] Please note that I have opted to discuss the second round of the Bank War prior to Nullification, as an extension of the first Bank War. The reality is that both issues roughly occurred at the same time, though Nullification was solved prior to the end of the Bank War.

[258] Robert Remini provides an excellent account of the bond issue in, Robert Remini, *Andrew Jackson: The Course of American Democracy*, 1833-1845 (New York: Harper & Row, 1984), 52-3.

then noted "the failure of the bank to perform its duties," explained that the secretary of the treasury was looking into the matter, but added, "I recommend the subject to the attention of Congress, under the firm belief that it is worthy of their serious investigation." He closed by stating that if problems are discovered, the BUS "is no longer a safe depository of the money of the people."[259]

Jackson followed his address with a letter to his young friend, the Tennessee congressional representative James K. Polk, who became a key ally in the continuing attack on the BUS: "the hydra of corruption is only *scotched, not dead*, and the intent is…to destroy the vote of the people lately given at the ballot boxes, and to rally around the recharter the present session of congress two thirds An investigation kills it and its supporters *dead*. Let this be had—call upon the sec' of the Treasury who must agree with me that an investigation by Congress is absolutely necessary."[260] Always with an eye toward political maneuvering, Jackson believed that a movement would be made to congressionally override his veto. One way to stop such a tactic was by casting further doubt, which Jackson really did entertain, on the bank's operations.

The House of Representatives began the investigation on January 31, 1833, and after three weeks concluded that the deposits were safe. As a member of the committee, Polk wrote a dissenting minority report in which he argued that the BUS had acted improperly on a number of occasions. Jackson relied far more heavily on Polk's than the House's report and began a movement against the bank by querying his cabinet on March 19th about the feasibility of removing government deposits from the bank.[261] It is important to clarify that Jackson was not advocating the immediate withdrawal of federal monies from the BUS. Rather, the term "removal" meant that new deposits would be shifted to state banks and the deposits still remaining in the BUS would be withdrawn over a period of time as the government needed the money.

Most important to Jackson were the opinions of Roger Taney, the attorney general, and Louis McLane, the secretary of the treasury. Taney wrote the president on April 29th, announcing, "the conduct of the Bank of the United States appears to have been such that the Executive Branch of the Government

---

[259] Andrew Jackson, "Fourth Annual Message," December 4, 1832, T*he American Presidency Project*, http://www.presidency.ucsb.edu.
[260] Andrew Jackson to James K. Polk, December 16, 1832, in *Correspondence, vol. 4*, 501.
[261] Andrew Jackson to the Members of the Cabinet, March 19, 1833, in *Correspondence, vol. 5*, 32-3.

may lawfully withdraw from it the deposites of the public money, and that the public interest requires it to be done." McLane came to a different conclusion. In a lengthy letter written on May 20th, the secretary, in a mindful and respectful tone, explained that he did not question the constitutionality of the bank and that removal of the deposits would be "an arbitrary exercise of authority" and "the only justification of the Secretary of the Treasury in making this order is his just sense of responsibility for the safety of the public money; and it must therefore be admitted that where the House of Representatives by so large a vote have declared the money to be safe in the Bank of the United States, no such responsibility could well exist."[262]

Jackson was not surprised by McLane's view and even noted in pencil on the letter that "There are some strong points in this view—all ably discussed."[263] Nonetheless, on the whole he believed that the deposits should be removed and understood that McLane would be an obstacle in doing so. The secretary was removed from his position and transferred to that of secretary of state. In fairness to Jackson, the repositioning was not solely, perhaps even primarily, about the bank. Secretary of State Edward Livingston desired appointment as minister to France, and McLane had done an admirable job while previously serving as minister to England and opening the West Indies trade to American shipping. For Jackson, McLane made a perfect replacement for Livingston. The movement to the state department, then, was hardly a punishment for McLane's support of the bank. Indeed, he wrote his opinion of the bank and deposit removal fully aware of the transfer and even acknowledged such in his letter to the president. Still, the reassignment of the pro-bank McLane could only aid Jackson in his mission for removal.

Into the treasury department came William Duane, an anti-bank man from Pennsylvania, where the BUS main branch was located, and whose father had been a staunch Jeffersonian opponent of the first bank. Jackson expected no difficulties from Duane, and wrote him two letters on June 26th, one directing him to make arrangements for depositing federal monies in designated state banks around the country, and another lengthy letter explaining Jackson's views on the bank and the recent history related to its re-charter and veto.[264] On July 10th Duane responded, explaining that though he disapproved of the bank's re-charter, he thought it unnecessary and unjust to change government

---

[262] Roger Taney to Andrew Jackson, April 29, 1833, in *Correspondence, vol. 5*, 67-71; Louis McLane, May 20, 1833, in *Correspondence, vol. 5*, 75-101.
[263] Louis McLane, May 20, 1833, in *Correspondence, vol. 5*, 101.
[264] Andrew Jackson to William Duane, June 26, 1833, in *Correspondence, vol. 5*, 111-13, 113-128.

policy by placing federal deposits in state banks. Jackson responded calmly with a series of letters and meetings, to which Duane ultimately replied on July 22nd: "I have already, both in writing and verbally, had the honor to state to you, that, after the fullest consideration, which I had been able to give to the subject, I do not, under existing circumstances, feel myself justified in substituting state banks for the bank of the United States, as the depository of public money."[265]

Jackson left shortly thereafter for vacation, allowing Amos Kendall, a member of his Kitchen Cabinet and an important agent in the deposit issue, to wrangle with Van Buren, McLane and others about the timing of the deposit changes. Then, on September 8, the president wrote to Vice-President Van Buren, insisting that if a delay occurred in shifting the deposits to state banks it "would be to do the very act it [BUS] wishes, that is, to have it in its power to distress the community, destroy the state Banks, and if possible corrupt congress and obtain a two thirds, to recharter the Bank." Jackson closed by announcing, "is it possible that your friends hesitate, and are overawed by the power of the Bank. it cannot overawe me. I trust in my God and the virtue of the people."[266] Two days later, Jackson called a meeting of the cabinet and made clear his opinions on deposits. Duane, once again demurred that Congress must comment on the issue. Jackson's mind was now made up. Duane should remove the deposits or resign his office. Writing to Roger Taney, the pesident insisted, "If Mr. Duane will not agree to carry into effect these conclusions and remain, the sooner he withdraws the better—it is known what my determination is, and if he cannot act with me, on that determination, he ought to withdraw."[267] Jackson even considered transferring Duane to serve as minister to Russia, but he refused to resign or accept a different office.

Jackson was left with little choice. He called his cabinet together once again, on September 18, and had delivered to them a virtual manifesto of his views on the bank and his decision to halt any further deposits in the institution. He advised Duane that the act was done under the president's authority. Just two days later a notice appeared in the Washington *Globe* announcing that public monies would be deposited in state banks beginning on October 1st. Then came a standoff between Jackson and Duane, who refused to resign and insisted that the president actually dismiss him. Jackson obliged on the 23rd: "your further services as Secretary of the Treasury are no longer

---

[265] William Duane to Andrew Jackson, July 22, 1833, in *Correspondence, vol. 5*, 141-2.
[266] Andrew Jackson to Martin Van Buren, September 8, 1833, in *Correspondence, vol. 5*, 182-3.
[267] Andrew Jackson to Roger Taney, September 15, 1833, quoted in Remini, *Andrew Jackson: The Course of American Democracy*, 95.

required."[268] Roger Taney was moved to the treasury department and carried out the president's directives on deposits in what became known as the "Pet Banks."

Jackson's commitment to removal was steadfast, almost maniacal. He was so insistent on killing the bank that all sense of decorum and finesse was lost. A critic had once charged that Jackson was like an "exasperated rhinoceros, wreaking his fury on every object that presents itself," and his actions to secure a final death blow to the BUS was certainly akin to a bull in a china shop. Even Robert Remini acknowledged that Jackson's treatment of Duane had been "mishandled" and exhibited "bad judgment." "The President did everything wrong." Historian Sean Wiletnz has concurred, remarking that "Jackson also complied exactly with his opponents' image of him as a reckless and vengeful autocrat."[269]

Yet Jackson was not incorrect in his appraisal of the bank's excessive power. He had made cogent arguments in his veto message. The BUS wielded far too much power over the American economy and possessed a monopoly of sorts over government funds and how they could be used to spur or contain the overall financial health of the nation. Jackson understood the fundamental and constitutional problems posed by the bank. It was his single-mindedness, the arrogance in carrying out *his* superior directives and *knowing* that he was correct, above and beyond his many able advisors who counseled caution, which made removal a political mess. Jackson simply lacked any sense of political decorum or compromise. He preferred to kill the bank, to win through sheer determination, rather than push it into a slow but likely death following the veto. Moreover, removal alienated other Democrats and threatened to divide the still developing party. Equally troubling was Jackson's decidedly weak solution of utilizing state banks for the deposits, even though this is what had been done in the aftermath of expiration of the first Bank of the United States in 1811.[270]

The BUS had managed to use its considerable influence to provide a stable currency and counteract the over-extension of paper money. Jackson assumed that state banks would manage a similar restraint. They did not, and it caused for a period of time wild speculation. Additionally, Nicholas Biddle

---

[268] Paper Read to the Cabinet, September 18, 1833, in *Correspondence, vol. 5*, 192-203; dismissal quoted in Remini, *Andrew Jackson: The Course of American Democracy*, 102.

[269] Snelling, *A Brief and Impartial History of The Life and Actions of Andrew Jackson*, 95; Remini, *Andrew Jackson: The Course of American Democracy*, 104; Wilentz, *Andrew Jackson*, 104.

[270] Sean Wilentz, in *The Rise of American Democracy*, provides an excellent explanation of the Bank War and the economic and political issues involved. See chapter 13 in particular.

was hardly willing to go down without a fight. In response to removal, Biddle restricted and called in loans. The result was a general reduction in currency and a financial panic. Biddle snorted, "This worthy President thinks that because he has scalped Indians and imprisoned Judges, he is to have his way with the Bank. He is mistaken."[271] Yet in directing such a dire and mean spirited financial retaliation against Jackson, Biddle actually proved the president's point about the bank's immense and dangerous economic power and Biddle was ultimately forced to lighten the restrictions.

The second round of the Bank War also had profound effects regarding the development of political parties. Prior to 1833, those opposed to Jackson had belonged to one of several differing groups. The National Republicans were still around, and the Anti-Masons had nominated their own candidate for president in 1832. The anger over Jackson's removal of the deposits, however, caused these two groups, and some Democrats upset with the president's actions, to coalesce into a new political party. The Whigs, as they came to be known, organized in opposition to King Andrew I. The name Whig harkened back to the English Commonwealth, when opponents decried the power of the King. Clay and his fellow anti-Jacksonians chose the term as a protest and rallying cry to defend liberty from executive usurpation. In a three-day speech in December of 1833, Clay played to a packed Senate, announcing, "We are in the midst of a revolution, hitherto bloodless, but rapidly tending toward a total change of the pure republican character of the government, and to the concentration of all power in the hands of one man. The powers of Congress are paralyzed, except when in conformity with his will."[272] To some extent, the address was reminiscent of Clay's "military chieftain" speech in the House when he attacked Jackson for invading Florida during the Seminole Campaign. Both addresses provided dire warnings concerning Jackson's power and the future of the nation.

In order to stop the president's aggressive usurpation, Clay advocated a Senate censure, condemning Jackson for his high-handed and "illegal" removal of the deposits. This was ultimately done in March of 1834 and was the first and only time a president has ever been censured. Congress considered this action when President William Jefferson Clinton lied under oath about his sexual relations with Monica Lewinsky, but instead opted for impeachment. This, in fact, is what Jackson argued Congress should attempt

---

[271] Nicholas Biddle to Joseph Hopkinson, February 21, 1834, quoted in Remini, *Andrew Jackson: The Course of American Democracy*, 108.

[272] Henry Clay, "On the Removal of the Deposits," December 26, 1833, in Watson, ed., *Andrew Jackson vs. Henry Clay*, 214-222.

with him. In a lengthy response to the Senate censure, which consisted of a passage in the Senate Journal essentially stating that "on this day Andrew Jackson was censured," Jackson insisted that the censure was unconstitutional and that the only real power possessed by Congress was impeachment. Jackson was correct. The censure carried no legitimate power. It was merely politics, and was ceremoniously repealed some three years later when Senator Thomas Hart Benton of Missouri, one of Jackson's leading supporters, organized a vote to "expunge" it. The action consisted of making a black box and "x" through the censure resolution, and writing "expunged" next to it. Such were the politics of the early republic.

Jackson ultimately weathered the removal and censure storm. Clay, Calhoun, and Daniel Webster lambasted the president in Congress, but he was also ably defended by Benton, John Forsyth, and other Jacksonian stalwarts. In many ways, the second round of the Bank War helped to stabilize the Democratic Party by clarifying the policy lines the Jackson forced his supporters to follow. He made abundantly clear his views on the bank and what must be done to protect the people. Benton had scoffed at Clay's charges of Jackson being a king, retorting that the president had saved the nation from Czar Nick, referring to bank president Nicholas Biddle.

That Jackson could be portrayed by Democrats as the savior of the republic and harbinger of democracy, while Whigs could at the very same time refer to him as King Andrew I and the greatest danger to the fledgling nation, strikes at the very heart of the competing visions and the politicking of early America. Democrats and Whigs had very real policy differences over internal improvements, banks, tariffs, and westward expansion. As the party lines became more clearly drawn, these differences became more apparent. This stands in stark contrast to the rather loosely defined Democratic coalition at the start of Jackson's presidency. The Whigs, in addition to differences in economic policy, rallied around steadfast opposition to Jackson himself. This was largely in response to Jackson's rather freewheeling use of power and his firm belief that the presidency was particularly invested with power. He also believed that he was the only truly elected national representative of the people – senators at this time were appointed or elected by state legislatures, representatives were elected by the people within individual states, and judges were appointed. In this sense, Jackson insisted that he was acting in conformity with the people's will in killing the bank. The outcome in the election of 1832 cemented such a belief. Because all of this occurred within, and was really a defining factor in the rise of the second American party system, Jackson's dual image has been forever influenced by the competing party views of his day. He was either a hero or a despot depending on one's party views.

How have historians viewed the Bank War? Remini insisted that Jackson, "exerted renewed leadership over the nation and the party by virtue of his victory over the BUS, and he breathed new power and authority into the presidency. Far more important, the Bank War provided a powerful assist in moving the Republic further down the road to democracy. The war was constantly described by the Democratic press as an effort to stop the few from robbing the many. Quite simply, they said, it was a contest between democracy and aristocracy." Wilentz concurred, explaining, "To some observers, Jackson's attack on the Bank was but the latest example of his habitual lashing out against anyone or anything he thought had insulted his honor....[But] Jackson raised principled and considered objections to the Bank as an unconstitutional aberration and an affront to popular sovereignty."[273]

James C. Curtis came to markedly different conclusions. Writing of "self-righteous indignation" and that Jackson "desperately sought vindication," Curtis focused intently on the meaning of Jackson's statement to Van Buren that "the Bank is trying to kill me." "Jackson did not strengthen the presidency, nor did he intend to," argued Curtis. Rather, "Without Andrew Jackson, without his fears, his anger, his boldness, his ambivalence, there might never have been a war at all." Whereas Curtis' is correct in noting that a Bank War may have never occurred had it not been for Jackson's opposition, to assert that Jackson possessed no larger constitutional, fiscal, or democratically oriented objections defies Jackson's own writings about the bank. For his part, Andrew Burstein has written, "The Bank of the United States was perfectly well managed," and noted, in reference to the infamous "the Bank is trying to kill me" quote, that "These words seem to suggest that Jackson could not separate an attack on himself from an attack on 'the people'." Donald Cole offered a more comprehensive consideration of Jackson's conduct, but also concluded that the Bank War revealed "a far less independent, composed, and authoritative" Jackson than previously argued, and that his letters with Van Buren "leaves a picture of a rather unsure president craving friendship, needing someone to confide in, and seeking approval without asking for much in return."[274]

---

[273] Remini, *Andrew Jackson: The Course of American Democracy*, 178; Wilentz, *Andrew Jackson*, 75.
[274] Curtis, *Andrew Jackson and the Search for Vindication*, 130-1, 111; Burstein, *The Passions of Andrew Jackson*, 199-200; Cole, *The Presidency of Andrew Jackson*, 194-5.

There is no question that Jackson personalized his battles, both military and political. Yet it seems that some have read a little too closely between the lines by attempting to divine the "real" meaning of Jackson's statements, while at the same time discounting other writings. There is plenty within his letters to reveal that Jackson had real policy concerns regarding the bank. Moreover, it is clear that Jackson was not so "unsure" or intent on "seeking approval" that he failed to stand by his own convictions no matter the difficulties it might cause within his party or the potential friction with Van Buren or members of the presidential cabinet. Jackson's actions alone reveal that he was steadfast in his views. Clearly antagonized, in part by Biddle's interference in the 1832 election, Jackson desired a final, crushing blow to end the BUS once and for all. The president was far more apt to go for the jugular and finish the fight quickly than engage in a more nuanced, politically-minded dance to defang the "monster bank." When it came to the BUS, Jackson was hardly a compromiser or politically tactful, but it is hard to fathom how his actions reveal uncertainty or weakness. His lack of experience, really his lack of interest in the art of legislation or compromise, was without question a liability that often created problems. Yet the other side of the coin is that he could act decisively and not bargain away his principles. This was just the sort of thing he viewed as corrupt and in need of reform.

THE NULLIFICATION CRISIS

Nullification was the greatest domestic crisis to ever face the Union prior to the outbreak of the Civil War. South Carolina, through Calhoun's "Exposition and Protest" and the state's subsequent Nullification convention, challenged not only the law making power of Congress, but the perpetuity of the Union itself. Though the government possessed the constitutional right to regulate trade and raise money through tariffs, it was unconstitutional, argued Calhoun, to aid one section of the nation – the industrial North – at the expense of another section – the agricultural South. Those involved in agriculture had traditionally opposed tariffs both because they caused retaliatory regulations from other governments on items that farmers exported, but also because northern industry benefitted from protection and also raised their domestic prices on products that farmers needed. In all, the tariff was good for the North and bad for the South.

To argue, however, that a state could nullify an act of Congress was something of a stretch. Yet this is where Calhoun's political genius shined.

Basing his ideas in part on the foundations of the Virginia and Kentucky Resolutions – which had been written by James Madison and Thomas Jefferson, respectively, in opposition to the Alien and Sedition Acts – Calhoun insisted that because the people of the states had joined in convention to ratify the Constitution, they could also join together and declare a law null and void. Further, the people could end their association with the Union through the same type of convention. Surely, he insisted, if the people could join in convention to ratify, they could also join in convention to essentially de-ratify or secede. Madison and Jefferson had never gone as far as Calhoun. They merely advocated a theory of "state interposition" or "nullification," but never offered a process through which it could be carried out. Calhoun defined that process, and more, by advocating the right of secession should the government attempt to force a state into compliance with a nullified law.

Calhoun and South Carolina nullifiers had hoped in 1828 that the "Exposition" would be enough to force tariff reform. They also believed that Calhoun's close association with Jackson would be a source of help, and, notwithstanding that, Calhoun might be the next president. These hopes disappeared in the midst of the Eaton and Seminole Affairs, when the president and vice-president had a falling out that resulted in Calhoun's resignation, his banishment from the Democratic Party, and a return to Washington as a South Carolina senator in total opposition to Jackson. In the midst of this increasingly bad blood, the two men had attended a Jefferson birthday celebration in April of 1830 at which it was customary to deliver toasts. Jackson reportedly leered at Calhoun and thundered, "Our Union. It must be preserved." The word "Federal" Union was later added to the quote. The force of the proclamation was immediate and all turned to Calhoun for the next toast: "The Union. Next to our liberty, the most dear."[275]

Nor was it merely Jackson who focused on the threat of Nullification and the Union's future. In January of 1830, senators Robert Hayne of South Carolina and Daniel Webster of Massachusetts debated one another for several days about the legality of Nullification and the supposed right of secession, with Webster insisting that the nation's very liberty was tied to the Union's existence. With matters growing more serious and the ejection of Calhoun from the president's circle of influence, nullifiers began actively organizing a South Carolina convention to nullify the tariff. This was done in November of 1832 when an Ordinance of Nullification was passed and a date of February 1, 1833 set as for when tariffs would no longer be collected in the state.

---

[275] A wonderful account of this episode is told in James, *The Life of Andrew Jackson*, 539.

Jackson's position on Nullification was simple: as president, he had a duty to see that the laws were faithfully executed; no state had the authority to nullify a federal law; the Union was perpetual; secession and rebellion were the same; there existed no constitutionally based right to secede; he would use force if necessary to carry out the nation's laws. The underlying issues related to Nullification were not nearly as simple as Jackson's views. The founding of the Union had been fraught with concern over states' rights versus that of the federal government, an issue that was debated right up to the start of the Civil War. Jackson had traditionally been considered a defender of states' rights, especially regarding the right of Georgia to control the Cherokee Indians. The right to secede, however, was a decidedly different matter, even though New York, Virginia, and Rhode Island had all included clauses in their ratification of the Constitution allowing them to withdraw at a future date. Jackson's uncompromising stance on Nullification was one of the first (Daniel Webster's debate with Hayne was the other) major declarations on the perpetuity of the Union. When Abraham Lincoln prepared his "First Inaugural Address" and challenged the idea of secession, he turned to Jackson, Webster, and the Declaration of Independence to prove the Union's origins and perpetuity.

Though Jackson had kept a fairly close eye on the happenings in South Carolina, it was not until the fall of 1832 that he expressed wider concerns. In a September 11 letter to Secretary of the Navy Levi Woodbury, the president warned of potential dangers and that the fort in Charleston needed to be prepared for an attack, especially if nullifiers attempted to infiltrate the officers and soldiers stationed there: "While I will not admit the probability of things in the South coming to a desperate issue, yet it behoves us to be ready for any emergency." He requested Woodbury to engage in confidential communication with Secretary of War Lewis Cass to prepare for any problems. Jackson also wrote to Cass, stating, "The Secretary of War will forthwith cause secrete and confidential orders to be Issued to the officers commanding the Forts in the harbor of charleston So Carolina to be vigilant to prevent a surprise in the night or by day, against any attempt to seize and occupy the Fts. by any Set of people under whatever pretext the Forts may be approached."[276] Jackson later discussed quietly transferring officers and soldiers who might pose loyalty problems. In all of these considerations the old General revealed his still formidable military skills.

---

[276] Andrew Jackson to Levi Woodbury, Secretary of the Navy, September 11, 1832, *Correspondence, vol. 5*, 474-5; Andrew Jackson to Lewis Cass, Secretary of War, October 29, 1832, *Correspondence, vol. 5*, 483.

Nor did Jackson think solely about military preparations. He also dispatched George Breathitt to South Carolina in the guise of a postal inspector to ascertain what was occurring within the state. The president's letter to Breathitt not only instructed his mission, but defined Jackson's position on his own duties as chief executive:

> "The recent movements in So Carolina have awakened in my bosom the most painful sensations, and although nothing of serious and dangerous character may result from them, it becomes my duty to ascertain, as far as practicable, to what extremity the nullifyers intend to proceed, and to counteract, to the extent of authority vested in the executive and the high obligations incumbent upon him, such of the movements as tend to defeat the collection of revenue imposed by the united states, and thus render null and void the laws of congress on this subject....You will collect all the information touching the subject intrusted to your inquiries that you can obtain, which may be serviceable to the government. Perceiving, as you must, the highly delicate and confidential character of your business, it is not necessary to give you caution as to your conduct."[277]

Jackson also corresponded with Joel R. Pointsett, a key Unionist (a South Carolinian who opposed nullification), both informing him of Breathitt's mission and requesting Unionist preparations for potential hostilities. "It appears a crisis is about to approach," wrote the president, "when the government must act and that with energy. My own astonishment is that my fellow citizens of So, Carolina should be so far deluded, by the wild theory and sophistry of a few ambitious demagogues, as to place themselves in the attitude of rebellion against their government, and become destroyers of their own prosperity and liberty. There appears in their whole proceedings nothing but madness and folly. If grievances do exist there are constitutional means to redress them. Patriots would seek those means only." "The duty of the Executive is a plain one," he continued, "the laws will be executed and the union preserved by all the constitutional and legal means he is invested with and I rely with great confidence on the support of every honest patriot in So. Carolina who really loves his country and the prosperity and happiness we enjoy under our happy and peaceful republican government." Jackson added in a subsequent letter, "perpetuity is stamped upon the constitution by the blood

---

[277] Andrew Jackson to George Breathitt, November 7, 1832, *Correspondence, vol. 5,* 484-5.

of our Fathers—by those who atcheived as well as those who improved our system of free Government."[278]

In the midst of these clandestine preparations, Jackson also worked on the looming crisis by addressing the nullifiers directly, first through his December 4th "Annual Address" and again on December 10th through what has become known as the "Nullification Proclamation." Each statement was an expansion of ideas expressed in his private letters and as a result indicate the extent to which Jackson himself was the driving force behind the ideas in the declarations. In the "Annual Address," Jackson announced,

> "It is my painful duty to state that in one quarter of the United States opposition to the revenue laws has arisen to a height which threatens to thwart their execution, if not to endanger the integrity of the Union. What ever obstructions may be thrown in the way of the judicial authorities of the General Government, it is hoped they will be able peaceably to overcome them by the prudence of their own officers and the patriotism of the people. But should this reasonable reliance on the moderation and good sense of all portions of our fellow citizens be disappointed, it is believed that the laws themselves are fully adequate to the suppression of such attempts as may be immediately made. Should the exigency arise rendering the execution of the existing laws impracticable from any cause what ever, prompt notice of it will be given to Congress, with a suggestion of such views and measures as may be deemed necessary to meet it."[279]

The president also looked toward conciliating the nullifiers by directing a significant section of the "Address" to the tariff. Commenting on the quickly approaching payment of the national debt, he recommended that it was time to reduce the tariff and noted specifically, "In effecting this adjustment it is due, in justice to the interests of the different States, and even to the preservation of the Union itself." Jackson even commiserated on the difficulties of the protective system, announcing,

> "It [is] doubtful whether the advantages of this system are not counter-balanced by many evils, and whether it does not tend to beget in the minds of a large portion of our country-men a spirit of discontent and jealousy dangerous to the stability of the Union....A large portion of the people in one section of the Republic declares it not only inexpedient on these grounds, but as disturbing the equal relations of property by legislation, and therefore

---

[278] Andrew Jackson to Joel R. Pointsett, November 7, 1832, *Correspondence, vol. 5*, 485-6; Andrew Jackson to Joel R. Pointsett, November 7, 1832, *Correspondence, vol. 5*, 493-4.

unconstitutional and unjust. Doubtless these effects are in a great degree exaggerated, and may be ascribed to a mistaken view of the considerations which led to the adoption of the tariff system; but they are never the less important in enabling us to review the subject with a more thorough knowledge of all its bearings upon the great interests of the Republic, and with a determination to dispose of it so that none can with justice complain."[280]

Here was a clear attempt on Jackson's part to express understanding with the plight of South Carolina and direct Congress to consider problems connected to the tariff. In this sense, the "Address" was a model of patience and consideration. A mere six days later, however, the president left absolutely no doubt where he stood on the doctrines of Nullification and secession, or on the sanctity of the Union. "I, Andrew Jackson, President of the United States, have thought proper to issue this my PROCLAMATION, stating my views of the Constitution and laws applicable to the measures adopted by the Convention of South Carolina, and to the reasons they have put forth to sustain them, declaring the course which duty will require me to pursue, and, appealing to the understanding and patriotism of the people, warn them of the consequences that must inevitably result from an observance of the dictates of the Convention." Within the "Proclamation," Jackson announced forcefully, "I consider, then, the power to annul a law of the United States, assumed by one State, *incompatible with the existence of the Union, contradicted expressly by the letter of the Constitution, unauthorized by its spirit, inconsistent with every principle on which It was founded, and destructive of the great object for which it was formed.*"

In a lengthy appeal concerning patriotism, the nation's founding, and the balance between state sovereignty and federal power, Jackson concluded,

> "This, then, is the position in which we stand. A small majority of the citizens of one State in the Union have elected delegates to a State convention; that convention has ordained that all the revenue laws of the United States must be repealed, or that they are no longer a member of the Union. The governor of that State has recommended to the legislature the raising of an army to carry the secession into effect, and that he may be empowered to give clearances to vessels in the name of the State. No act of violent opposition to the laws hasyet been committed, but such a state of things is hourly apprehended, and it is the intent of this instrument to PROCLAIM, not only

---

[279] Jackson, *"Fourth Annual Message."*
[280] Jackson, *"Fourth Annual Message."*

that the duty imposed on me by the Constitution, " to take care that the laws be faithfully executed," shall be performed to the extent of the powers already vested in me by law or of such others as the wisdom of Congress shall devise and Entrust to me for that purpose; but to warn the citizens of South Carolina, who have been deluded into an opposition to the laws, of the danger they will incur by obedience to the illegal and disorganizing ordinance of the convention-to exhort those who have refused to support it to persevere in their determination to uphold the Constitution and laws of their country, and to point out to all the perilous situation into which the good people of that State have been led, and that the course they are urged to pursue is one of ruin and disgrace to the very State whose rights they affect to support."[281]

The "Proclamation" was like a thunder clap. If anyone doubted Jackson's resolve, a foolish thing to do, they no longer did once the address was reprinted throughout the nation. The president had made clear not only his intentions to enforce the tariff laws and crush the very ideas of Nullification and secession, but he offered important, and controversial, views on the nature of the Constitution and the origins of the Union, both of which challenged what some believed was the proper relationship between states' rights and those of the federal government. Jackson's position was bold and uncompromising. It also caused disputes within his own party, for not everyone agreed with his understanding of the Union and the government's power. In this sense, like in his views of the Bank, Jackson further outlined the policy on which his Democratic Party was based.

In many ways Jackson's decree awakened the nation to the seriousness of Nullification and the nation's legislators scrambled to work through a compromise that would avoid open conflict. The president had already been working behind the scenes to prepare militarily, gain intelligence, and lessen potential hostilities by removing the customs house in Charleston to ships in the harbor so that a conflict would not arise over the collection of tariffs. In Congress, members of the Democratic Party and the opposition worked to settle the controversy. Henry Clay, as he had during the Missouri Crisis, focused on compromise measures that could settle the issue. Calhoun also worked towards this end, realizing that a standoff with Jackson was a battle that he and the nullifiers could not win. Ultimately, a compromise was reached that reduced tariff duties over a period of time. On the same day that the compromise legislation was passed, Congress authorized the Force Bill, which

---

[281] Andrew Jackson, "Nullification Proclamation," December 10, 1832, *The Avalon Project*, Yale University, http://www.yale.edu/lawweb/avalon/presiden/proclamations/jack01.htm

gave Jackson the authority to use the military if necessary. In reality, he required no such bill, but it was a powerful statement of authority that balanced the fact that the nullifiers had won a portion of the battle by making the nation and Congress bend to their remonstrations over the tariff. The crisis essentially ended when Jackson signed both the Compromise Bill and the Force Bill on March 2, 1833.

Who ultimately won the nullification crisis? This is a disputed point among historians. Some argue that Calhoun and the nullifiers could claim victory.[282] The tariff would be reduced. Yet that was to be done over a period of time, with the main reductions not occurring for many years. In this sense, the Compromise Bill was far more about saving face than gaining tangible tariff reductions. More importantly, at least one historian has argued forcefully that Nullification was really about the constitutional power of the government and the nature of strict construction of the Constitution – essentially whether or not the Government could engage in acts not explicitly authorized by the Constitution.[283] Calhoun had argued that because the tariff served the North at the South's expense, it was unconstitutional. The southern fear was that if the federal government could pass an unconstitutional tariff they might also be able to abolish slavery, another act that was believed to be unconstitutional. Yet if the issue of making a statement about constitutionality was the true motivating factor behind Nullification, then the nullifiers gained no real victory by reducing the tariff. In doing so they essentially abandoned the argument about constitutionality and strict construction, and this was the main argument to protect slavery. As for the doctrine of Nullification, it was effectively killed by Jackson, though the belief in secession lived on until Lincoln killed it too.

For Jackson's part, he gained a reputation as a staunch patriot and defender of the Union. Yet his "Proclamation," with its arguments about the origins and perpetuity of the Union caused many, even in his own party, to cringe. Thus Nullification, like the Bank War, was filled with positives and negatives for the president. One thing, however, is certain: Jackson absolutely believed that the Union could not be broken and that as chief executive he had the duty and power to protect it. It is not unreasonable to question what president, until Lincoln, could have stood up to the nullifiers with such force and conviction.

---

[282] See in particular, Richard E. Ellis, *The Union at Risk: Jacksonian Democracy, States' Rights and the Nullification Crisis* (New York: Oxford University Press, 1987).

[283] William W. Freehling, *Prelude to Civil War: The Nullification Controversy in South Carolina, 1816-1836* (New York: Oxford University Press, 1965).

Historians have debated widely Jackson's actions regarding Nullification. Was he merely lashing out, attacking South Carolina because the arch villain John Calhoun was one of the leaders of the movement and Jackson had come to despise him? Did Jackson have any constitutionally minded scruples, or was this merely another challenge to his authority that required vindication? Did Jackson think strategically about how to deal with the crisis, or did he thunder and threaten, and by doing so worsen the situation? How much did the "Nullification Proclamation" represent the president's views versus those of its principal author, Secretary of State Edward Livingston?

As with all things Jackson, scholars have arrived at markedly different conclusions. James C. Curtis assured readers of a number of things: "In responding to nullification, the President followed no consistent political course, nor in the months ahead did he give much thought to the partisan consequences of his actions." "His determination and lack of flexibility jeopardized his party's efforts to arrange a political compromise." "The president did not intend to commit himself or his party to a new ideological course." "The president believed that nullifiers needed proof of executive determination, not a lesson in constitutional philosophy." "Andrew Jackson approached the nullification crisis with the determination of a crusader who had finally found the ultimate cause."[284]

Andrew Burstein was more favorably disposed to seeing something different in Jackson's response, noting, "His handling of the nullification crisis was arguably the noblest action Jackson took over the course of his two terms."[285] Robert Remini naturally filled out the portrait of a focused, intent Jackson who saved the nation:

> "Resolving the nullification controversy probably constituted Jackson's greatest victory as President....His policy—a combination of tariff reform and the Force Bill—was wise and practical....Of all the leading figures of the period, only Jackson had insisted on both measures as a combined package to solve the problem. And his "masterful statesmanship" played a crucial role in providing the final settlement that preserved the Union. Even more masterful was Jackson's ability to reassure the American people that in the White House sat a very determined President who knew what he was doing and had the means to prevent the breakup of the Union."[286]

---

[284] Curtis, *Andrew Jackson and the Search for Vindication*, 133, 138, 144.
[285] Burstein, *The Passions of Andrew Jackson*, 194.
[286] Remini, *Andrew Jackson: The Course of American Democracy*, 43.

Specialists on Nullification have also accorded Jackson credit for his determination and handling of the crisis. Richard E. Ellis wrote, "I have argued that Andrew Jackson was a clear, coherent, forceful, and even formidable constitutional thinker. His differences with the nullifiers were real and profound, and in certain ways irresolvable. One cannot explain the Old Hero's opposition to South Carolina's actions during the winter of 1832-33 simply in terms of his hatred for Calhoun, as is often done." Ellis also made the important point that Jackson's "Proclamation" was far more than a simple tirade against Calhoun and the nullifiers. It was, rather, a statement about the nation's origins and the actual doctrine of Nullification.[287] William W. Freehling agreed, insisting, "Any interpretation of the Calhoun-Jackson split which concentrates only on personal feuds misses the larger significance of the issues at stake. The President and Vice President clashed over crucial matters of public policy no less than petticoat politics and old Indian wars." Moreover, Freehling argued that Jackson did not approach the crisis with a "shoot from the hip" mentality, blustering and bullying his way through. Rather, Jackson was wary of utilizing the military: "The old general remained sensitive to the charge of being a military tyrant, and smothering an insurrection was an unpleasant business. The President was no less aware than the nullifiers were of the danger of antagonizing southern states by appearing the aggressor. Jackson preferred not to use armed force at all, and was determined that if war came, the nullifiers would be clearly to blame....Jackson endorsed ingenious means of avoiding bloodshed, and putting nullifiers in the wrong if hostilities did begin." When considering the Force Bill, Freehling concluded, "In the main Jackson requested, and Congress provided, means of avoiding the use of force rather than new authority for dragooning South Carolina."[288]

In terms of Jackson's influence on the "Nullification Proclamation," one can compare his many letters with the actual text and readily see his hand in determining the Proclamation's intent and direction. Moreover, days before releasing the decree Jackson wrote a note to Livingston, instructing him to add a section to the conclusion: "Let it receive your best flight of eloquence to strike to the heart and speak to the feelings of my deluded Countrymen of South Carolina. The Union must be preserved, without blood if this be possible, but it must be preserved at all hazards and at any price." He also required Livingston to change certain parts of the document because the secretary had not understood the president's notes and thus portions "were not

---

[287] Ellis, *The Union at Risk*, ix.
[288] Freehling, *Prelude to Civil War*, 191, 280, 284.

in accordance with his [the President's] views, and must be altered."[289] In light of such facts, it is difficult to reconcile the notion that Jackson was motivated solely by personal pique and a selfish desire for vindication. There was more to it than that. There was principle, weighty constitutional questions, and the very survival of the Union – all of which, in Jackson's own way, he had been committed to since he was a very young man.

CONCLUSION

Removal of federal deposits and Nullification were enough to fill out two full presidential terms, let alone comprise what was really just the beginning of his second term. Both were serious constitutional crises that Jackson met with resolve, even ferocity. He handled neither perfectly or delicately. One can commend his determination, yet criticize his bullish approach to problem solving. During the remainder of his term he continued to focus on the extinguishment of the national debt, trade relations in other parts of the world, spoliation claims against France and other nations – all of which were discussed in the previous chapter. Jackson also experienced the first ever attempted presidential assassination in January 1835. As he returned from a funeral, an out of work house painter named Richard Lawrence produced a pistol and fired. The cap exploded, but failed to ignite the gun powder. Jackson, always willing to do battle, lunged at Lawrence, who produced yet another pistol, with the same result. The powder failed to ignite. Though it was a misty, damp day, it is statistically remarkable that neither gun fired. Lawrence was captured, tried, and ultimately committed to an asylum.

This was not the only threat against Jackson. In May 1833 he was assaulted by Robert Randolph, a former Navy Lieutenant who had been dismissed, on Jackson's order, for theft. The president also received threatening letters: "You damn'd old Scoundrel…I will cut your throat whilst you are sleeping." As Robert Remini has rightly noted, because Jackson was both the first president to be assaulted and the first to suffer an assassination attempt it tells us something about how controversial he really was.[290] As I have noted throughout this book, Jackson's image embodied two very distinct ideas. He was both a hero and a despot. There was very little middle ground.

---

[289] Andrew Jackson to Edward Livingston, "For the conclusion of the Proclamation," December 4, 1832, *Correspondence, vol. 5*, 494-5; for evidence on Jackson's directives to Livingston, see, Longaker, "*Was Jackson's Kitchen Cabinet a Cabinet?*," 105.

[290] Remini, *Andrew Jackson: The Course of American Democracy*, 227, 60.

One either loved or hated Old Hickory. His intensity, his bluster, his personal conviction that he represented a new path for democracy in the name of the people embodied in Jackson an already formidable vanity, a self-righteousness that he was always correct. His belief that corruption existed within government and that a lack of principle and devotion to the public had resulted in serious threats to the Union spurred an almost fanatical zeal. This was a major component of Jacksonian Democracy.

The second round of the Bank War and Nullification fit perfectly within Jackson's larger conceptions of what he needed to do in order to safeguard the Union and further majoritarian rule. The BUS, in his view, was a corrupt institution, an unconstitutional monopoly that exercised dangerous power over the American economy. The only solution was to finish it through removal of the deposits. Nullification was an equally dangerous unconstitutional act, one that also threatened majority rule if one state could essentially determine that all the others were wrong about a law. Both issues were complex and controversial. Members of the president's own party did not agree with him on every aspect of his views or his approach to dealing with these problems. Historians will therefore continue to debate the merits and methods of Jackson's democratic and constitutional ideals. To determine, however, that Jackson had no such ideals, that he was motivated solely by personal pique and a need for vindication is short sighted and simplistic. Were there elements of defensiveness? Did Jackson personalize his battles? There is little doubt of this. It does not, however, mean that Jackson failed to be, as Richard Ellis insisted, a clear, forceful, coherent constitutional thinker.

Chapter 8

RETIREMENT

When Andrew Jackson retired from the presidency in 1837 and attended the inauguration of the newly elected president, Martin Van Buren, the stalwart senator from Missouri, Thomas Hart Benton, remarked on the overwhelming reaction to Jackson's presence: "It was the stillness and silence of reverence and affection; and there was no mistake as to whom this mute and impressive homage was rendered. For once, the rising was eclipsed by the setting sun."[291]

Jackson was a man beyond men. He had become far more than even he could have imagined when a young man trying to survive the rough and tumble existence of the Waxhaw frontier and the challenges of the American Revolution. The Battle of New Orleans had launched him to national fame and a path that led to the White House. By the time he left the presidency, Jackson had further enhanced his image as the Union's great defender. He was also a symbol of what the common man might achieve if given the opportunity, and in light of this and some of his policies, a symbol of democracy.

Yet he had also become a symbol of despotism and executive usurpation, King Andrew I, and inspired the coalescence of an entire political party that formed in direct opposition to his use of presidential power. It is doubtful that Jackson will ever shed the duality of these images; nor should he. Old Hickory could reach the heights of the most exalted patriotism and descend to the lowest of personal enmity. He was, as James Parton wrote so many years ago, "an atrocious saint."

If there was one thing that Jackson understood as he left the presidency, it was that the Union's future could only be maintained through constant vigilance and an acute attention to the dangers that surfaced at every turn. Though Jackson's methods were often questionable, even deplorable, his essential dedication to the nation's safety and survival cannot be questioned. He had grown up with the Union. Its birth pangs mirrored his own adolescent challenges. Neither was easy. Jackson and his family had shed a great deal of blood and he never forgot that fact. On this point, James C. Curtis and I agree. Jackson's Revolutionary War experience shaped his outlook. The difference in our interpretations, however, is Curtis' conclusion that Jackson was unable to grow beyond his experience, that he constantly sought vindication and viewed everything through the lens of a debilitating survivor's guilt. I argue that the evidence shows a Jackson who rose to the challenges of life with a sincere, intense belief in the Union and what needed to be done to safeguard it. Most of his policies, good or bad, can be traced to this basic rationale. Even in the last months of his life, while literally dying in his bed, he thought of little else beyond the nation's sanctity and perpetuity.

This vigilance inspired Jackson to follow in the steps of George Washington by offering a "Farewell Address" that expressed both his devotion to and fear for the nation. Both of these men, the first president and the seventh, offered their parting thoughts on the dangers that lay ahead for the United States. There is a remarkable similarity in the addresses. As he often did, Jackson tried to appear as the paternal father who counseled his children on what was best for the country's future and warn them of the dangers that lay beneath the surface.

Even though in the waning years of his presidency Jackson constantly wrote of his desire to live out the remainder of his days in simplicity at the Hermitage, he could never eschew himself of an interest and hand in politics. While in retirement he engaged in two major political battles. The first was connected to the Battle of New Orleans, the source of his national appeal. In 1815, federal judge Dominick Augustus Hall had fined Jackson $1,000 for contempt of court in relation to his imposition of martial law. In looking back at what he viewed as an otherwise brilliant career, the contempt fine still rankled Jackson. He meant to have the fine back, with interest, both to remove all blemish from the victorious battle and, just as importantly, to set a precedent for emergency powers in times of crisis.

The second battle involved the annexation of Texas, which had become an independent republic in 1836. Jackson always had an interest in making Texas part of the Union and during his presidency dispatched an envoy to negotiate

---

[291] Benton, *Thirty Years View*, vol. 1, 735.

with Mexico. Though nothing ultimately came of the matter in the 1830s, by 1843 there was considerable clamor for annexing the region. Jackson supported annexation, eventually breaking with Van Buren because he opposed it, and instead backed James K. Polk for the presidency in 1844. Jackson's influence in the matter was paramount, and once again revealed his still potent political power.

Finally, even after Jackson passed away in 1845, he continued to be recognized as a symbol, both good and bad. Cities around the nation held ceremonies commemorating his death, with Democrats and Whigs revealing that they were still unable to separate themselves from the political animosity that had surrounded Old Hickory. Thus even dead, he remained a political lightening rod. And as time marched on, Jackson's symbolism once again rose to the needs of the Union. When the Civil War broke out, Jackson was revered as the nation's great defender and many former Whigs turned Republican pointed out to wayward Democrats that their former leader would never have sanctioned the secession of southern states. With the looming clouds of war hovering over the nation, many prayed for another Jackson. They also reinvigorated the steadfast debate over the nation's security versus the people's liberties.

THE "FAREWELL ADDRESS"

Jackson's "Farewell Address" was produced in pamphlet form on the same day as Martin Van Buren's inauguration as president. With a resounding nationalism and constant evocations of "the people," Jackson defined his political philosophy as it related to governmental power. Within the nature of that power, he raised the constitutionality of a national bank, the use of paper money, and the extent to which tariffs could be imposed for the needs of raising revenue. These, after all, had been some of the battles that he waged during his eight years in office, and it is clear that Jackson felt compelled to warn the people of the still impending dangers that existed from "the moneyed power." In looking at Jackson's language in documents like the Bank Veto and "Farewell Address" it is easy to ascertain why historian Arthur Schlesinger, Jr., saw in his presidency a prototype Progressive who fought the corporations in defense of the common man.[292] Both addresses are replete with the language

---

[292] See Schlesinger, *The Age of Jackson*.

of a David and Goliath economic battle. There is little question that Jackson believed what he said.

And always, there was his confidence in the people: "In your hand is rightfully placed the sovereignty of the country, and to you everyone placed in authority is ultimately responsible. It is always in your power to see that the wishes of the people are carried into faithful execution, and their will, when once made known, must sooner or later be obeyed; and while the people remain, as I trust they ever will, uncorrupted and incorruptible, and continue watchful and jealous of their rights, the Government is safe, and the cause of freedom will continue to triumph over all its enemies."[293] Here was a model of Jackson's thoughts on democracy, the power and responsibilities of the people, and the strong but still tenuous foundations on which the nation rested.

To be sure, Jackson had not always been a staunch democrat. He was in his early years an aspiring aristocrat on a quest for wealth and political power, but in the aftermath of the 1824 election he came to realize the dangers of what he perceived as corruption. He became a true convert to majoritarian democracy, and though the right to vote and the expansion of the common man's rights rose in concert with Jackson's own rise to power, he came to embody and symbolize the successes and rights that so many others craved. His constant call to and comment on the "great body of the people" furthered the already significant move towards democracy in America.

Jackson's concerns about being "watchful and jealous," he also said "vigilant," harkened back to earlier Revolutionary era warnings about the people's virtue and the need to be wary of power and corrupting influences. Such ideas, what many historians consider to be the core of "republican ideology," were hardly the grumblings of an insecure and self-absorbed man who spied conspiracies at every turn. James C. Curtis' ideas regarding the "Farewell Address" point to this latter conclusion: "Inevitably, the address told the tale of injured innocence at war with the forces of corruption."[294] The problem was that corruption, or at least political intrigue did exist, and Jackson's address was chiefly designed to make the public aware. Thus he spent page after page focusing on the threat of sectionalism and what would happen to the Union should it be split along geographic lines. So too had Washington in his farewell. Jackson saw in the Nullification crisis the specter of even greater perils, and the address therefore offers a remarkable prescience for the coming of the Civil War: "If the Union is once severed, the line of

---

[293] Andrew Jackson, "Farewell Address," in Watson, ed., *Andrew Jackson vs. Henry Clay*, 239.
[294] Curtis, *Andrew Jackson and the Search for Vindication*, 178.

separation will grow wider and wider, and the controversies which are now debated and settled in the halls of legislation will then be tried on the fields of battle and determined by the sword." "In the union of these States," he insisted, there is a sure foundation for the brightest hopes of freedom and for the happiness of the people. At every hazard and by every sacrifice this Union must be preserved."

As always, Jackson's solution for such dangers was the vigilance and devotion of the people. He insisted that neither the Constitution nor the Union itself could be maintained "in opposition to public feeling." "The foundations must be laid," he insisted, "in the affections of the people, in the security it gives to life, liberty, and character, and property in every quarter of the country, and in the fraternal attachment which the citizens of the several States bear to one another as members of one political family, mutually contributing to promote the happiness of each other."[295] In making such arguments, Jackson not only revealed his belief in democracy and the will of the people, but in an over arching nationalism and devotion to the Union.

RETIREMENT AND THE REFUND

Jackson left for the Hermitage on March 7, only three days after Van Buren's inauguration. The General arrived home towards the end of the month, happy to live out the remainder of his life on the plantation that he and Rachel had built and on which his family resided. He was in poor health and constantly complained of "feebleness." At seventy-one, he still carried a bullet in his chest from the Dickinson duel (the Benton bullet had been removed during Jackson's presidency), suffered from congestive heart disease, failing kidneys, weakness from frequent blood-lettings, and a slow poisoning from mercury and calomel used as a medicinal. He wrote to his old friend Francis Blair, remarking, "I live in hopes of regaining my strength so that I can amuse myself in riding over my farm and visitting my good neighbors," and, always with a mind towards politics, added, "who, all but one, new born Whigg, formerly a friend, has cheered and welcomed my return—he like many other Whiggs I suppose are ashamed of their course and dislike to meet me."[296] Here was both the fixation on politics and the certainty of conviction that had carried Jackson through his life. Retirement did not change either. And so

---

[295] Jackson, *"Farewell Address,"* 239.
[296] Andrew Jackson to Francis P. Blair, April 2, 1837, in *Correspondence, vol. 6*, 472.

Jackson both sent and received numerous letters from around the nation, keeping apprised of politics and offering advice and warnings. He often wrote to President Van Buren, as well as various cabinet members, to learn of the goings on in Washington, constantly concerned that the policies he had worked so hard to put in place would not be lost in his absence.

It was during these years, in looking back over his career, that Jackson considered the $1,000 contempt fine that had been imposed so many years earlier. He had declared martial law in New Orleans, believing that it was the only way to save the city from British invasion, and ultimately arrested both a state senator and a federal judge. When the judge, Dominick Hall, returned after news of the peace treaty arrived, he hauled Jackson before the court and fined him. Jackson paid the money, but then traveled to Washington to meet with Secretary of War Alexander Dallas and President Madison to clear his name. Neither wanted to pursue the matter and the issue of martial law barely surfaced again until Jackson ran for the presidency in 1824 and again in 1828. Thus until he raised the matter in the 1840s, little mention of martial law had occurred in ensuing years. That changed quickly when Jackson wrote to his old friend, military aide, and political protégé Major Auguste Davezac de Castera, remarking, "no one has ever brought to [the] view of Congress the iniquity and injustice of the $1000 fine with costs imposed on me by a vindictive judge." Jackson continued, "Congress is the only body whose action could wipe this stain from my memory, by a joint resolution ordering the fine, with costs and interests, to be refunded." He finished the letter, noting, "this is the only imputation that has not been by Congress expunged from the record...I cannot but regret that this stain upon my name, shall be permitted to pass down to posterity."[297]

Davezac lost little time implementing the plan that Jackson devised. In January 1842 the major presented a motion in the New York legislature, where he served as a representative, to refund the fine. From that body's discussion of the issue Senator Lewis Field Linn of Missouri began a national movement to return Jackson's money. The result was a two year battle that stretched over three sessions of Congress in which Democrats and Whigs debated Jackson's use of martial law, the term's meaning, its constitutionality, and its potential for future use.

The debates revealed a variety of things: Jackson, even in retirement and feeble, still wielded tremendous political skill and power. His letters make clear that he ushered the refund bill through the Congress, with the help of his

---

[297] "General Jackson's Fine," *The Daily Globe*, March 12, 1842.

political foot soldiers, and made it a major party battle. That battle illustrated Jackson's continued duality: his symbolic appeal and the steadfast loathing that many had for him. Democrats held him up, once again, as the Union's great defender, while Whigs launched into more tirades against Jackson the defiler of the Constitution. For Jackson, the refund was both personal and Union-minded. Indeed, most of Jackson's political career had been generated by a blend of personal desire and principled conviction. Never believing that the fine had been fair or legal, he desired vindication for the blemish on his military record. At the same time, his constant concern for the Union's future convinced him that a precedent was needed for the future use of extraordinary power in times of emergency. At the start of the refund debates he wrote to his senatorial benefactor Lewis Linn, questioning, "I ask what general hereafter, if Neworleans was again threatened with invasion, let the real necessity be what it might, and the most energetic measures for its defense necessary, would hazard the responsibility, of adopting those energetic measures by which the Country could alone be defended, whilst the record of the fine and loss stared him in the face, inflicted upon me by an unjust judge for declaring martial law."[298]

At the core of Jackson's belief were two imposing ideological convictions: the sanctity of the Union, and that the military could subvert civil liberties if doing so was imperative to that sanctity. The second of these beliefs struck hard against the Constitution, but has, throughout the history of our nation, been a source of great debate. Can a government subvert its own laws in order to ultimately save the nation itself? A troubling proposal, and one that can rarely be answered adequately, Jackson is the man who first brought it forth for national discussion. He is also the man who forced a precedent and in doing so established a source of emergency powers that subsequent presidents have utilized in times of national crisis: Abraham Lincoln in the Civil War; Franklin D. Roosevelt in World War II; George Bush in the aftermath of 9/11 and during the Iraq War.[299]

As much as the debates were over a significant ideological and constitutional dilemma, they also descended to the lowest levels of party intrigue and political power. Here is where Jackson's symbolism became a tool manipulated by Democrats and Whigs to serve their wider electoral needs during congressional elections and the coming 1844 presidential contest. The 1840 election had marked the first presidential victory for Whigs, who had

---

[298] Andrew Jackson to Louis F. Linn, March 12, 1842, *Correspondence, vol. 6*, 144.
[299] For more on the history of Jackson and martial law, and how it was both a political and ideological battle, see Warshauer, *Andrew Jackson and the Politics of Martial Law*.

finally awoken to Democratic campaign strategies of fine tuned political organization and the use of campaign symbols. The Democratic defeat revealed organizational problems within the party, not the least of which was the loss of its greatest unifying symbol when Jackson retired in 1837. Though the Democrats had dominated the national political scene for years, the party was now in trouble and the bill to refund Jackson's fine came in the midst of this political gloom.

Whigs were also in something of a political mess. They had successfully elected William Henry Harrison in 1840, only to watch him die within a month of taking office and be succeeded by John Tyler, who was really a Democrat and placed on the ticket solely to draw crossover votes. Now, in the midst of the refund debates, Whigs viewed everything through the lens of partisan maneuvering and were quick to sniff out a campaign ploy, charging that the refund bill was merely a ruse to bring the old Hero before the people once again and in doing so aid a faltering Democratic Party.

Although this was not the actual impetus of the bill, (Jackson had devised the refund legislation without this goal in mind) it did not take Democrats long to embrace such a strategy. Writing to Jackson at the outset of the refund battle, Francis Blair, the General's long-time friend, political advisor, and editor of the Washington based *Democratic Globe*, understood that the bill could be used to ignite the passions and nationalism of the people: "I think it a good occasion to renew the impression on the public mind...[of] your glorious efforts in the last act of the war....A revival of your military triumphs will give it [the Democratic party] strength in its present contest with Federalism."[300]

Thus a bill that was ostensibly about the constitutionality of martial law and establishing a future precedent for emergency powers was subsumed by partisan strategizing that hinged on Jackson's symbolic image as either a hero or a despot. Jackson and his allies in the Democratic Party played the game well, passing the House bill on January 8, 1844, the anniversary of Jackson's New Orleans victory, and the Senate bill a little over a month later, on February 14. It was another skillful political victory for Jackson and showed his still potent popularity and power.

---

[300] Francis P. Blair to Andrew Jackson, June 30, 1842, *Jackson Papers*, Library of Congress. Blair and Jackson repeatedly referred to Whigs as Federalists, a name that was linked to elitism and, during the war of 1812, traitorous activity.

TEXAS

The refund was not the only major issue that occupied Jackson's retirement. He wanted Texas in the Union. He always had, and in order to secure that desire he sent during his presidency Minister Anthony Butler to negotiate an arrangement with Mexico. Jackson believed that Texas was actually a part of the Louisiana Purchase and had been negotiated away by John Quincy Adams in the 1819 Transcontinental Treaty with Spain. Even after that treaty, neither nation had surveyed the border, the Sabine River, and established exact boundaries. By the 1830s, Mexico had gained its independence from Spain and encouraged Americans to settle in Texas.

In the fall of 1833 Butler wrote to the president expressing his dismay at dealing with the Mexican government. Officials were suspicious of Butler because upon his arrival a Mexico City newspaper announced that he was there to purchase Texas for up to $5 million. Thus his mission was compromised from the start and he was looked at with disdain for the presumed belief that he could waltz into Mexico and essentially demand the annexation of Texas. When negotiations went poorly, Butler wrote to Jackson and suggested outright bribery to secure the territory, then wrote again arguing that the United States simply take Texas through a quick military expedition. "I will Negotiate or fight as you think best," wrote Butler. "I say that my preference is for the latter. We have abundant cause for quarrel and it would cost less by one half, aye two thirds to take, than to purchase the Territory."[301] Jackson replied with, as he put it, "astonishment," scolding Butler for not sending the letter in cipher in case it was intercepted, and then for construing "that my private letters authorised you to apply to corruption [bribery], when nothing could be farther from my intention than to convey such an idea." He continued, "The case is a plain, clear one—you are authorised to give five millions of dollars for the cession of Texas as far west as the Grand Desert."[302]

Butler responded with a less than glowing letter concerning the "mexican character" and insisted that "those who are known to possess intimate knowledge of the policy and views of this Governmt. indicates most clearly that we need indulge no hope of obtaining Texas by amicable arrangement unless we first shew our strength." Again, Butler recommended taking at least a portion of the territory by force, with himself leading the expedition. Upon

---

[301] Colonel Anthony Butler to Andrew Jackson, October 2, 1833, in *Correspondence, vol. 5*, 215-16.

[302] Andrew Jackson to Colonel Anthony Butler, November 27, 1833, in *Correspondence, vol. 5*, 228-30.

receiving the communiqué, Jackson wrote a comment on the letter: "A. Butler: What a scamp. Carefully read. The Secretary of State will reiterate his instructions to ask an extension of the treaty for running boundary line, and then recall him, or if he has recd. his former instructions and the Mexican Govt. has refused, to recall him at once."[303] Butler ultimately met with the president and was allowed to return to Mexico, where he continued his nefarious plots. He was later recalled as minister, but remained in Mexico in an attempt to close his interminable negotiations.

In October of 1835, American settlers in Texas took matters into their own hands by taking up arms and eventually proclaiming independence on March 2, 1836. The United States remained neutral, and Jackson refused to annex Texas under the circumstances of its independence, concerned that it might look like he and America had acted dishonorably by encouraging the Texans and essentially stealing the territory. Still, on his last day in office Jackson recognized Texan independence. If he could not secure it as part of the Union, at least he could pave the way for that possibility. What is particularly remarkable about Jackson's dealings with Texas is that he refused to do whatever was necessary to annex the territory. As a diehard expansionist, he coveted the region yet would not go to the same lengths that he had been willing to in order to take Indian lands, when bribery and military force proved quite effective. For Jackson, the difference seemed to be in dealing with a sovereign nation as opposed to "uncivilized" Indian tribes. Still, he had had no qualms about invading Florida in 1818 with the hope the United States would keep the territory.

When the opportunity for annexation arrived in 1843, Jackson was literally dying. He suffered hemorrhages, could barely walk from the swelling in his legs and shortness of breath, and continued to weaken himself with bloodlettings and medicine such as mercury and calomel. Nevertheless, propped up in his bed, he breathed fire for the Union. As he had always argued regarding foreign territories that bordered the United States, security was the primary concern. He had believed this when he confiscated Indian lands and invaded Florida. Texas fit into exactly the same rationale. Thus Jackson urged Democrats to annex the region. "I viewed, and still view the Texas of the utmost importance to the safety of the U. States, and particularly Neworleans," wrote the General, closing, "My debility is too great to follow the subject further." He expanded on his concerns in subsequent letters: "We must regain

---

[303] Colonel Anthony Butler to Andrew Jackson, February 6, 1834, and March 7, 1834, in *Correspondence, vol. 5,* 244-47; 249-53.

Texas, *peaceably if we can, forcibly if we must*," insisted Jackson. "Great Britain forming a treaty with Texas...might obtain the right on the event of war with us, or prospect of war...take possession of Memphis and Baton Rouge, before we could raise and organize an army, possess herself of Neworleans and reduce our fortifications, and having command of the ocean, could keep the country a long time, and it would cost oceans of blood, and millions of mony to regain it." Jackson ended, "I write under great pain."[304]

In early 1844, Robert J. Walker, an ardent expansionist and senator from Mississippi, wrote to Jackson: "*Dear Sir*, I write to you confidentially and in haste. I think the annexation of Texas depends *on you*. Much as you have done for your country, this would be the crowning act." Walker implored Jackson to write Sam Houston, the president of Texas and one of the General's protégés, and convince him to support an annexation treaty. Walker added to the letter his great esteem for Jackson and the principles on which he had governed: "It is now more than twenty years, since I had the honor to present your name, for the Presidency, to the *first* democratic meeting in the union, and to have supported you from that day to this, and as I grow older, I feel every day, increased, and increasing confidence, in the wisdom of the great measures of your administration."[305]

Jackson did as asked. He had a long and close relationship with Houston, who always addressed him as "*Venerated Friend*" and credited Jackson with the development of Houston's democratic ideals: "To you General, I feel myself *vastly* indebted for many principles, which I have never abandoned thro' life. One is a holy love of country, and a willingness to make every sacrifice to its honor and safety! Next a sacred regard for its constitution and law, with an eternal hostility and opposition to all Banks!" When Jackson wrote to Houston about annexation, he promptly wrote back: "So far as I am concerned or my hearty c[o]peration required, I am determined upon immediate annexation to the United States....Now, my venerated friend, you will perceive that [T]exas is presented to the United States, as a bride adorned for her es[p]ousals." Houston warned, however, that should the U.S. Senate reject the treaty, Texas would be forced to seek support elsewhere.[306]

---

[304] Andrew Jackson to Aaron V. Brown, February 9, 1843, in *Correspondence, vol. 6*, 201-2; Andrew Jackson to Major William B. Lewis, September 18, 1843, in *Correspondence, vol. 6*, 228-30.
[305] Robert J. Walker to Andrew Jackson, January 10, 1844, in *Correspondence, vol. 6*, 255.
[306] Sam Houston to Andrew Jackson, January 31, 1843, in *Correspondence, vol. 6*, 187-90; Sam Houston to Andrew Jackson, February 16, 1844, in *Correspondence, vol. 6*, 261.

Jackson anxiously awaited news concerning annexation, writing to Francis Blair, "I hope that annexation of Texas may be promptly done, or necessity must arise to compel Texas to make terms with great Britain, which may destroy our revenue and endanger New Orleans. Feeble as I am, I cannot refrain from writing you on this subject believing it to be all important to the safety, and prosperity of our country." He ended the letter, "Day before yesterday I had to bleed. I am better from it, how long I cannot say....I am very feeble."[307]

Then disastrous news arrived. On the very same day, Henry Clay and Martin Van Buren released public letters opposing annexation. The presumptive party nominees for the approaching 1844 presidential election, neither man wanted to engage the potential sectional rift that Texas might bring. Some in the nation believed that annexation was primarily about protecting and expanding slavery, and this belief was confirmed when John Calhoun wrote a letter to the British minister in Washington, Richard Pakenham, stating exactly that. Both letters, Clay's and Van Buren's, were troubling. Jackson thus penned a note to Blair: "I am truly filled with regret, and I must be candid—I am fearful his V.B. letter will loose [sic] him many western and southern votes at the Baltimore convention....I am very feeble, but excited by the subject, mortified at Mr. V.B. letter...for there is no evidence of ever the time being more propitious than the present....P.S. When you view the incoherence of my letter you will easily see the state of my health."[308]

Jackson had a difficult decision to make. He still possessed considerable political clout, and should he openly abandon Van Buren for the nomination, the New Yorker's chances were pretty much doomed. Nonetheless, Jackson coveted Texas and believed that Van Buren had done himself in: "The whole democracy was united on Mr. V.Buren as strong as the Rocky mountains, until his illfated letter was published." Jackson therefore wrote an open letter to the Nashville *Union* in which he advocated annexation, insisting, "My aim is to give to this country the strength to resist foreign interference. Without Texas we shall not have this strength. She offers this Key to us on fair and honorable terms. Let us take it and lock the door against future danger." He ended, "I cannot close these remarks without saying that my regard for Mr. Van Buren is so great, and my confidence in his love of country is strengthened by so long and intimate an acquaintance, that no difference in sentiment on this subject

---

[307] Andrew Jackson to Francis Blair, March 5, 1844, in *Correspondence, vol. 6,* 272.
[308] Andrew Jackson to Francis P. Blair, May 7, 1844, in *Correspondence, vol. 6,* 285.

can change my opinion of his character."[309] Confidence or not, Jackson abandoned Van Buren. The Little Magician, as he was often called, failed to receive the Democratic nomination when the convention met in Baltimore on May 27, 1844. It instead went to Jackson's chosen man, James K. Polk of Tennessee. His nickname was "Young Hickory," a tribute to the use of Jackson's symbolic appeal.

The maneuverings swirling around Texas annexation were intense. In addition to toppling Van Buren, Democrats worried about John Calhoun and the belief that he might attempt to break away the South and Texas into a separate confederacy. To such threats, Jackson insisted to the newly nominated Polk, "Every democrat must put his face against any meeting of *Disunion*, or nullification. we must and will have Texas, with, and in our *glorious Union*. The Federal union must be preserved."[310] Clearly the ghost of Nullification and concerns over perpetuity of the Union still haunted the aged Jackson. It was these very threats that he had focused upon in his "Farewell Address."

Even after openly abandoning Van Buren, Jackson's work was still not done. Supporters beseeched him to write President Tyler and secure his withdrawal from the presidential contest so that there would be no difficulties for Polk, most importantly that the Democratic Party would not split its vote and hand the election to Henry Clay. In return for stepping out of the race, Tyler was assured that he and his supporters would be welcomed back into the Democratic fold. Jackson responded to the entreaties with characteristic clarity and political skill, writing to Polk that such a tactic was foolish and "would be seized upon as a bargain and intrigue for the Presidency. Just as Adams and Clays bargain. Let me say that such a letter from any of your friends would damn you and destroy your election." He closed, "I am now writing scarcely able to wield my pen, or to see what I write"[311] Notwithstanding such admonitions, Jackson engaged the matter anyway. He did not, however, write directly to Tyler. Rather, he wrote to friends, and to Secretary of the Navy John Y. Mason: "With much frankness I give you my opinion of the course that Mr. Tyler ought to pursue with regard to the Presidency, if he expects to retire in the confidence of the democracy; and adding to his popularity....If Mr. Tyler ever expects to be before the democracy for any public office he must withdraw from the canvass *now*. If he does not, he will retire forsaken by

---

[309] Andrew Jackson to Francis P. Blair, May 11, 1844, in *Correspondence, vol. 6*, 285; Andrew Jackson to the Editors of the Nashville Union, May 14, 1844, in *Correspondence, vol. 6*, 289-91.
[310] Andrew Jackson to James K. Polk, June 29, 1844, in *Correspondence, vol. 6*, 299.
[311] Andrew Jackson to Polk, July 26, 1844, *in Correspondence, vol. 6*, 303-4.

the true democracy of this union, never to be able to regain their confidence, when by now retiring he carries home with him the confidence and respect of all the democracy of the Union....My dear sir I am exhausted, and must close."[312]

Jackson's political power and skill were unmistakable. A mere three weeks after making his views known, President Tyler bowed to the grey eminence of the Hermitage: "your views as to the proper course for me to pursue in the present emergency of public affairs has decided me to withdraw from the canvass." A month later, Tyler wrote Jackson again, requesting his influence to convince Andrew Jackson Donelson, the General's nephew and personal secretary, to accept an emergency appointment as minister to Texas because the other minister had died. Tyler wanted Donelson "from the fact of his being intimate with President Houston and above all being a member of your family and in your close confidence."[313]

Jackson's involvement in the annexation of Texas could not have been more complete. Donelson accepted the mission, and finally, after the Senate had at first rejected the annexation treaty on June 8, 1844, Congress voted in February of 1845 by joint resolution to accept Texas into the Union. "I congratulate you, Dear General, on the success of the great question which you put in action," wrote Blair. Jackson responded: "This may be the last letter I may be able to write you. But live or die I am your friend—(and never deserted one for *policy*)....May god's choicests blessings be bestowed upon you and yrs. thro life, is the prayer of yr. sincere friend." Yet Jackson did not die immediately, and followed with another letter in which he expressed his satisfaction: "I not only rejoice, but congratulate my beloved country Texas is reannexed, and the safety, prosperity, and the greatest interest of the whole union is secured by this act, This great and national act. The Federal Union must be preserved....I am quite unwell to day, but my Joy was such that I could not refrain from letting you know it."[314]

Jackson delivered Texas, literally as he lay dying. Still his preeminent concern was the Union. Ironically, Texas was arguably the entering wedge that divided the nation and sent it spiraling over the next few years towards the Civil War. Jackson, however, did not see that. In reading his letters it is

---

[312] Andrew Jackson to John Y. Mason, August 1, 1844, in *Correspondence, vol. 6*, 305-6.

[313] President John Tyler to Andrew Jackson, August 18, 1844, in *Correspondence, vol. 6*, 315; President John Tyler to Andrew Jackson, September 17, 1844, in *Correspondence, vol. 6*, 319-20.

[314] Francis P. Blair to Andrew Jackson, February 28, 1845, in *Correspondence, vol. 6*, 375; Andrew Jackson to Francis P. Blair, March 9, 1845, in *Correspondence, vol. 6*, 378; Andrew Jackson to Francis P. Blair, March 10, 1845, in *Correspondence, vol. 6*, 378.

impossible to deny his intense nationalism and devotion to the Union. These were not merely the masked entreaties of a petty, insecure man with no vision for the country. Was Jackson old, did he grumble and cast aspersions? Did he personalize battles and believe that conspiracies existed around every corner? Yes. Yet it is an enormous mistake to conclude, as have historians like Curtis and Burstein, that Jackson had no larger goals than satisfying his own vanity. He constantly looked to the security of the Union and the stability of the Democratic Party, making sure, for example, that Tyler withdrew. His dying breaths were "The Federal Union must be preserved." Even his Last Will and Testament exuded devotion to the Union. Bequeathing a sword to Andrew Jackson Donelson, the old man admonished "that he fail not to use it when necessary in support and protection of our glorious Union, and for the protection of the Constitutional rights of our beloved country should they be assailed by foreign enemies or domestic traitors."[315]

DEATH

Andrew Jackson died on June 8, 1845. News of his passing spread quickly and cities throughout the nation held commemorations. President Polk issued a statement on June 16, declaring, "Andrew Jackson is no more!...His country deplores his loss, and will ever cherish his memory." The president ordered all business in the executive departments suspended for one full day, as "a tribute of respect to the illustrious dead." George Bancroft, serving as the secretary of the navy and war departments, issued a general order on the same day. In grand style and with lofty praise, he heralded Jackson as "first in natural endowments and resources, not less than first in authority and station. The power of his mind impressed itself on the policy of his country, and still lives, and will live forever in the memory of its people....Heaven gave him lengths of days and filled them with deeds of greatness." All troops under Bancroft's command were ordered to wear black crepe on the left arm and sword for six months. On the day after receipt of the order, all naval vessels and military posts were ordered to fly their flags at half-staff and salute guns were to be

---

[315] Jackson bequeathed other swords, always with the same message. To the son of his long-time friend General John Coffee, Jackson stated: "wield it in the protection of the rights secured to the American citizens under our glorious constitution against all invaders whether foreign foes, or intestine traitors." To his grandson, Andrew Jackson III, the general stated, "always use it in defense of the constitution and our glorious Union and the perpetuation of our

fired at specified times throughout the day. The nation's capital held a large ceremony on June 27 in front of the Washington Monument, where Bancroft once again showered visitors with words of Jackson's prowess.[316]

The nation's largest commemoration, however, was held in its most populous city – New York. On June 24 40,000 people marched in the procession and ten times that number, some 400,000, paid respects while the nearly five mile long funeral train, in which dozens of military, civic, and private organizations, marched through the streets. Everywhere, businesses and private residences displayed the traditional signs of mourning; black crepe and pictures of the deceased abounded. All places of business were closed and literally thousands of flags in the city and on ships in the harbor fluttered at half-staff. The residents of Brooklyn and Staten Island were ferried over on additional boats so they too could take part in the grand ceremonies. One newspaper reported that the streets in Brooklyn were "virtually deserted." The commemoration was, arguably, the largest in the nation's history up to that time.[317]

In large letters the *New York Evening Post* announced the "DEATH OF GEN. JACKSON": "The decease of this great man leaves a wide blank in the affections of the American people. No one, since the days of Washington, ever occupied so high a place in the hearts, and no name will go down to posterity so identified with the greatness, the glory and prosperity of the American people." Yet the *Post* did not leave the matter with a simple tribute to the departed. Jackson was too much a political, partisan symbol for that. The battles of the era were still too close at hand, and Jackson, even in his dying days, had engaged in vigorous support for the Democratic Party and denunciation of Whigs. Thus the *Post* seized the opportunity to make a partisan attack: "The halo of his glory shone far into the East. The growlings of party hate, and the aspersions of disappointed office seekers or partisans removed from the place at his accession to power, were not heard beyond the waters of the Atlantic. The violent animosity of the thousands who were thwarted in their eager pursuit after inordinate wealth, or who suffered in the

---

republican system, remembering the motto 'draw me not without occasion nor sheath me without honor.'" See Jackson's Will, June 7, 1843, in *Correspondence, vol. 6*, 221-2.

[316] "By the President of the United States," *New York Herald*, June 17, 1845; *New York Morning News*; George Bancroft, "Eulogy," in *Monument to the Memory of General Andrew Jackson: Containing Twenty-five Eulogies and Sermons Delivered on the Occasion of His Death*, ed. Benjamin M. Dusenbery, (Philadelphia: n.p., 1848), 33-51. Numerous Democratic papers published Bancroft's eulogy in its entirety. See for example, *New York Evening Post*, June 25, 1845; *New York Morning News*, July 2, 1845.

[317] Warshauer, *"Contested Mourning."*

enjoyment of well earned fortune by the financial measures of his administration did not reach foreign ears." In one short paragraph the *Post's* editors had championed Jackson's use of rotation in office (called the spoils system by his opponents), as well as his controversial bank policies, and dismissed Whig concerns as "murmurs" and "lurking hostility." The paper continued: "Before this generation passes away, the memory of Andrew Jackson will be universally revered, and all will unite in speaking of him to their children and their children's children as the greatest and best of men."[318] The belief that generations living beyond the partisan battles of the day would come to appreciate Jackson's superior leadership and his importance to the era was a common theme among Democratic papers.

Democrats also expected Whigs to either mourn Jackson or stand in muted silence. Death, they insisted, was no time for party rancor. Yet, given the partisanship of the period, and attacks like the one in the *Post*, this was impossible. The degree of Jackson's continuing partisan importance outlived even the fiery General. Many New York Whigs treated the news of Jackson's demise with suspicion and scorn. When some engaged in back-handed slaps or outright opposition to Jackson's memory, Democrats lashed out, decrying such acts as un-American, mean spirited, and lacking decorum. They attempted to hold Whigs to the fire of public opinion (Democrats of course attempted to shape that opinion), insisting that men who could attack Jackson during a time of grieving were not true Americans.

Yet Democrats themselves were largely responsible for Jackson's continued recognition as a political symbol. The Whig sponsored Middletown *Constitution* of Connecticut understood the traditional Democratic strategy all too well, announcing, Jackson's "friends have for so long a time paraded his name before the public eye as a pattern for the 'democracy,' and have so long kept him in the political field, even to the moment of his departure, that we cannot regard him in the light which, we would had he been content to keep in that place which both his years and the custom of society demanded of him."[319]

Whigs argued that Democrats were attempting to make political capital out of New York's commemoration. Democrats repeatedly announced that citizens from all parties and walks of life, regardless of "party spirit," should come forth to show respect for Jackson, the greatest man of the age. Yet there remained Democrats and Whigs who jumped at the opportunity to capitalize on and cross swords over the General's demise. The leading Whig newspaper

---

[318] "Death of Gen. Jackson," *New York Evening Post*, June 17, 1845.
[319] "Death of General Jackson," *The Constitution*, June 25, 1845. For more on Connecticut's treatment of Jackson's death, see Warshauer, *"Ridiculing the Dead."*

in the city, and arguably the nation, Horace Greeley's *Tribune*, did not hesitate to offers its views of Jackson. Though acknowledging that he "loved and sought to serve his country," Greeley declared, "we shower no indiscriminate, unmeaning eulogies on the departed....We shudder at the deprivation of public morals and corruption of popular suffrage which has been created by his most wanton and unprovoked Proscription of political opponents throughout his Presidential career—when we reflect on the long array of usurpations and acts of violence which marked his rule, and the terrible legacies of disorder, crime and calamity they have left to the present and future generations, we rejoice and are thankful that we never, never for one moment aided or consented to his most unfortunate elevation." Here was hardly the lack of "party spirit" that Democrats professed to desire. Rocked by such militant declarations, the *Post* ineffectually responded: "the *Tribune*...of this city, disgraces itself by an ebullition of party spleen and impotent malignity."[320]

Such sentiments were not expressed by the *Tribune* alone. Other Whig newspapers from across the state joined in the condemnation of Jackson, though they did not engage in quite the level of acrimony engendered by Greeley. Some even acknowledged the General's service as a "gallant soldier." *The Advocate*, based in Batavia, just east of Buffalo, announced, "we never praised him while living, and we cannot flatter him dead." The editor continued, noting that Jackson's military exploits had "showered additional luster upon our country's annals," but added, "in a civil career [he]...sanctioned acts most unhappy to the honor and welfare of the country he so heroically defended." Though hoping that the "evil" done by Jackson would be "buried with him," *The Advocate* stated, with not a little irony, that it would be "an ungracious task to review with the slightest censure the history of one over whom the grave...has so lately closed."[321]

That some Whigs refused to "forgive and forget" tells us much about the party's foundation. Its very nature was wrapped up in hating Jackson. To yield from this position for any reason, even death, undermined not only party ideology, but, perhaps more importantly, its origins. As historian Michael Holt noted, "the Whig party began simply as a collection of the disparate foes of Andrew Jackson, and the party's name symbolized its opposition to the

---

[320] "Death of Gen. Jackson," *New York Tribune*, June 17, 1845; *New York Evening Post*, June 18, 1845.
[321] "Death of Gen. Jackson," *The Advocate*, June 17, 1845.

monarchical usurpations of King Andrew I."[322] There existed among Whigs a very tangible concern that stepping back from condemning Jackson, even for a brief moment, might condone some of his presidential acts, influence future generations, and potentially damage the Whig Party.

Aside from Democratic and Whig party maneuvering, the extent to which the people of New York honored Jackson revealed his still astounding popularity. As does the fact that so many children in the years that followed were bestowed with the General's name. John William Ward attempted to define Jackson's meaning to the people of the nineteenth century in his seminal 1953 work, *Andrew Jackson Symbol for an Age*. Yet Ward presented only a Democratic vision of the General at a time when party animosity was rampant. Jackson possessed at least two images: hero and despot.[323]

JACKSON AND LINCOLN[324]

When Jackson died, one newspaper announced that he "was the embodiment of a grand idea—the impersonation of an era—the energy of a principle."[325] That principle, or at least the component of it that espoused the perpetuity of the Union, became ever more important when Abraham Lincoln faced secession and war. Into these perilous times, Jackson's name arose again, heralded as the type of leader needed in such an emergency. His famous "Nullification Proclamation" was reprinted and a new biography released, which, according to historian Kenneth M. Stampp, was to "provide a worthy example of how a brave soldier-President had dealt with an earlier crisis." The *New York Herald* announced, "the times demand a Jackson," and the *Chicago Tribune* declared, "Mr. Lincoln will have a precedent in Old Hickory for doing just that thing which the emergency requires."[326]

---

[322] Michael F. Holt, *The Political Crisis of the 1850s* (New York: W.W. Norton & Co., 1983), 23; see also, Michael F. Holt, *The Rise and Fall of the American Whig Party* (New York: Oxford University Press, 1999), 28.
[323] Ward, *Andrew Jackson: Symbol for an Age*.
[324] I am particularly indebted to an undergraduate student at Central Connecticut State University, Todd Jones, for his excellent paper "'*Our Federal Union: It Must Be Preserved:*' Abraham Lincoln and the Memory of Andrew Jackson During the Secession Crisis of 1860-1861," for much of the information that follows. Used with permission.
[325] *New York Evening Post*, June 18, 1845.
[326] Kenneth M. Stampp, *And the War Came: The North and the Secession Crisis, 1860-1861* (Baton Rouge: Louisiana State University Press, 1950), 243; Courtland Canby, ed., *Lincoln and the Civil War: A Profile and a History* (New York: George Braziller, Inc., 1960), 39; "A Good Precedent," *Chicago Tribune*, December 3, 1860, 2.

Jackson's strength was also cited as a negative reference for the outgoing Democratic President James Buchanan. He was "no man for the emergency, no Jackson." Buchanan's lack luster response to secession made many northern Unionists hope for just "an hour of Jackson!" In December of 1860 when Buchanan was reluctant to send soldiers to Fort Moultrie in Charleston, South Carolina, even his top army commander, General Winfield Scott, wrote him, stating that Andrew Jackson did not delay for a moment to reinforce the fort in 1832.[327] Everywhere Buchanan turned he met the ghost of Andrew Jackson, and the comparisons between the two presidents never put Buchanan in a favorable light.

As for Lincoln, he was viewed as the Jackson-like president so many northerners desired. In May of 1860, prior to his election, the *Hartford Daily Courant* announced, "Lincoln is said to be a compound of Andrew Jackson and Henry Clay. He has the iron will of the former, and the eloquence and geniality of the latter." In October, the *Courant* added, "There is reason to believe that Mr. Lincoln will be our next President, and make a second Andrew Jackson in office. He has the nerve enough to do his duty." [328]

When Lincoln was ultimately elected, the comparisons grew. The New York *Courier and Enquirer* declared, "Mr. Lincoln…is not the man to shrink from the performance of any duty. Like Jackson he…will not be wanting in the hour of trial." A November editorial in the *Wisconsin Daily State Journal* predicted, "[secession] will find in ABRAHAM LINCOLN as prompt and as decided an opponent as it found in ANDREW JACKSON."[329] In a personal letter to Lincoln, one J. Medill insisted that Lincoln should stop the "expected" secession of Maryland before his inauguration and "show them they had a second Jackson to deal with." In January, Joseph Butler sent Lincoln a letter telling him to "be like General Jackson who made Calhouns [sic] neck feel *Rather uneasy*." Shortly after inauguration, Lincoln commented on the possible secession of Maryland, which prompted the *Hartford Courant* to announce, "It is Jackson's style; and let us hope it will prove to be Lincoln's style."[330]

---

[327] Stampp, *And the War Came*, 54, 61, 58.

[328] *Hartford Daily Courant*, May 28, 1860, 2; *Hartford Daily Courant*, October 25, 1860, 2.

[329] Kenneth M. Stampp, "Lincoln and the Strategy of Defense in the Crisis of 1861," *The Journal of Southern History 11* (1945): 315; *Wisconsin Daily State Journal*, November 17, 1860, in Howard Cecil Perkins, ed., *Northern Editorials on Secession, Vol. I*, (Gloucester: Peter Smith, 1964), 181.

[330] J. Medill to Abraham Lincoln, December 31, 1860, in David C. Mearns , ed., *The Lincoln Papers, vol. 2,* (Garden City: Doubleday & Company, Inc., 1948), 363; Joseph Butler to Abraham Lincoln, January 10, 1861, *The Abraham Lincoln Papers*, Library of Congress,

Even southerners concerned themselves with the Jacksonian Lincoln, with the *Charleston Mercury* warning "he will certainly play the Andrew Jackson." Once Fort Sumter was bombarded and the war began in earnest, the *Mercury* offered a poetic barb to both Jackson and Lincoln:

> "When on his trembling knees arose the doughty President. Now, by old Andrew Jackson's shade, and by the oaths he swore, And by his hickory stick, and by the thunder of his snore, And by the proud contempt he showed for Carolina gents, And English grammar," quoth old Abe, "them's jist my sentiments."[331]

As Lincoln battled to maintain the Union that Jackson had so stubbornly defended, the comparison between the two continued. In the aftermath of Lincoln's second inauguration, one author noted that Lincoln was the first president to win a second term since Jackson, and that "Abraham Lincoln stands pledged before his countrymen to complete the great work which was in the heart of Jackson to do."[332]

The connection between Old Hickory and Old Abe also made its way into the imagery and popular art of the time. One such example was a picture of Lincoln and vice-president Hannibal Hamlin on an envelope, and underneath Jackson's famous statement, "Our Federal Union: It must be preserved." Historians have also noted a particular portrait of Lincoln which "bears a striking resemblance to several period paintings of Old Hickory," adding, "to modern eyes…there is more Jackson than Lincoln to it….The times seemed to demand a Jackson to face down southern secession threats." Lincoln also prominently displayed a portrait of Jackson in the oval office of the White House.[333]

Beyond the imagery and symbolism of the Jackson-Lincoln connection, Lincoln actually gained tangible insights and benefits from the General. Facing secession, the newly elected president sat down to write his "Inaugural

---

http://www.memory.loc.gov/ammem/alhtml/malhome.html; Hartford Daily Courant, April 26, 1861, 2.

[331] *Charleston Mercury*, February 26, 1861, in Herbert Mitgang, ed., *Lincoln As They Saw Him* (New York: Rinehart & Company, 1956), 233; Charles Edward Leverett, Jr., "Fort Sumter: A Heroic Poem in Three Cantos," from the *Charleston Mercury*, May 18, 1861, in Mitgang, *Lincoln As They Saw Him*, 263-264.

[332] Benjamin Barondess, *Three Lincoln Masterpieces: Cooper Institute Speech, Gettysburg Address, Second Inaugural* (Charleston: Education Foundation of West Virginia, Inc., 1954), 58.

[333] Harold Holzer, Gabor S. Boritt, and Mark E. Neely Jr., *The Lincoln Image: Abraham Lincoln and the Popular Print* (Chicago: University of Illinois Press, 2001), 53.

Address" with a copy of Jackson's "Nullification Proclamation" at hand to help define Lincoln's ideas about the origins of the Union and its perpetuity. Lincoln also utilized Daniel Webster's reply to Robert Y. Hayne in the famous Hayne-Webster Debates of 1830, as well as the Declaration of Independence.[334] Lincoln also turned to Jackson when justifying the use of martial law and suspension of habeas corpus during the Civil War. Jackson had been the first to utilize both measures, and Lincoln held the General up to Democrats who complained of constitutional violations:

> "After the Battle of New Orleans and while the fact that the treaty of peace had been concluded was well known in the city, but before official knowledge of it had arrived, General Jackson still maintained martial or military law....It may be remarked—first, that we had the same Constitution then as now; secondly, that we then had a case of invasion, and now have a case of rebellion; and, thirdly, that the permanent right of the people to public discussion, the liberty of speech and of the press, the trial by jury, the law of evidence, and the *habeas corpus* suffered no detriment whatever by the conduct of General Jackson, or its subsequent approval by the American Congress."[335]

The use of Jackson's unionism and devotion to the nation, even in justifying violations of the Constitution in extraordinary times, could hardly be more complete. As he had been among Democrats in his own day, Andrew Jackson's name was synonymous with the perpetuity of the Union during the Civil War and Abraham Lincoln benefited from that association. And Lincoln fully understood it, creating a postage stamp during the war with Jackson's image on it. Nor were these uses of Jackson merely some sort of fictionalized, heroic, storybook figures. He had stood for the Union, from the time he was a teenager during the Revolution to his last entreaties for Texas. Few, if any, Americans embodied a greater love for the nation or deserved more credit in maintaining it than Jackson.

---

[334] William H. Herndon and Jesse W. Weik, *Herndon's Life of Lincoln* (Cleveland: Fine Editions Press, 1949), 386.

[335] Abraham Lincoln to Erastus Corning and others, 12 June 1863, Roy P. Basler et al., eds., *Collected Works of Abraham Lincoln, vol. 6* (New Brunswick: Rutgers University Press, 1953-55), 268-269.

Conclusion

Andrew Jackson recognized the possibility of the Union's demise. His parting words to the people, as evidenced by his "Farewell Address," warned them that dangers existed and only vigilance and mutual forbearance could save the nation. Yet even after he left the presidency, the aged and dying old man could not break from his political activities and concerns for the country to which he had devoted himself. Into his final months and weeks, he penned letter after letter. His two primary missions in retirement were refunding his $1000 contempt fine for imposing martial law, and thereby setting a precedent for emergency powers, and his long desire to annex Texas. He achieved both. In doing so, Jackson maintained principles that he had spent a lifetime developing. In reading his letters, it is difficult to understand how anyone could conclude that Jackson failed to have principles, or that he did not maintain a vision for the country. One does not have to agree with all that Jackson did, as a general or as president, to accord him his due in this regard. If Jackson lashed out at others and constantly believed that someone was attempting to thwart his activities, it was because he had spent a lifetime in politics actually dealing with such attempts. He was a partisan lightening rod, even in the end, as is clear from the Democratic and Whig reactions to his death. After he gasped his last breath, the party embers that had grown up directly around him still burned brightly. Nor had the fire connected to his image diminished by the 1860s. Rather, with the Civil War, Old Hickory became, once again, relevant, symbolic, a force in America.

Conclusion

Historians will continue to disagree about Andrew Jackson. To some extent, that is the nature of history as a profession. Scholars come to the study of the past with competing ideas and interpretations about people and events. They are also influenced by the contemporary society in which they live and often see the past through the lens of the present. These factors complicate the already difficult task of judging Jackson. As noted in the introduction and throughout this work, Jackson needs to be assessed by the social, ethical, and political standards of the time in which he lived. Any attempt to understand his views on slavery and the treatment of Native Americans, for example, is doomed if we attempt to do so according to post-Civil Rights Era beliefs. Accepting such a reality does not mean that Jackson or any of the Founding Fathers should be let off the hook for their reprehensible social and racial views. Rather, the point is to better understand the context in which those views were allowed to proliferate and never permit it to occur again. The point of understanding history is to learn from the past so that we do not repeat the same mistakes. No matter, that as human beings we do not often seem capable of embracing such an idea.

Readers must also recognize that even by the standards of his own day Jackson was an incredibly polarizing figure. The Second American Party System developed directly around his image, Democrats lauding him as the nation's great defender and Whigs castigating him as King Andrew I. Though these competing views were certainly exacerbated by partisan wrangling, there was without question truth in both parties' arguments.

Jackson was indeed the nation's champion, second only to Washington. The Hero of New Orleans, as he was often called, or more simply – the General – had secured his symbolism with the astonishing victory over the

British in 1815. It carried him to the White House, where, after the disturbing outcome of the 1824 election and the Corrupt Bargain, he preached majority rule, the will of the people, and promised to root out corruption. Such messages became as much a part of Jackson's symbolic appeal as his military nationalism. As a true commoner, born in a log cabin and orphaned at an early age, he rose up in a deferential, aristocratic society, became a lawyer, then a major land owner, a political force, and ultimately president. In doing so, he revealed, in both his actions and his constant mantra "the people," that a simple man could achieve anything in America. Hence the reason the era is known as the Age of Jacksonian Democracy or the Age of the Common Man.

The competing problem, however, is that Jackson was anything but simple or common. As James Parton accurately explained so many years ago, Jackson was a jumble of complexity. Most historians have acknowledged this ever since. In order to achieve what he did, the great General crushed civil liberties in New Orleans, periodically violated international treaties and the Constitution, ran roughshod over his political enemies, and generally did whatever *he* thought was right, regardless of legality or propriety. Is there any wonder why some in the nation looked at Jackson with fear and disdain, believing that he was a dangerous "military chieftain"?

Historians will therefore continue to debate Jackson's actions and legacy. Yet that debate should be based on the policies that he put forth and on his larger views about the Union and democracy. And herein lay one of the difficulties related to studies of Jackson in the late twentieth and early twenty-first century. Scholars like James Curtis and Andrew Burstein have created a simplistic, monolithic image of Jackson when nothing could be further from the truth. Jackson was certainly no saint; he embodied much of the worst in nineteenth century America. Yet he was also remarkably symbolic of the period. He held serious, deadly serious views about the preservation of the Union and the rights of the people, neither of which can be explained or understood by the notion that he viewed everything from the perspective of a traumatized boy who constantly sought vindication. As one reviewer of Curtis' book put it, Jackson "behaved less like a man seeking vindication for a traumatic past than like a new Messiah, sure that he could do no wrong....He seems less often seeking for vindication than grasping for power."[336]

On the whole, Jackson's actions, good or bad, were based on larger principles. This, to be sure, was not always the case. His periodic bursts of

---

[336] Charles Wiltse, review of James Curtis, Andrew Jackson and the Search for Vindication, *American Historical Review* 64 (1977): 143.

anger, his brawl with the Benton brothers, for example, revealed the worst of his rough, intolerant backwoods upbringing and penchant to solve problems with violence. Such episodes, however, were not the norm and should not be used to explain away the larger complexities that Jackson embodied. He engaged in real ideological battles in his day and mapped out real policies and philosophies to engage those battles. His policy towards Native Americans represented larger concerns about national security and foreign influence. The Bank War revealed serious constitutional questions regarding governmental power and that of economic institutions within the nation. Jackson crushed Nullification, the most serious domestic threat up to the Civil War, and in doing so advocated a strident nationalism that embodied a vigorous defense of the Union's perpetuity.

As twenty-first century Americans struggle to understand the meaning of democracy and freedom in light of serious economic and foreign policy challenges, we must not forget that Americans of Jackson's day confronted similar difficulties. Granted, social, political, and economic views have evolved considerably, but contextually for the time periods, there are many similarities. Maybe this is what makes so relevant the continued study of Jackson and the age that bears his name. He embodied much that was positive and negative in American society. His actions and symbolism were both good and evil. Perhaps it is best to understand Andrew Jackson as an imperfect hero, a principled despot.

BIBLIOGRAPHY

A History of the Life and Public Services of Major General Andrew Jackson. n.p., 1828.

Abernethy, Thomas Perkins. *From Frontier to Plantation in Tennessee: A Study in Frontier Democracy.* Chapel Hill: University of North Carolina Press, 1932. Reprint, University, AL: University of Alabama Press, 1967.

──────────────. *The Burr Conspiracy.* New York: Oxford University Press, 1954.

Adams, Henry. *History of the United States of America During the Administrations of Thomas Jefferson.* New York: Library of America, 1986.

Adams, Henry, ed. *The Writings of Albert Gallatin,* vol. 2. New York: Antiquarian Press, 1960.

Adams, John Quincy. *Memoirs of John Quincy Adams, Comprising Portions of His Diary from 1795 to 1848.* Edited by Charles Francis Adams. 12 vols. Philadelphia: J.B. Lippincott and Co., 1874-1877.

Adams, David Wallace. *Education for Extinction: American Indians and the Boarding School Experience, 1875-1928.* Lawrence: University Press of Kansas, 1995.

Address from a Meeting of Democratic Citizens of the City of Philadelphia, opposed to the election of General Jackson. Philadelphia: John Binns, 1827.

Allgor, Catherine. *Parlor Politics: In Which the Ladies of Washington Help Build a City and a Government.* Charlottesville: University Press of Virginia, 2000.

Ammon, Harry. *James Monroe: The Quest for National Identity.* New York: McGraw-Hill, 1971. Reprint, Charlottesville: University Press of Virginia, 1990.

An Address to the People of the United States, on the Subject of the Presidential Election: with a special reference to the nomination of Andrew Jackson, containing public sketches of his public and private character. --By a citizen of the United States. n.p., 1828.

An Impartial & True History of the Life & Services of Major-General Andrew Jackson. n.p., 1828.

"Andrew Jackson and Judge D.A. Hall, Report of the Committee of the Senate (Of The State of Louisiana, 1843)," *Louisiana Historical Quarterly* 5 (1922): 509-570.

Aronson, Sidney H. *Status and Kinship in the Higher Civil Service: Standards in Selection in the Administrations of John Adams, Thomas Jefferson, and Andrew Jackson.* Cambridge: Harvard University Press, 1964.

Bailyn, Bernard. *The Origins of American Politics.* New York: Vintage Books, 1968.

_____. *To Begin the World Anew: The Genius and Ambiguities of the American Founders.* New York: Alfred A. Knopf, 2003.

Bancroft, Frederic. *Calhoun and the South Carolina Nullification Movement.* Baltimore: John Hopkins Press, 1928. Reprint, Gloucester, MA: Peter Smith, 1966.

Banner, Stuart. *How the Indians Lost Their Land: Law and Power on the Frontier.* Cambridge: Harvard University Press, 2005.

Barondess, Benjamin. *Three Lincoln Masterpieces: Cooper Institute Speech, Gettysburg Address, Second Inaugural.* Charleston: Education Foundation of West Virginia, Inc., 1954.

Basler, Roy P. et al., eds., *Collected Works of Abraham Lincoln,* vol. 6. New Brunswick: Rutgers University Press, 1953-55.

Bassett, John Spencer. *The Life of Andrew Jackson.* New York: Macmillan Co., 1925.

Belohlavek, John M. *"Let the Eagle Soar!": The Foreign Policy of Andrew Jackson.* Lincoln: University of Nebraska Press, 1985.

Benton, Thomas Hart. *Thirty Years View*, vol. 1. New York: D. Appleton and Co., 1856.

Bodenhorn, Howard. *A History of Banking in Antebellum America: Financial Markets and Economic Development in an Era of Nation-Building.* Cambridge: Cambridge University Press, 2000.

Booraem, Hendrik. *Young Hickory: The Making of Andrew Jackson*. Dallas: Taylor Trade Publishing, 2001.

Boucher, Chauncey Samuel. *The Nullification Controversy in South Carolina*. Chicago: University of Chicago Press, 1916.

Bowers, Claude G. *The Party Battles of the Jackson Period*. Boston: Houghton Mifflin Co., 1922.

Brands, H.W. *Andrew Jackson: His Life and Times*. New York: Doubleday, 2005.

Bragaw, Stephen. "Thomas Jefferson and the American Indian Nations: Native American Sovereignty and the Marshall Court," *Journal of Supreme Court History* 31, no. 2 (2006): 155-180.

Breen, T.H. *The Marketplace of Revolution: How Consumer Politics Shaped American Independence*. New York: Oxford University Press, 2004.

Brooks, Philip Coolidge. *Diplomacy in the Borderlands: The Adams-Onis Treaty of 1819*. University of California, 1939; reprint: New York: Octagon Books, 1970.

Bryan, Charles F., Jr. "The Prodigal Nephew: Andrew Jackson Donelson and the Eaton Affair." *East Tennessee Historical Society's Publications* 50 (1978), 92-112.

Buchanan, John. *Jackson's Way: Andrew Jackson and the People of the Western Waters*. New York: John Wiley and Sons, 2001.

Buckler, Melton F. *Aaron Burr: Conspiracy to Treason*. New York: Wiley, 2002.

Byker, Carl. "The Two Andrew Jacksons: Was 'Old Hickory' a Great President or an American Hitler?" *Los Angeles Times*, December 12, 2008.

Caldwell, Mary French. *Andrew Jackson's Hermitage: The Story of a Home in the TennesseeBlue-Grass Region*. Nashville: Ladies' Hermitage Association, 1949.

_____. *General Jackson's Lady: A Story of the Life and Times of Rachel Donelson Jackson*. Nashville: Ladies' Hermitage Association, 1936.

Calhoun, John C. *The Papers of John C. Calhoun*. Edited by Robert L. Meriwether. 28 vols. to date. Columbia: Published by the University of South Carolina Press for the South Caroliniana Society, 1959-.

_____. *Union and Liberty: The Political Philosophy of John C. Calhoun*. Edited by Ross M. Lence. Indianapolis: Liberty Fund, 1992.

Canby, Courtland. ed., *Lincoln and the Civil War: A Profile and a History*. New York: George Braziller, Inc., 1960.

Capers, Gerald Mortimer. *John C. Calhoun, Opportunist: A Reappraisal*. Gainesville: University of Florida Press, 1960.

Cave, Alfred A. "Abuse of Power: Andrew Jackson and the Indian Removal Act of 1830." *Historian* 65 (December 2003): 1330-53.

Cheathem, Mark R. *Old Hickory's Nephew: The Political and Private Struggles of Andrew Jackson Donelson*. Baton Rouge: Louisiana State University Press, 2007.

Clay, Henry. *The Papers of Henry Clay*. Edited by James F. Hopkins and Mary W.M. Hargreaves. 11 vols. Lexington: University of Kentucky Press, 1959-1992.

Clay, Thomas H. "Two Years with Old Hickory." *Atlantic Monthly* 60 (August 1887), 187-99.

Coffin Handbill: Some Account of Some of the Bloody Deeds of GENERAL JACKSON. Philadelphia: John Binns,1828.

Coit, Margaret L. *John C. Calhoun: American Portrait*. Boston: Houghton Mifflin Co., 1950.

Cole, Donald B. "The Age of Jackson: After Forty Years." Review of *The Age of Jackson*, by Arthur M. Schlesinger, Jr. *Reviews in American History* 14 (March 1986): 149-59.

_____. *A Jackson Man: Amos Kendall and the Rise of American Democracy*. Southern Biography Series. Baton Rouge: Louisiana State University Press, 2004.

_____. *The Presidency of Andrew Jackson*. American Presidency Series. Lawrence: University Press of Kansas, 1993.

Coleman, Michael C. *American Indian Children at School, 1850-1930*. Jackson: University Press of Mississippi, 1993.

Cooper, William J., Jr. *The South and the Politics of Slavery, 1828-1856*. Baton Rouge: Louisiana State University Press, 1978.

Copeland, Gary W. "When Congress and the President Collide: Why Presidents Veto Legislation," *The Journal of Politics* 45, no. 3 (August 1983): 696-710.

Crockett, Davy. *A Narrative of the Life of Davy Crockett, by Himself*. Reprint, Lincoln: University of Nebraska Press, 1987.

Cumfer, Cynthia. "Local Origins of National Indian Policy: Cherokee and Tennessean Ideas about Sovereignty and Nationhood, 1790-1811." *Journal of the Early Republic* 23 (Spring 2003): 21-46.

Curtis, James C. *Andrew Jackson and the Search for Vindication*. Boston: Little, Brown, 1976.

Dangerfield, George. *The Awakening of American Nationalism, 1815-1828.* New York: Harper and Row, 1965.

Debo, Angie. *The Road to Disappearance.* Norman: University of Oklahoma Press, 1967.

Dusenbery, B.M., comp. *Monument to the Memory of General Andrew Jackson: Containing Twenty-five Eulogies and Sermons Delivered on Occasion of His Death.* Philadelphia: James A. Bill, 1848.

Earle, Jonathan H. *Jacksonian Antislavery and the Politics of Free Soil, 1824-1854.* Chapel Hill: University of North Carolina Press, 2004.

Eaton, Clement. *Henry Clay and the Art of American Politics.* The Library of American Biography. Boston: Little, Brown and Co., 1957.

Eaton, Margaret. *The Autobiography of Peggy Eaton.* With a preface by Charles F. Deems. New York: Charles Scribner's Sons, 1932. Reprint, New York: Arno Press, 1980.

Egerton, Douglas R. "An Update on Jacksonian Historiography: The Biographies," *Tennessee Historical Quarterly* 46 (1987): 79-85.

Elkins, Stanley, and Eric McKitrick. *The Age of Federalism.* New York: Oxford University Press, 1993.

Ellis, Richard E. *The Union at Risk: Jacksonian Democracy, States' Rights, and the Nullification Crisis.* New York: Oxford University Press, 1987.

Erikson, Eric M. "The Federal Civil Service under President Jackson," *Mississippi Valley Historical Review* 13 (March 1927): 517-40.

Fanning, Charles. *New Perspectives on the Irish Diaspora.* Carbondale: Southern Illinois University Press, 2000.

Feller, Daniel. *The Public Lands in Jacksonian Politics.* Madison: University of Wisconsin Press, 1984.

Finkleman, Paul, ed., *Congress and the Emergence of Sectionalism: From the Missouri Compromise to the Age of Jackson.* Columbus: Ohio University Press, 2008.

Fish, Carl Russell. *The Civil Service and the Patronage.* New York: Longman, Green, and Co.,1904.

Foreman, Grant. *Indian Removal: The Emigration of the Five Civilized Tribes of Indians.* Norman: University of Oklahoma Press, 1972.

Formisano, Ronald P. "Toward a Reorientation of Jacksonian Politics: A Review of the Literature, 1959-1975." *Journal of American History* 63 (June 1976): 42-65.

Freehling, William W. *The Nullification Era: A Documentary Record.* New York: Harper and Row, 1967.

_____. *Prelude to Civil War: The Nullification Controversy in South Carolina, 1816-1836*. New York: Harper and Row, 1966.

Freeman, Joanne B. *Affairs of Honor: National Politics in the New Republic*. New Haven: Yale University Press, 2001.

Frelinghuysen, Theodore. *Speech of Mr. Frelinghuysen, of New Jersey, Delivered in the Senate of the United States, April 6, 1830, on the Bill for an Exchange of Lands with the Indians Residing in Any of the States or Territories, and for Their Removal West of the Mississippi*. Washington, D.C.: Printed and published at the Office of the National Journal, 1830.

Friedman, Reuben. *Scabies – Civil and Military: Its Prevalence, Prevention and Treatment*. New York: Froben Press, 1941.

Genovese, Michael A. *The Power of the American Presidency, 1789-2000*. New York: Oxford University Press, 2001.

Goldsmith, William M. *The Growth of Presidential Power: A Documented History*. vol. 1, *The Formative Years*. vol. 2, *Decline and Resurgence*. New York: Chelsea House Publishers, 1974.

Govan, Thomas P. *Nicholas Biddle: Nationalist and Public Banker, 1786-1844*. Chicago: University of Chicago Press, 1959.

Green, Michael D. *The Politics of Indian Removal: Creek Government and Society in Crisis*. Lincoln: University of Nebraska Press, 1982.

Griffen, Patrick. *The People with No Name: Ireland's Ulster-Scots, America's Scotch-Irish, and the Creation of a British Atlantic World*. Princeton: Princeton University Press, 2001.

Hall, A. Oakey. "Andrew Jackson: His Life, Times and Compatriots. First Paper – Andrew Jackson's Private Life." *Frank Leslie's Popular Monthly* 44 (November 1897).

Hammond, Bray. *Banks and Politics in America from the Revolution to the Civil War*. Princeton: Princeton University Press, 1957.

_____. "Jackson's Fight with the 'Money Power.'" *American Heritage* 7 (June 1959): 8-11, 100-103.

Hay, Robert B. "The Case for Andrew Jackson in 1824: Eaton's Wyoming Letters," *Tennessee Historical Quarterly* 29 (1970): 139-151.

Hayne, Rob. Y. "Letters on the Nullification Movement in South Carolina, 1830-1834." *American Historical Review* 6 (July 1901): 736-65.

Healy, Gene. *The Cult of the Presidency: America's Dangerous Devotion to Executive Power*. Washington, D.C.: Cato Institute, 2008.

Herndon, William H. and Jesse W. Weik. *Herndon's Life of Lincoln*. Cleveland: Fine Editions Press, 1949.

Hickey, Donald R. *The War of 1812: A Forgotten Conflict*. Urbana: University of Illinois Press, 1989.

Hine, Robert V. and John Mack Faragher. *The American West: A New Interpretive History*. NewHaven: Yale University Press, 2000.

Hinsdale, Mary L. *A History of the President's Cabinet*. Ann Arbor: University of Michigan Press, 1911.

Hofstadter, Richard. *The American Political Tradition and the Men Who Made It*. New York: Alfred A. Knopf, 1948.

_____. *The Idea of a Party System: The Rise of Legitimate Opposition in the United States, 1780-1840*. Berkeley: University of California Press, 1970.

Holt, Michael. *The Political Crisis of the 1850s*. New York: W.W. Norton & Co., 1983.

_____. *The Rise and Fall of the American Whig Party*. New York: Oxford University Press, 1999.Holzer, Harold. Gabor S. Boritt and Mark E. Neely Jr. *The Lincoln Image: Abraham Lincoln and the Popular Print*. Chicago: University of Illinois Press, 2001.

Hone, Philip. *The Diary of Philip Hone, 1828-1851*. Edited by Allan Nevins. 2 vols. New York:Dodd, Mead and Co., 1927.

Hopkins, James F. "Election of 1824." In *History of American Presidential Elections, 1789-2001*, edited by Arthur M. Schlesinger, Jr. and Fred L. Israel, 347-409. Vol. 1.Philadelphia: Chelsea House Publishers, 2002.

Houston, David Franklin. *A Critical Study of Nullification in South Carolina*. New York: Longmans, Green, and Co., 1896. Reprint, Gloucester, Mass.: Peter Smith, 1968.

Howe, Daniel Walker. *What Hath God Wrought: The Transformation of America, 1815-1848*. New York: Oxford University Press, 2007.

Hughes, Emmet John. *The Living Presidency: The Resources and Dilemmas of the American Presidential Office*. New York: Coward, McCann and Geoghegan, 1873.

Jackson, Andrew. *Correspondence of Andrew Jackson*. Edited by John Spencer Bassett. 7 vols. Washington, D.C., Carnegie Institution of Washington, 1926-1935.

_____. *Legal Papers of Andrew Jackson*. Edited by James W. Ely, Jr., and Theodore Brown, Jr. Knoxville: University of Tennessee Press, 1987.

_____. *The Papers of Andrew Jackson*. Edited by Sam B. Smith and Harriet Chappell Owsley. Vols. 1-6. Knoxville: University of Tennessee Press, 1980, 1984, 1991, 1994, 1996, 2002.

James, Marquis. *Andrew Jackson: Portrait of a President*. Indianapolis: Bobbs-Merrill Co., 1938.

_____. *The Life of Andrew Jackson, Complete in One Volume*. Indianapolis: Bobbs-Merrill Co., 1938.

Jefferson, Thomas. *The Writings of Thomas Jefferson*, Edited by Albert Ellery Bergh, vol. 10, Washington, D.C.: The Thomas Jefferson Memorial Association, 1907.

Jennings, Francis. *The Invasion of America: Indians, Colonialism, and the Cant of Conquest*. New York: W. W. Norton & Company, 1976.

_____. *Empire of Fortune: Crowns, Colonies and Tribes in the Seven Years War in America*. New York: W. W. Norton & Company, 1990.

Kanon, Tom. "The Other Battle of New Orleans: Andrew Jackson and the Louisianans," *Gulf South Historical Review* 2d ser., 17 (Spring 2002): 41-61.

Kaplan, Edward S. *The Bank of the United States and the American Economy*. Westport: Greenwood Press, 1999.

Kendall, Amos. "Anecdotes of General Jackson." *United States Magazine and Democratic Review* 11 (September 1842): 272-74.

_____. *Autobiography of Amos Kendall*. Edited by William Stickney. Boston: Lee and Shepard, 1872.

Kennedy, Roger G. *Burr, Hamilton, and Jefferson: A Study in Character*. New York: Oxford University Press, 1999.

Knott, Stephen F. *Secret and Sanctioned Covert Operations and the American Presidency*. New York: Oxford University Press, 1996.

Laski, Harold J. *The American Presidency: An Interpretation*. New York: Harper and Brothers, 1940.

Latner, Richard B. "The Eaton Affair Reconsidered," *Tennessee Historical Quarterly* 35 (Fall 1977): 330-51.

_____. "The Kitchen Cabinet and Andrew Jackson's Advisory System," *The Journal of American History* 65, no. 2 (September 1978): 367-388.

_____. *The Presidency of Andrew Jackson: White House Politics, 1829-1837*. Athens: University of Georgia Press, 1979.

Lee, Henry. *A Biography of Andrew Jackson: Late Major-General of the Army of the United States*. Edited by Mark A. Mastromarino. Occasional Pamphlet, no. 3. Knoxville: Tennessee Presidents Trust, 1992.

Lee, Jong R. "Presidential Vetoes from Washington to Nixon," *The Journal of Politics* 37, no. 2 (May 1975): 522-46.

Levy, Leonard W. *Jefferson and Civil Liberties: The Darker Side*. Chicago: Ivan R. Dee, 1989.

Leyburn, James G. *The Scotch-Irish: A Social History*. Chapel Hill, The University of North Carolina Press, 1962).

Longaker, Richard P. "Was Jackson's Kitchen Cabinet a Cabinet?" *The Mississippi Valley Historical Review* 44, no. 1 (June 1957): 94-108.

Magliocca, Gerard N. *Andrew Jackson and the Constitution: The Rise and Fall of Generational Regimes*. Lawrence: University Press of Kansas, 2007.

Mahon, John K. "British Command Decisions Relative to the Battle of New Orleans," *Louisiana History* 6 (Winter, 1965): 53-76.

Marszalek, John F. *The Petticoat Affair: Manners, Mutiny, and Sex in Andrew Jackson's White House*. New York: Free Press, 1997.

McKay, David. "Presidential Strategy and the Veto Power: A Reappraisal," *Political Science Quarterly* 104, no. 3 (Autumn 1989): 447-61.

Meacham, Jon. *American Lion: Andrew Jackson's White House Years*. New York: Random House, 2008.

Mearns, David C. ed., *The Lincoln Papers,* vol. 2. Garden City: Doubleday & Company, Inc., 1948.

Meyers, Marvin. *The Jacksonian Persuasion: Politics and Belief*. Stanford: Stanford University Press, 1957.

Miller, Douglas T., ed. *The Nature of Jacksonian America*. New York: John Wiley and Sons, 1972.

Miller, Kerby. *Emigrants and Exiles: Ireland and the Irish Exodus to North America*. New York: Oxford University Press, 1985.

Mitgang, Herbert. ed., *Lincoln As They Saw Him*. New York: Rinehart & Company, 1956.

Mooney, Chase C. *Slavery in Tennessee*. Bloomington: Indiana University Press, 1957.

Mugleston, William F. "Andrew Jackson and the Spoils System: An Historiographical Survey," *Mid-America* 59 (1977): 113-125.

Murray, Robert K. and Tim H. Blessing, "The Presidential Performance Study: A Progress Report," *Journal of American History* 71, No. 3 (December 1983): 535-555.

Nagel, Paul C. *John Quincy Adams: A Public Life, A Private Life*. New York: Alfred A. Knopf, 1997.

Neustadt, Richard E. *Presidential Power: The Politics of Leadership*. New York: John Wiley and Sons, 1960.

Niven, John. *John C. Calhoun and the Price of Union: A Biography*. Baton Rouge: Louisiana State University Press, 1988.

_____. *Martin Van Buren: The Romantic Age of American Politics*. New York: Oxford University Press, 1983.

O'Brien, Michael. *In Bitterness and Tears: Andrew Jackson's Destruction of the Creeks and Seminoles*. Westport: Praeger, 2003.

Owsley, Jr., Frank L. "Role of the South in the British Grand Strategy in the War of 1812," *Tennessee Historical Quarterly* 31 (Spring, 1972): 22-38.

_____. *Struggle for the Gulf Borderlands: The Creek War and the Battle of New Orleans, 1812-1815*. Gainesville: University of Florida Press, 1981.

Parsons, Lynn Hudson. *John Quincy Adams*. Madison: Madison House, 1998.

Parton, James. *Life of Andrew Jackson*. 3 vols. Boston: Ticknor and Fields, 1860.

Patterson, James T. "The Rise of Presidential Power Before World War II." *Law and Contemporary Problems* 40 (Spring 1976): 39-57.

Perkins, Howard Cecil. ed., *Northern Editorials on Secession*, vol. I. Gloucester: Peter Smith, 1964.

Perry, Lewis. Review of *Fathers and Children: Andrew Jackson and the Subjugation of the American Indian*, by Michael Paul Rogin, *History and Theory* 16, no. 2 (May, 1997): 174-195.

Pessen, Edward. *Jacksonian America: Society, Personality, and Politics*. Rev. ed. Homewood, IL: Dorsey Press, 1978. Reprint, Urbana: University of Illinois Press, 1985.

_____, ed. *Jacksonian Panorama*. The American Heritage Series. Indianapolis: Bobbs-Merrill Co., 1976.

Peterson, Merrill D. *The Great Triumvirate: Webster, Clay, and Calhoun*. New York: Oxford University Press, 1987.

_____. *Olive Branch and Sword: The Compromise of 1833*. Baton Rouge: Louisiana State University Press, 1982.

Powell, Edward Payson. *Nullification and Secession in the United States: A History of the Six Attempts During the First Century of the Republic*. New York: G.P. Putnam's Sons, 1898.

Prince, Carl E. *The Federalists and the Origins of the U.S. Civil Service*. New York: New York University Press, 1977.

Proceedings of the Anti-Jackson Convention, Held at the Capitol in the City of Richmond: With their Address to the People of Virginia. Richmond: Franklin Press, 1828.

Prucha, Francis Paul. "Andrew Jackson's Indian Policy: A Reassessment." *Journal of American History* 56 (December 1969): 527-39.

Ratner, Lorman A. *Andrew Jackson and His Tennessee Lieutenants: A Study in Political Culture* Westport: Greenwood Press, 1997.

Reilly, Robin. *The British at the Gates: The New Orleans Campaign in the War of 1812*. New York: Putnam, 1974.

Remini, Robert V. *Andrew Jackson and His Indian Wars*. New York: Viking, 2001.

_____. *Andrew Jackson and the Bank War: A Study in the Growth of Presidential Power*. New York: W.W. Norton & Company, 1967.

_____. *Andrew Jackson and the Course of American Democracy, 1833-1845*. New York: Harper and Row, 1984.

_____. *Andrew Jackson and the Course of American Empire 1767-1821*. New York:Harper and Row, 1981.

_____. *Andrew Jackson and the Course of American Freedom, 1822-1832*. New York: Harper and Row, 1981.

_____. *The Battle of New Orleans: Andrew Jackson and America's First Military Victory*. New York: Viking, 1999.

_____. *The Election of Andrew Jackson*. Philadelphia: J.B. Lippincott, 1963.

_____. "Election of 1832." In *History of American Presidential Elections, 1789-2001*, edited by Arthur M. Schlesinger, Jr. and Fred L. Israel, 493-574. Vol. 2. Philadelphia: Chelsea House Publishers, 2002.

_____. *Henry Clay: Statesman for the Union*. New York: W.W. Norton, 1991.

_____. *John Quincy Adams*. New York: Times Books, 2002.

_____. *The Legacy of Andrew Jackson: Essays on Democracy, Indian Removal, and Slavery*. Baton Rouge: Louisiana State University Press, 1988.

_____. *The Life of Andrew Jackson*. New York: Harper and Row, 1966.

Robertson, Lindsay G. *Conquest by Law: How the Discovery of America Dispossessed Indigenous Peoples of Their Lands*. New York: Oxford University Press, 2005.

Rosen, Deborah A. "Wartime Prisoners and the Rule of Law: Andrew Jackson's Military Tribunals during the First Seminole War," *Journal of the Early Republic* 28, no. 4 (Winter, 2008): 559-595.

Rossiter, Clinton. *The American Presidency*. New York: Harcourt, Brace, 1956.

Satterfield, Robert Beeler. *Andrew Jackson Donelson: Jackson's Confidant and Political Heir.*Bowling Green, KY: Hickory Tales, 2000.

Satz, Ronald N. *American Indian Policy in the Jacksonian Era.* Lincoln: University of Nebraska Press, 1974.

_____. Review of *Andrew Jackson and His Indian Wars*, by Robert V. Remini. *Journal of American* History 90 (December 2003): 1013-14.

Schlesinger, Arthur M. *Life Magazine,* 25 (1 November 1948): 65-66.

Schlesinger, Arthur M., Jr. "Rating the Presidents: Washington to Clinton," *Political Science Quarterly* 112, No. 2 (Summer, 1997): 179-190.

_____. *The Age of Jackson.* Boston: Little, Brown and Co., 1945.

_____. ed. *The Election of 1828 and the Administration of Andrew Jackson.* Philadelphia: Mason Crest Publishers, 2003.

Sellers, Charles. *The Market Revolution: Jacksonian America, 1815-1846.* New York: Oxford University Press, 1991.

Sellers, Charles Grier Jr., "Andrew Jackson versus the Historians," *Mississippi Valley Historical Review* 44 (March 1968): 615-634.

Sheehan, Bernard W. *Seeds of Extinction: Jeffersonian Philanthropy and the American Indian.* New York: W.W. Norton, 1974.

Silbey, Joel H. *Martin Van Buren and the Emergence of American Popular Politics.* Lanham: Rowman and Littlefield, 2002.

Snelling, J. A *Brief and Impartial History of The Life and Actions of Andrew Jackson.* Boston: Stimpson and Clapp, 1831.

Somit, Albert. "Andrew Jackson as Administrative Reformer," *Tennessee Historical Quarterly* 13 (September 1954): 205-223.

Smith, Margaret Bayard. *The First Forty Years of Washington Society in the Family Letters ofMargaret Bayard Smith.* Edited by Gaillard Hunt. New York: Frederick Ungar Publishing Co., 1965. Reprint of the 1906 edition.

Smith, William E. "Francis P. Blair, Pen-Executive of Old Hickory," *The Mississippi Valley Historical Review* 17, no. 4 (March 1931): 543-556.

Stampp, Kenneth M. *And the War Came: The North and the Secession Crisis, 1860-1861.* Baton Rouge: Louisiana State University Press, 1950.

_____. "Lincoln and the Strategy of Defense in the Crisis of 1861," *The Journal of Southern History* 11 (1945): 315.

Stannard, David. *American Holocaust: The Conquest of the New World.* New York: OxfordUniversity Press, 1993.

Stenberg, Richard R. "Jackson's 'Rhea Letter' Hoax," *The Journal of Southern History* 2, No. 4, (November, 1936): 480-496.

_____. "The Jefferson Birthday Dinner, 1830." *The Journal of Southern History* 4 (August 1938): 334-45.

Story, William W. ed., *Life and Letters of Joseph Story*, vol. 1. Boston: Charles C. Little and James Brown, 1851.

Sumner, William Graham. *Andrew Jackson*. vol. 17. Boston: Houghton Mifflin Co., 1899.

Swisher, Carl Brent, ed. "Roger B. Taney's 'Bank War Manusript.'" Parts 1, 2. *Maryland Historical Magazine* 53 (June, September 1958): 103-130, 215-237.

The Letters of Wyoming, to the People of the United States, on the Presidential Election, and In Favour of Andrew Jackson. Philadelphia: S. Simpson & J. Conrad, 1824.

Toplovich, Ann. "Marriage, Mayhem, and Presidential Politics: The Robards-Jackson Backcountry Scandal," *Ohio Valley History* 5, no. 4 (Winter 2005): 3-22.

Van Buren, Martin. *The Autobiography of Martin Van Buren*. Edited by John C. Fitzpatrick. Washington, D.C.: U.S. Government Printing Office, 1920. Reprint, New York: A.M. Kelley, 1969.

Walker, Arda. "The Educational Training and Views of Andrew Jackson." *East Tennessee Historical Society's Publications* 16 (1944): 22-29.

Wallace, Anthony F.C. *Jefferson and the Indians: The Tragic Fate of the First Americans*. Cambridge: Belknap Press of Harvard University Press, 1999.

_____. *The Long, Bitter Trail: Andrew Jackson and the Indians*. A Critical Issue. New York: Hill and Wang, 1993.

Ward, John William. *Andrew Jackson, Symbol for an Age*. New York: Oxford University Press, 1953.

Warshauer, Matthew. *Andrew Jackson and the Politics of Martial Law: Nationalism, Civil Liberties and Partisanship*. Knoxville: University of Tennessee Press, 2006.

_____. "Andrew Jackson: Chivalric Slave Master" *Tennessee Historical Quarterly,* 65 (Fall 2006): 203-229.

_____. "Contested Mourning: The New York Battle over Andrew Jackson's Death," *New York History* 87, no. 1 (Winter 2006): 29-65.

_____. "Ridiculing the Dead: Andrew Jackson and Connecticut Newspapers," *Connecticut History* 20, no. 1 (Spring 2001): 13-31.

_____. "The Passions of Andrew Burstein: A Review of *The Passions of Andrew Jackson*," by Andrew Burstein, *Tennessee Historical Quarterly* 38, no 4 (Winter 2003): 366-373.

Watson, Harry L. *Andrew Jackson vs. Henry Clay: Democracy and Development in Antebellum America*. New York: Bedford, 1998.

──────. *Liberty and Power: The Politics of Jacksonian America.* New York: Noonday, 1990.

──────. "Old Hickory's Democracy." *Wilson Quarterly* 9 (Autumn 1985): 101-33.

White, Leonard D. *The Jacksonians: A Study in Administrative History, 1828-1861.* New York:Macmillan Co., 1954.

Wilentz, Sean. *Andrew Jackson.* New York: Times Books, 2005.

──────. *The Rise of American Democracy: Jefferson to Lincoln.* New York: W.W. Norton, 2005.

Wiltse, Charles M. *John C. Calhoun.* vol. 1, *Nationalist, 1782-1828.* vol. 2, *Nullifier, 1829-1839.* Indianapolis: Bobbs-Merrill Co., 1944, 1949.

Wyatt-Brown, Bertram. *Southern Honor: Ethics and Behavior in the Old South.* New York: Oxford University Press, 1982.

──────. *The Shaping of Southern Culture: Honor, Grace, and War, 1760s-1880s.* Chapel Hill: University of North Carolina Press, 2001.

Young, Mary E. "Indian Removal and Land Allotment: The Civilized Tribes and Jacksonian Justice." *American Historical Review* 64 (October 1958): 31-45.

INDEX

A

Adams, John, xii, 123, 190
Adams, John Quincy, ii, x, 63, 80, 82, 88, 90, 95, 97, 111, 112, 169, 189, 197, 198, 199
adulthood, 3, 9
Age of Jacksonian Democracy, 104, 106, 186
ambition, xxi, 10, 19, 25, 27, 41, 87, 91, 99
Appalachian Mountains, 14, 19, 42
Arthur, Chester Alan, ii
atrocities, 83, 128
attorney general, 20, 113, 141

B

Bank of the United States, xxxi, 111, 121, 124, 131, 132, 135, 137, 140, 141, 144, 147, 196
Bank War, xxxi, xxxii, 4, 131, 132, 134, 138, 139, 140, 144, 145, 146, 147, 155, 159, 187, 199, 201
banking, 132, 135
Battle of New Orleans, xxii, xxv, 47, 63, 67, 71, 161, 162, 182, 196, 197, 198, 199
bluster, 110, 128, 159
boldness, 60, 70, 147
bravery, 6, 13, 51, 58

Buchanan, James, 180
Burr Conspiracy, 35, 37, 62, 189
Burr, Aaron, 35, 37, 45, 191
Bush, George Herbert Walker, xii

C

cabinet, 63, 80, 95, 112, 113, 114, 115, 116, 117, 118, 119, 133, 135, 141, 143, 148, 166
Charles Town, 7, 9, 10, 11, 15
Cherokee, xxvii, 43, 128, 150, 192
childhood, 2, 32, 127
children, 5, 9, 35, 38, 43, 46, 47, 54, 58, 78, 79, 95, 103, 105, 162, 177, 179
Civil War, xxxii, 49, 132, 139, 148, 150, 155, 157, 163, 164, 167, 174, 179, 182, 183, 187, 191, 194
Clay, Henry, 192
Cleveland, Grover, xi
Clinton, William Jefferson, xii, 145
coalition, 111, 112, 133, 134, 135, 138, 146
commitment, xxx, 10, 23, 35, 36, 60, 99, 100, 137, 144
community acceptance, 22
connections, 11, 14, 21, 24, 27, 114, 118
Constitution, ix, xiii, 61, 62, 69, 72, 82, 83, 96, 98, 104, 105, 106, 111, 120, 121, 124, 125, 134, 138, 149, 150,

153, 154, 155, 165, 167, 177, 182, 186, 197
constitutional crises, 158
contradictions, xxi, xxv, 26
conviction, xxxii, 17, 26, 38, 51, 52, 65, 88, 130, 155, 165, 167
Coolidge, Calvin, xi
Corrupt Bargain, 88, 95, 98, 100, 101, 106, 109, 137, 186
corruption, xx, 88, 97, 99, 100, 101, 103, 104, 109, 120, 121, 122, 123, 134, 135, 137, 141, 159, 164, 169, 178, 186
Creek Indians, 41, 48, 50, 61
Creek War, 41, 44, 47, 50, 57, 58, 59, 78, 87, 130, 138, 198
cross-border raids, 83

D

death, xx, xxxi, 1, 3, 5, 7, 8, 9, 10, 26, 29, 30, 31, 35, 38, 45, 51, 56, 58, 79, 111, 114, 115, 144, 163, 177, 178, 183
Democratic Party, 119, 133, 134, 146, 149, 154, 168, 173, 175, 176
despotism, xxv, 60, 102, 161
divorce, 21, 22, 23
Duane, William, 142, 143
duel, xxxii, 15, 16, 21, 22, 28, 29, 30, 31, 33, 35, 70, 87, 165
duplicity, 36
duty, 10, 24, 45, 51, 52, 53, 64, 68, 71, 81, 91, 97, 135, 137, 140, 150, 151, 152, 153, 154, 155, 180

E

Eaton Affair, 115, 116, 117, 118, 119, 133, 135, 138, 191, 196
Eisenhower, Dwight David, xii
electoral votes, xii, 88, 96, 103
emergency powers, 62, 162, 167, 168, 183
ethnic cleansing, xxviii, 42, 131
European powers, 60, 126, 135

F

Farewell Address, 162, 163, 164, 165, 173, 183
federal deposits, 132, 138, 143, 158
Fillmore, Millard, xi
fiscal policy, 135
fisticuffs, 13
Florida, xii, 24, 47, 48, 59, 61, 62, 63, 65, 74, 75, 76, 77, 78, 80, 82, 83, 87, 88, 89, 90, 94, 102, 105, 109, 118, 126, 145, 170, 192, 198
foreign influence, 59, 65, 83, 126, 187
foreign trade, 135
Franklin, Benjamin, 14

G

Garfield, James, xii
Georgia, xii, 43, 59, 61, 74, 82, 83, 95, 112, 130, 150, 196
governorship, 28, 29, 90, 91
Great Britain, 24, 42, 77, 106, 119, 127, 171

H

Harrison, Benjamin, xii
Harrison, William Henry, ii, xii, 168
Henry Clay, xxxii, 10, 36, 38, 80, 81, 82, 87, 88, 89, 94, 96, 99, 105, 112, 124, 133, 137, 138, 145, 154, 164, 172, 173, 180, 192, 193, 199, 201
hero, xx, xxii, xxv, 41, 46, 62, 74, 80, 81, 94, 95, 102, 106, 138, 147, 158, 168, 179, 187
heroism, xxii, xxv, 60, 106
honor, xx, xxv, 13, 15, 16, 28, 29, 30, 31, 32, 34, 54, 81, 143, 147, 171, 176, 178
honor culture, 32
Hoover, Herbert, ii
Horseshoe Bend, 55, 57

I

ideology, 135, 164, 178
image, xxii, xxvii, 3, 92, 105, 109, 127, 137, 144, 146, 158, 161, 168, 182, 183, 185, 186
inauguration, 88, 104, 107, 115, 121, 161, 163, 165, 180, 181
Indian policy, xxviii, xxix, 42, 128, 131, 135
Indian sovereignty, xxix
Indians, xxvii, xxviii, xxix, xxx, 9, 13, 16, 24, 27, 42, 43, 47, 48, 49, 50, 55, 57, 59, 61, 63, 64, 65, 74, 75, 77, 78, 80, 83, 89, 105, 120, 121, 126, 128, 129, 131, 135, 138, 145, 150, 189, 190, 193, 194, 196, 201
insecurities, 28, 37, 119
insecurity, 9, 31, 38
intensity, xxiv, 26, 159
internal improvements, xxxii, 111, 120, 121, 124, 135, 146

J

Jackson-Dickinson duel, 29
Jacksonian Era, xx, 128, 200
Jay Treaty, 24
Jefferson, Thomas, ii, xi, xxvi, xxvii, xxix, xxx, 35, 37, 49, 77, 89, 94, 112, 122, 123, 126, 130, 131, 149, 189, 190, 191, 196
Johnson, Andrew, xi
Johnson, Lyndon Baines, xi
jury trials, 20

K

Kennedy, John F., xii
Kentucky, 21, 30, 36, 38, 81, 82, 89, 94, 96, 98, 99, 103, 124, 133, 149, 192

L

land fraud, 28
land holdings, 26, 34
law practice, 20
legal services, 25
legality, 62, 69, 149, 186
letters, xvii, 33, 34, 48, 53, 67, 79, 80, 92, 93, 96, 115, 118, 123, 138, 142, 147, 148, 152, 157, 158, 166, 169, 170, 172, 174, 176, 183
Lincoln, Abraham, xi, xxvi, xxxii, 139, 150, 167, 179, 180, 181, 182, 190, 195
lobbying, 27
Lyncoya, 43, 48, 49, 50

M

Madison, James, ii, xi, 132, 149
Manifest Destiny Era, 60
Marshall, John, 37, 132
martial law, xxv, 41, 44, 61, 62, 65, 69, 71, 73, 74, 76, 83, 88, 94, 102, 109, 138, 162, 166, 167, 168, 182, 183
McKinley, William, xi
Mexican War, 60
military service, ix, xii, 27, 95
Monroe, James, xi, xxx, 63, 65, 66, 71, 73, 75, 76, 79, 91, 130, 190
morality, xxxi, 84, 102
mother, xxiv, 1, 2, 4, 7, 9, 10, 11, 15, 32, 48, 57, 103, 111
multiculturalism, xxvii
mutual forbearance, 183

N

Nashville, xxv, 14, 16, 19, 20, 21, 29, 32, 33, 35, 42, 45, 46, 47, 48, 51, 58, 92, 93, 172, 173, 191
national debt, xxxii, 120, 121, 123, 124, 125, 135, 140, 152, 158
national security, xxix, 84, 135, 187
nationalism, xxii, xxx, 62, 63, 74, 82, 83, 87, 88, 90, 91, 93, 109, 126, 163, 165, 168, 175, 186, 187
Native Americans, xxiv, xxvii, xxviii, xxix, 42, 43, 47, 60, 128, 129, 135, 185, 187

Index

New Orleans, xviii, xxv, 36, 41, 44, 45, 51, 61, 62, 63, 64, 65, 66, 67, 68, 69, 70, 71, 72, 73, 74, 80, 81, 83, 87, 88, 91, 94, 102, 105, 109, 138, 166, 168, 172, 185, 186, 199
Nickajack Expedition, 24
Nixon, Richard, xi
North Carolina, 5, 6, 11, 13, 14, 20, 21, 22, 30, 113, 189, 193, 197, 202
Nullification, xxxi, xxxii, 4, 118, 120, 138, 139, 140, 148, 149, 150, 152, 153, 154, 155, 156, 157, 158, 159, 164, 173, 179, 182, 187, 190, 191, 193, 194, 195, 198

O

Old Hickory, xxviii, 2, 46, 76, 80, 93, 94, 117, 127, 133, 159, 161, 163, 179, 181, 183, 191, 192, 200, 202

P

partisanship, xx, xxii, 177
party policy, 135
personal conviction, 159
personality, xxiii, xxv, xxxiii, 1, 3, 5, 7, 15, 21, 46, 92, 99, 100, 126
Philadelphia, xx, xxii, 25, 90, 93, 97, 102, 103, 176, 189, 192, 193, 195, 199, 200, 201
Pierce, Franklin, xii
political power, 2, 19, 29, 41, 87, 119, 163, 164, 167, 174
popularity, xxi, 27, 35, 41, 55, 62, 63, 83, 87, 91, 94, 95, 103, 168, 173, 179
presidential assassination, 158
prestige, xiii, 23, 38, 88
principles, x, 125, 134, 148, 171, 183, 186
problem solving, 110, 158
property holding, 23
propriety, 15, 21, 32, 186

R

racial tolerance, xxvii

Reagan, Ronald, xi
remarriage, 22
reputation, xvii, 10, 12, 16, 21, 27, 30, 32, 33, 38, 58, 104, 111, 114, 155
residency, 23
resolution, 23, 24, 38, 54, 68, 146, 166, 174
retirement, 120, 162, 166, 169, 183
Revolution, xix, xxiv, xxvi, 1, 6, 7, 9, 10, 17, 19, 26, 33, 35, 38, 41, 56, 106, 132, 161, 182, 191, 194, 200
Robards, 21, 22, 23, 34, 35, 103, 201
Roosevelt, Franklin D., xi, xiii, 167
Roosevelt, Franklin Delano, ii, xxvi, 110
Roosevelt, Theodore, ii, xi, xxvi

S

Second American Party System, xx, 28, 185
self-defense, 62, 80, 83, 109, 135
Senate, x, 24, 25, 59, 73, 80, 82, 91, 92, 93, 119, 145, 168, 171, 174, 190, 194
settlers, 42, 43, 47, 57, 58, 61, 83, 84, 89, 129, 130, 170
slaughter, 48, 58, 78, 83, 129
slave holdings, 26, 27
slaveholder, xxvii, xxxi, 26
slaves, xxxi, 26, 31, 34, 49
South, xxviii, xxx, xxxi, xxxii, 4, 7, 30, 47, 63, 65, 67, 78, 79, 83, 101, 111, 112, 117, 120, 130, 138, 139, 140, 148, 149, 150, 151, 153, 154, 155, 156, 157, 173, 180, 190, 191, 192, 194, 195, 196, 198, 202
spoliation agreements, 126, 135
symbolism, 109, 137, 163, 167, 181, 185, 187

T

Taft, William Howard, xii
tariffs, 111, 117, 135, 146, 148, 149, 154, 163
Tecumseh, 47
Tennessee militia, 27, 45

territorial expansion, 84
Texas, xii, 60, 127, 162, 169, 170, 171, 172, 173, 174, 182, 183
theft, 121, 135, 158
trade relations, 158
Treaty of Fort Jackson, 41, 59, 60, 61, 79
Truman, Harry S., xi, xxvi
Tyler, John, ii, xi, 168, 174

U

understanding, iv, xxvii, xxxi, xxxii, xxxiii, 2, 3, 5, 19, 33, 38, 76, 92, 99, 100, 105, 119, 124, 153, 154, 185
Union, x, xxii, xxv, xxvi, xxix, xxxi, xxxii, xxxiii, 10, 19, 36, 37, 59, 60, 81, 99, 105, 117, 129, 136, 137, 139, 140, 148, 149, 150, 152, 153, 154, 155, 156, 157, 159, 161, 162, 163, 164, 165, 167, 169, 170, 172, 173, 174, 175, 179, 181, 182, 183, 186, 187, 191, 193, 198, 199

V

Van Buren, Martin, xii, 117, 131, 133, 135, 138, 143, 161, 163, 172, 198, 200, 201
violence, xxiii, xxx, 5, 7, 10, 12, 13, 19, 28, 30, 31, 33, 34, 39, 46, 79, 94, 102, 178, 187

Virginia, xii, 22, 36, 81, 102, 149, 150, 181, 189, 190, 198
vision, xix, xxv, xxvi, xxxii, 74, 80, 84, 88, 99, 124, 175, 179, 183

W

War of 1812, xxii, 41, 42, 44, 45, 54, 57, 62, 63, 82, 91, 97, 131, 195, 198, 199
Washington, George, ii, x, xi, xxvi, 14, 44, 74, 80, 112, 129, 131, 162
weakness, xxix, 38, 54, 116, 125, 148, 165
wealth, 25, 26, 38, 134, 164, 176
Webster, Daniel, 133, 146, 149, 150, 182
West, xv, xxviii, xxix, 19, 20, 24, 25, 36, 45, 46, 48, 81, 82, 83, 94, 96, 99, 111, 124, 127, 129, 130, 142, 181, 190, 194, 195
White House, xiii, xxiv, xxvi, 2, 63, 87, 101, 103, 105, 109, 110, 114, 115, 116, 126, 133, 134, 156, 161, 181, 186, 196, 197
Wilson, Woodrow, xi, xxvi
Wirt, William, 138

Z

Zachary Taylor, xii